Discard

Work this summer in a variety of interesting temporary assignments.

Kelly Services offers summer employment opportunities in over 100 different job classifications for college students and educators. Temporary work assignments include typists, secretaries, bookkeepers, word processors and a variety of marketing and light industrial assignments.

Kelly Services has over 450 branches coast to coast with offices in Puerto Rico, Canada, England and France.

See the White Pages for the office nearest you.

KELLY SERVICES — The "Kelly Girl" People

1981

Summer Employment Directory

of the United States

30th Edition

Edited by
Barbara Norton Kuroff
Assistant Editor
Joan Lynne Bloss

Writer's Digest Books 9933 Alliance Road
Cincinnati, Ohio 45242

Summer Employment Directory. Copyright 1981. Published by Writer's Digest Books, 9933 Alliance Road, Cincinnati, Ohio 45242. Printed and bound in the United States of America. All rights reserved. No part of this book may be reproduced in any manner whatsoever without written permission from the publisher, except by reviewers who may quote brief passages to be printed in a magazine or newspaper.

30th Edition

Library of Congress Catalog Card Number 54-33991
International Standard Serial Number 0081-9352
International Standard Book Number 0-89879-034-4(Paperback)
0-89879-035-2 (Hardbound)

Contents

Introduction

How would you like to spend this summer on a private island off the coast of Washington teaching French to children; working as a research assistant for the U.S. government in Washington, D.C.; picking strawberries in Utah; herding cattle on a ranch in Wyoming; or as an actor in a New England theater? These diverse and exciting jobs—and many more—are in this book.

The purpose of *Summer Employment Directory* of the United States is to list available jobs, particularly for students and teachers, during summer vacation and other breaks from school. All the job information comes directly from the employers.

This year—and this is *Summer Employment Directory*'s 30th year of publication—we've asked employers about the "hidden assets" of working for them. The answers are myriad—from travel allowances to homecooked meals—and can be found in the new "Fringe Benefits" section of most individual listings. We were especially pleased to see how many employers offer college credit (or are willing to arrange college credit) with their jobs.

Another new feature this year is the placement of the number of jobs available in each state based on the listings in this book just under respective state headings. An accurate total was not available in some states since government agencies, temporary employment agencies and some other employers find it hard to estimate the number of employees they need for the summer. A plus has been added to job totals for those states and indicates that there are even more jobs available than the total shown.

We've also added a whole new job category—Government—to our standard categories; this means jobs located in Washington, D.C. as well as in regional offices. And for the first time we have jobs for farm labor contractors who plant, harvest and, in some cases, process America's crops. Listings for individual contractors can be found in the Business and Industry sections.

We hope the listings in this book and the new features we've added will make your selection of a summer job easier and in line with your career goals.

— The Editors

Using Your Summer Employment Directory

Summer Employment Directory is divided into two parts. The first part offers articles that give you basic information on how to apply for a job and the second part lists actual job openings in all parts of the United States for the summer of 1981.

The articles tell you how to write a letter of application, what to put in your resume, and how to prepare for an interview. They also give inside tips from employers on what they look for in an applicant, information on summer jobs in the federal government, and data needed by foreigners wishing to work in the U.S.

The second and largest part of *SED* contains state-by-state listings of job openings in the U.S.—and some in Canada—in resorts, amusement parks, offices, summer theaters, summer camps, restaurants and many other businesses that need help in the summer. After the listings by state is a U.S.A. section for organizations or firms with nationwide locations.

Within each section, jobs are categorized according to the type of business or organization offering the job. The major categories are Business and Industry; Government; Commercial Attractions; National Parks; Expeditions, Guide Trips; Resorts, Ranches, Restaurants, Lodging; Summer Camps; and Summer Theaters. Don't limit your search to one category. For instance, if you want to cook, you should look at the listings under the subhead Resorts, Ranches, Restaurants, Lodging; but you can also find jobs for cooks under Summer Camps, National Parks and Commercial Attractions.

"Late Arrivals," the last part of SED, lists in alphabetical order job opportunities that arrived in our office too late to be included within state listings. This section allows us to accept listings from employers right up until press time and gives you even more choices from which to select your summer job.

The information in each listing comes directly from the employers themselves. Look for these details:

●Name of the company, organization or facility, and its location
●Type of positions open; the number of openings often are given also
●Salaries
●Whether the employer supplies room and board
●Dates of employment; pay particular attention to end-of-season dates, as they may conflict with other schedules you may have
●Name and address to send application; this may differ from the name and location given at the top of the listing
● How to apply; unless stated otherwise, send a letter and resume
● Skills or degree of education that may be required to fill the job
● Fringe benefits includes considerations other than salary, but equally important in choosing a summer job: college credit availability, transportation allowance, bonuses, chance to further your career goal, and more.

● College credit *available* means college credit is offered for completion of some positions within a facility. College credit *possible* indicates that, although college credit has not been recently offered to employees, the employer would be willing to cooperate with students wishing to arrange such credit with their college or university.

Buying a copy of *Summer Employment Directory* won't guarantee that you'll get a job. However, we do guarantee that all employers listed have indicated that they want to be in the book and are thus actively looking for summer/seasonal help. All await your application.

Job Hunting

Applying for a Job

Most of the employers listed in *Summer Employment Directory* require you to write a cover letter and attach a resume to apply for a job. Some also will want to interview you either over the phone or in person. The letter, resume and interview weigh heavily on your chances of being hired. It is important therefore to approach all three in a professional manner.

The Cover Letter

Introduce yourself to the employer in your cover letter. Remember that the letter you write will be his or her first impression of you and that it must reflect your most positive qualities in a succinct and imaginative way. You must inspire the employer to take special notice of your application and make him want to read your resume to find out more about you.

What information should you include in a letter? First, keep in mind that you're presenting your qualifications, not the story of your life. Do not waste the employer's time with irrelevant biographical data or by repeating all of the information you have presented on your resume. However, if there is any one particular qualification that you think makes you an outstanding candidate, display it prominently on both the letter and resume. For example, if you are applying for a job as a counselor at a tennis camp and you are the current Amateur Athletic Union champ, don't be shy about letting the employer know who you are.

In your letter, you should introduce yourself, explain why you are writing, and invite the employer to consider your qualifications and contact you. Include your name, address and telephone number on the letter as well as on the resume.

The tone of your letter does not have to be stiffly formal; learn to be yourself. Use your imagination to arouse the curiosity of the reader to learn more about you. Be careful with humor, however; it's better to be deadly serious than to try to be funny and fail. Unless you're applying to be a clown, keep your feet on the ground and your jokes to yourself.

After you've written the letter, read it to yourself to get a feeling for the impression you have created. Do you make yourself sound shy or unsure of yourself? Are you too boastful and brash? How should you present yourself? Remember not to let yourself be defensive, as this person did:

> I'd like to apply for the job of cabin counselor I saw listed in *SED*. I
> don't have any experience as a counselor, but I think I could do

Sample Cover Letter

123 First Avenue
Cincinnati OH 45299
February 2, 1981

Ms. Mary W. Shelley
Camp Xanadu
Round Pond ME 04566

Dear Ms. Shelley:

I would like to apply for the position of nature specialist at Camp Xanadu that you list in Summer Employment Directory of the United States.

I am majoring in education in biology in college, and I have had experience as a summer camp counselor. I have several ideas for a summer nature/education program for children that I would like to discuss with you.

The enclosed resume gives the details of my educational and employment background. Please call or write me if you have any questions about my qualifications. Also, I would appreciate receiving any additional materials necessary for applying for work at Camp Xanadu.

Thank you for your consideration of my application. I'm looking forward to your reply.

Sincerely,

Sinclair Lewis

Sinclair Lewis
(123)456-7890

Enclosures: resume
             photograph
             self-addressed, stamped envelope

the job if you gave me a chance. I'm not sure what I'm qualified to
do, but if you don't think I would be a good counselor maybe you
could give me a job in maintenance or in the kitchen.

Why should the employer trust the care of children to such a sniveling coward?
Be positive! Before you write your letter, think carefully about the job you want
and consider what qualities the employer might need in an employee. Then,
think of the reasons why you would be the *best* person to fill those needs. Convince yourself. Then, sit down at the typewriter and convince the employer:

I'm writing to apply for the job of cabin counselor I saw listed in
SED. I love children and, as the oldest of four in our family, have
had lifelong experience in caring for them. I have many special interests and abilities, listed on my resume, that I want to share, and
I am sure that I could be a good addition to your counseling staff.

A word of warning: don't list fictitious qualifications just to make yourself look
good on paper. Employers value honest, flexible applicants who desire experience and growth over those who exaggerate their suitability.

Don't use a mass-produced cover letter. Instead, compose a separate letter
for each job. Use white bond or good quality typing paper (no flowers, toadstools or happy faces, please!) and a standard business-letter format. When you
are satisfied with the image you present in the letter, proofread it with a critical
eye on spelling, grammar and writing style. Poor spelling—especially if you misspell the name of the employer or his company—will tell the reader you are
careless with details.

Employers put a premium on neatness. If at all possible, your letter should be
typed, although a *neat* letter, handwritten in ink, can serve your purpose also.
Keep typing errors to a minimum, even if it means retyping the letter once or
twice. Keep a carbon of each letter you send so that you will have an accurate
record of whom you've contacted.

The Resume

There is no one best format for a resume, but all good resumes begin with the
applicant's name, address, telephone number and date of birth. The rest of the
resume should be divided into at least five other categories: education, work experience, special interests, personal data and references.

Education: List your most important educational experiences—best subjects,
college major, activities and honors. Some employers also like to know how
much of your education you financed yourself, either through work or scholarships. If you've finished or are nearly done with college, drop any mention of
your high school days from your resume unless the information relates directly
to the job you want. For example, it is all right to say you were president of the
high school ecology club if you're applying to be a scientific aide for the Environmental Protection Agency. You don't have to report grade point averages or
class standings if they are not above average.

Work experience: This is a problem for those writing a first resume; obviously, they have little work experience to report. In that case, stress your abili-

Sample Resume

RESUME

Sinclair Lewis

123 First Avenue   telephone 123/456-7890
Cincinnati, Ohio 45299

PERSONAL DATA: Born 10/1/60, single, excellent health.

CAREER OBJECTIVE: I plan to teach biology and general science at the high
school level.

EDUCATION: Will complete second year of college at State University this
spring, majoring in education in biology. Maintaining a 3.2 grade point
average. 80% of tuition paid by athletic scholarship. Lettered in
tennis; also member of Alpha Beta Gamma social fraternity and the
university's ecology club.

WORK EXPERIENCE: June 6 to August 12, 1980 tennis counselor at Green Woods
Summer Camp in Oshkosh, Maine. Responsible for giving tennis lessons
to children ranging from 9 to 14 years of age. Also organized and
supervised in-camp tennis tournament. Assisted camp athletic director
to care for camp's equipment.

September 8, 1978 to May 15, 1980, worked part-time in campus book
store. Unpacked new books and kept them in stock on shelves. After
first year was promoted to assistant store manager.

PERSONAL INTERESTS: Enjoy golf and many other sports. Jog three miles a
day. Have been active in Sierra Club and other organizations involved
in saving natural resources.

REFERENCES:

Ms. Jane Gray, Manager, Campus Bookstore, 111 East West Street,
Cincinnati, Ohio 45299; 123/456-7890.

Mr. L. John Silver, Director, Green Woods Summer Camp, Box 1, Oshkosh,
Maine 12345; 123/456-7890.

Dr. Clara Barton, Professor of Biology, 123 Taft Hall, State University,
Cincinnati, Ohio 45299; 123/456-7890.

Dr. Joseph Blow, Professor of Biology, 456 Taft Hall, State University,
Cincinnati, Ohio 45299; 123/456-7890.

ties. You can also include volunteer work and major tasks you have tackled at home, such as painting the house. Let the employer know you haven't been idle, even if no one has been paying you for your work.

Persons who have had jobs should list the most recent first. List employers' names, addresses and the dates of your employment, and describe your duties on each job briefly. You may give details about your military experiences here or put them in a separate section.

Special interests: Let your individuality show through. List hobbies, favorite leisure and sports activities, and organizations you belong to outside of school. Special skills you have acquired through your interests can add to your qualifications for a job. For example, many camps hire specialty counselors who are proficient in music, crafts or swimming.

References: Though references might seem like an insignificant footnote to your resume, they are a vital part of your presentation. It is typical for an employer to regard the comments of a reference as a key factor in choosing an employee. List at least three persons not related to you who can testify to your good character and conscientiousness; former employers or co-workers are best. Be sure to get permission from your references before you use their names. List each individual's name, address (with Zip Code) and phone number so that the employer can easily contact the reference.

Personal data: Use your judgment. Employers usually don't need to know your height and weight unless the job you're applying for is unusually physical or requires a slender appearance. Obviously, being slim is an asset if you want to be an exercise instructor at a weight-reducing camp or a canoe guide along a whitewater river. Let the employer know you're in excellent health if the job requires stamina, and also let him know if you have any limitations or handicaps that might interfere with your work.

Your marital status may or may not be important to the employer, but you should mention it. The employer does not need to know your parents' occupations or other personal data about your family. Since many employers ask to see a photo of an applicant, it is convenient, though certainly not expected, to have a small photograph printed on your resume. However, this kind of resume costs more than the standard kind, and attaching a wallet-size photo to your resume is just as acceptable. Note that it's better to send no photo at all than a snapshot of you romping with the family dog. The employer should not require you to send a photograph, since such a requirement has often been used to discriminate against racial minorities.

Career objectives are appearing more frequently on resumes, usually just before the educational category. If you have already made a career decision—and especially if it ties in with the summer job you are applying for—by all means include in it your resume.

If you're applying for more than one job, you don't have to retype your resume every time you apply. A good, *clean* photocopy on standard paper stock is acceptable. Standard paper stock is white and similar to bond or good quality typing paper. Don't use a copier that copies on a waxy or cheap-looking, off-color paper. A copying or duplicating service should be able to give you 20 copies for around $2. Coin-operated copiers generally give you less than quality photocopies and are usually more expensive.

If you need 100 copies or more, consider having your resume printed by an offset process. Your resumes can be printed on any kind of paper, including the highest-quality bond or even a colored paper stock. The copying service will need a clean copy with no obvious corrections typed on white paper (no onionskin) using a new ribbon. Use an electric typewriter if one is available. The copying service will make a photographic plate of your resume and use the plate to print copies in the same way most newspapers and magazines are printed. Cost for the 100 copies should only be $5-10.

When mailing your resume and letter to the employer, it is courteous to enclose a stamped, self-addressed envelope for his reply.

The Interview

Not every employer listed in this book will want to interview you before hiring you, because of the distance involved in many cases. Those who do require an interview may rely on his or her impression of you in the interview far more than on what you have written in your letter or resume.

Most interviewees have two major questions about the interview process: What should I say, and what should I wear?

Don't go into an interview without preparation, planning *only* to answer the questions the interviewer asks. The interviewer may not have a clear idea of what he wants to say, and silence is deadly during an interview. Find out whatever you can about the organization you may be working for before the interview, and don't be shy about displaying your knowledge: "Your theater's production of 'Under the Yum-Yum Tree' was a big success last year," or "I understand that the Girl Scouts stress work on badges and campcraft skills in their camping program" are comments that tell the employer you've taken an interest in his or her theater or summer camp.

Think of the employer's needs again when you explain to him why you want the job you're interviewing for. "I want to work for a summer camp because I want to spend the summer outdoors, not cooped up in an office," is a poor response. It doesn't tell the employer what you can do for him, only what you want for yourself. Think of ways to relate the job to your personal interests or career goals. "I'm majoring in art education, and I have some great ideas for a children's summer crafts program, such as . . ." will tell your employer that you're ready to take on the job.

If you're nervous, just remember that the person interviewing you has been in your position himself, and he won't hold sweaty palms and a catch in your voice against you. However, try to avoid fidgeting in your chair, playing with objects on his or her desk, scratching yourself frequently, or any other action that might distract the interviewer from what you are saying to him. A small but crucial technique to use is to look the interviewer in the eyes when speaking or listening to him.

Take the job into consideration when deciding what to wear. It probably won't be necessary to wear a business suit if you're interviewing to be a trail guide, truck driver or camp counselor. The most important part of your appearance when you're interviewing for a job is cleanliness.

For an outdoors job, a simple dress or good pants and blouse would be a good choice for women; men can interview in shirt and slacks, possibly also a sports coat. Women should remember that there are still a few people who are negative toward women wearing pants, however. For an office job, of course, your best businesslike outfit is necessary.

An employer should tell each applicant being considered for a job when to expect a decision. If that date passes and you haven't heard, call the employer to ask about your application. He should understand your anxiety, and your call will serve to show that you're interested in the job. However, you should not call the employer several times before the agreed upon date. Such harrassment usually works against your chances for getting the job.

It's also a good idea to write a thank-you letter to an employer after an interview to let him know that you enjoyed speaking to him and that you hope he keeps you in mind for the job. A paragraph or two will suffice.

To Get More Information

For more tips on job hunting, see the newest edition (revised 1980) of *What Color Is Your Parachute?* by Richard Nelson Bolles. This manual, published by Ten Speed Press, describes a systematic approach to making career decisions, as well as numerous sources for help in the job search. *Guerrilla Tactics in the Job Market*, by Tom Jackson, emphasizes techniques for researching and choosing a market, making contacts and interviewing. It is published by Bantam. Another source is Burdette E. Bostwick's *Resume Writing: A Comprehensive, How-to-Do-It Guide*, which was revised in October, 1980, and published by Wiley-Interscience. Although it is about resumes, Bostwick's book also deals with cover letters and gives many good examples of letters and resumes.

Inside Tips From Employers

This year the summer employer, whether he operates out of executive offices in a metropolitan area or a summer camp in the woods, is seeking employees willing to contribute more than just time to a job.   Our *Summer Employment Directory* questionnaires show that employers, although they clearly value the "standard" qualifications, are looking even beyond an applicant's talents and abilities to find abstract qualities, such as dedication and motivation.

Nevada Brown, Associate Executive Director of Camp Fire, Inc. in Denver, Colorado, says, "I want special people for a special experience and I am choosy. Of course qualifications, experience and special talents are important, but originality as well as attitude, enthusiasm, interest and the tone of the cover letter always catch my eye. Sloppiness [in a cover letter and resume] implies lack of initiative to me."

Another practice that shows lack of motivation, according to Mrs. Silas B. Ragsdale, Jr. of Camp Stewart for Boys in Texas, is submitting an "obviously duplicated application or resume which has been sent to many people. We tend to discard those," she says.

Nevada Brown and others agree that applications and letters written in pencil are too much trouble to handle. Taking the few extra minutes to type your application and resume shows the employer that your initiative is strong. In the words of Stephen Feinstein, Director of Camp Samoset II in Maine, "I am impressed by the care and concern an applicant takes in completing an application because it evidences a real desire." The care that Feinstein speaks of can be reflected in as simple a step as carefully reading and following the employer's instructions. Many employers are unimpressed by applicants who forget to enclose a photo if requested or who give incomplete information about themselves or references. By the same token, adding optional information—extracurricular activities, club memberships, pertinent awards—to an application form can give a favorable impression, points out Martin Silverman, Director of Camp Kippewa for Girls, Maine.

Other employers from different parts of the U.S. point out still more of those abstract qualities that are desirable in an applicant.

"I'm interested in their motivation—why a camp?", says Suzanne B. Marfak, Director/Secretary of Camp Waredaca, Gaithersburg, Maryland.

Hal Watman of Camp Hadar, Connecticut, is impressed by applicants who show "creativity and verbal enthusiasm," while "interest in outdoor life and a genuine love of children" are characteristics sought by Jan Kater of Camp Sunapee in New Hampshire.

Employees with "an interest in seeing a new area and working in a new situation" appeal to Dorothy Mackin of Imperial Hotel and Imperial Players, Cripple Creek, Colorado. Maude Katzenbach of Camp Fire-Potomac Area Council in Washington, D.C., agrees that being able to work in different situations is important. She says, "Willingness to accept responsibility cheerfully, reliability and the ability to cope with the unexpected count more than anything else."

James Congdon of Brush Ranch in New Mexico says he is influenced by "very little on the application form. It is the response from references and the interview with the applicant that matter the most."

In a personal interview you must draw on your own inner resources to convey your abstract qualities of enthusiasm and commitment to the employer. There's no need to put on an act, however—just be truly interested in the job and let the employer see your willingness to work.

The interview can easily work to your advantage, since the interest and enthusiasm that employers seek is often easiest to show in person through body language, facial expressions and your voice.

The attitude of a successful job applicant is best summed up by Mike Olsen of Camp Foster YMCA, Spirit Lake, Iowa. He looks for persons who show "personal excitement in the opportunity."

Working for the Federal Government

The United States federal government offers many summer jobs that involve the use of both brains and brawn, and with educational and skill requirements ranging from none to a Ph.D. However, the first page of a booklet published by the U.S. Office of Personnel Management—"Summer Jobs: Opportunities in the Federal Government," hereafter called Announcement No. 414—annually carries this stern warning:

"Opportunities are very limited. There are many more applicants than there are positions available. Therefore, you would be wise not to apply for summer work solely with the federal government."

If you are employed by Uncle Sam, you can have the opportunity to gain valuable professional experience in your summer months as well as earn a salary. You could be an agricultural or scientific aid for the Department of Agriculture; a computer aid with the Environmental Protection Agency; an engineering aid with the National Aeronautics and Space Administration; or a graphic designer for the Department of the Treasury.

Other positions offer adventure. The Forest Service, for example, has openings in national parks and forests for aids and technicians in such areas as conservation, fire control, surveying, physical and biological science and recreation. Other government departments have openings for legal aids, veterinarian trainees and journalists.

To obtain information—deadline dates, forms needed, positions open—about all government summer jobs, get a copy of Announcement No. 414 from any Federal Job Information Center (FJIC). Copies of No. 414 for summer 1981 were available in December 1980.

Some federal jobs require applicants to apply as early as January. Late applications are never accepted. You may apply directly for jobs in some government agencies, and you can find a list of these in booklet No. 414. Also for the first time the *Summer Employment Directory* has specific jobs listed under **Government** in the District of Columbia and other state sections.

The Office of Personnel Management has classified government summer jobs into five groups. Jobs in Group I are mostly clerical positions on the level of GS-1 through GS-4. Jobs in Group II, which are also in grades GS-1 through GS-4, involve technical, nonclerical work. These jobs require some college or experience in specific occupational fields.

Jobs in Group III are in grades GS-5 or above and involve technical, professional and administrative work. Some of these positions require four years of college; others a master's or doctoral degree. In many cases, persons with four years of college must supply proof of acceptance into graduate school to obtain a Group III job.

Group IV positions are for laborers and tradesmen. This group includes such jobs as printing plant worker, animal caretaker and carpenter's helper.

Two special government programs are listed under Group V. The Summer

Employment for Needy Youth program provides jobs for young people from low-income families and for youths who need incomes from summer jobs in order to return to school in the fall. To apply, contact the nearest Bureau of State Employment Services. If there is no State Employment Services office in your area, contact any Federal Job information Center for information on referral procedures.

A limited number of outstanding undergraduate and graduate students nominated by their colleges are selected annually to participate in the Federal Summer Intern Program, which offers internships related to administrative, professional or technical career fields. Most internships are located in Washington DC, although a few are in other parts of the country. The grades involved range from GS-4 to GS-11. Students may not file applications directly; if you would like to participate, contact your college placement office. For more information, see Announcement No. 414 and *1981 Internships*, published by Writer's Digest Books.

If You Are Not a U.S. Citizen

If you are not a U.S. citizen, you can still apply for any job in the *Summer Employment Directory* unless the employer states otherwise. some employers specify in their listings that they would like to hire foreign college and university students. If an employer in the U.S. offers you a job, however, be sure that he is willing to obtain and file the correct forms *before* you come to the U.S. so that you will be able to get a work permit when you arrive to take the job.

The paperwork involved is long and time consuming, but you will not be able to come to the U.S. on a visitor's visa and get authorization to work after you arrive. Regulations are enforced strictly, and certification must be shown on your visa, which will be validated upon arrival in the United States, *before* your employer can allow you to begin work for him.

When an employer decides to hire you, he must obtain Form 1-129B (Petition to Classify Nonimmigrant as Temporary Worker or Trainee) and an H-2 Labor Certification from his local Immigration and Naturalization office. He must also obtain Form MA 7-50B (Application for Labor Certification) from either the same department or the Bureau of State Employment Services.

The H-2 classification is given to an individual coming into the U.S. for a temporary period to perform a temporary service or temporary labor. An individual with exceptional abilities—for example, a professional athlete or entertainer—receives an H-1 classification. Trainees are classified as H-3.

Form MA 7-50B is completed and filed with the Bureau of State Employment Services, to be processed and returned to the employer. When the form is received, he submits it, together with Form 1-129B and the H-2 Temporary Alien Labor Certification, to the U.S. Department of Immigration office having jurisdiction in the area in which you will work. There is a $15 fee for filing a temporary visa petition.

Your employer must have completed and filed these forms before you can receive a visa to enter the U.S. You have two responsibilities: First, obtain a passport before leaving for the U.S.; second, upon your arrival in the U.S., have Form I-94 (Arrival-Departure Record) endorsed by the immigration officer to show the period of authorized stay. Form I-94 is your work permit; a summer employer cannot hire you legally unless you can show authorization as an H-2 worker. For more information, contact your nearest U.S. consulate.

If you are Canadian, you will not need a passport to enter the U.S. from a place within the Western Hemisphere. You will, however, need to comply with all other regulations.

These strict regulations are intended to give citizens of the U.S. the first chance at jobs. Therefore, the number of temporary summer workers admitted to the United States from other countries depends a great deal on the level of unemployment in the U.S. at that time. When unemployment is high, there will be few permits to work granted; the policy is relaxed as unemployment decreases. If you write to an employer listed in the book, be certain that the employer also understands the regulations involved and that he is willing to take the time to do the paperwork.

Persons who attend school in the United States, but who are citizens of another country would usually be classified F-1 nonimmigrant students. An F-1 nonimmigrant who would like to take a summer job in the U.S. should check with his local Immigration and Naturalization office although the general rule is that an F-1 student is not granted permission to work.

SED lists a few jobs in Canada. As in the U.S., foreign workers are permitted to enter Canada to take seasonal jobs only when the jobs cannot be filled by Canadians. The number of aliens given authorization to work varies somewhat from province to province.

A job offer from a Canadian employer must be presented by the employer to the nearest Canada Employment Center (CEC) office. If the CEC agrees that no qualified Canadian resident is available to fill the job, the Canadian office nearest your home will be notified. That office will contact you and ask you to come in to be interviewed and to apply for Employment Authorization. The interview will determine if you are qualified for the job and if you may enter Canada temporarily under Canada's immigration laws.

If your application is approved, you will receive a visa and an Employment Authorization to cover the particular job for a predetermined amount of time.

The Employment Authorization must be issued before you enter Canada; you will not be allowed to enter Canada to look for a job. In all but a few exceptional cases, persons who have entered Canada already on a visitor's visa will not be able to obtain authorization to work. For more information, contact the nearest Canadian consulate.

British Universities North America Club (BUNAC) administers a student exchange program between Britain and the United States that has been approved by the U.S. International Communications Agency. For details on jobs write to BUNAC, 30/31 Store Street, London WCIE 7BS, England. The telephone number is 01-637-7686.

Camp America, another exchange program recognized by the U.S. International Communications Agency, arranges for European and Australian university students to work as counselors in U.S. summer camps. For more information, write Camp America, 37 Queen's Gate, London SW7 5HR, England, or telephone 01-589-3223.

Abbreviation Chart

The following are some common abbreviations used in the book and also the U.S. Postal Service's two-letter state codes used in the listing addresses:

Abbreviations

ACA	American Camping Association
ALS	Advanced Life Saving
ARC	American Red Cross
BUNAC	British University North American Club
CAA	Camp Archery Association
CIT	Counselor-in-training
EMT	Emergency Medical Technician
EOE	Equal Opportunity Employer
LIT	Leader-in-training
LPN	Licensed Practical Nurse
LSC	Life Saving Certificate
NRA	National Riflery Association
RN	Registered Nurse
SCI	Small Craft Instructor
SASE	Self-addressed, stamped envelope
SLS	Senior Life Saving
WSI	Water Safety Instructor

State Codes

AK	Alaska
AL	Alabama
AR	Arkansas
AZ	Arizona
CA	California
CO	Colorado
CT	Connecticut
DC	District of Columbia
DE	Delaware
FL	Florida
GA	Georgia
HI	Hawaii
IA	Iowa
ID	Idaho
IL	Illinois
IN	Indiana
KS	Kansas
KY	Kentucky
LA	Louisiana
MA	Massachusetts
MD	Maryland
ME	Maine
MI	Michigan
MN	Minnesota
MO	Missouri
MS	Mississippi
MT	Montana
NC	North Carolina
ND	North Dakota
NE	Nebraska
NH	New Hampshire
NJ	New Jersey
NM	New Mexico
NV	Nevada
NY	New York
OH	Ohio
OK	Oklahoma
OR	Oregon
PA	Pennsylvania
PR	Puerto Rico
RI	Rhode Island
SC	South Carolina
SD	South Dakota
TN	Tennessee
TX	Texas
UT	Utah
VA	Virginia
VI	Virgin Islands
VT	Vermont
WA	Washington
WI	Wisconsin
WV	West Virginia
WY	Wyoming

The Jobs

Alaska

42 jobs available

Expeditions, Guide Trips

America & Pacific Tours, Inc. (A&P), Located in Anchorage.
Alaskan tour guide service. Openings for college students, teachers and foreign
students from June 1 through August 31. Needs 10 Japanese speaking tour
guides, $1,000/month plus overtime. "Room and board is not included but we
will assist in locating housing in Anchorage with close access to our offices. Our
groups are all Japanese ranging from age 20 up. We also have specialty groups
ranging from commercial filming to government officials. Applicant must speak
fluent Japanese, should be outgoing, and willing to work long hours for which
they will be properly paid. Our season is short with many groups, so be ready to
do hard but enjoyable work." Send resume and letter by April 30. Apply to
Keizo Sugimoto, President, Dept. SED, Box 1068, Anchorage AK 99510; tel.
907/272-9401.
Fringe Benefits: Training on Alaska.

Government

National Transportation Safety Board, Jobs available at the
regional office in Anchorage. Applications must be made to Washington DC
office. See Washington DC office (District of Columbia section) for descriptions
of jobs available and how to apply information.

Resorts, Ranches, Restaurants, Lodging

Cripple Creek Resort, Located in Ester, Alaska. Hotel and restaurant
in restored gold camp. Openings for college students and teachers from May
15 to Labor Day (except bartenders-waiters work May 1 to September 10).
"Unless you can fill dates of employment please do not apply." Needs 5
bartender-waiters, $500-700/month plus tips; 4 dining room waiters,
$500/month plus tips; 3 office workers and maids, $450/month; 3 kitchen
helpers, $500/month. "Applicants may do any or all of the job descriptions, so
are trained in all phases at the start." Salaries include room and board, plus
transportation one way if contract is completed. Applicants "must be
personable and able to live with others harmoniously." Resort is tourist oriented
but has a substantial local clientele. Send resume by February. Apply to Donald

W. Pearson, Dept. SED, 17 Galloway Drive, Concord CA 94518; tel.
415/676-5894.

McKinley KOA Kampground, Located in Healy. Family
campground with grocery store, automotive repair shop, propane service and
garage (with wrecker service). Openings for college students, teachers and local
applicants from May 15 to September 15 (June 1 to September 5 for
recreation director and bus driver). Needs 3 store clerks (minimum age 19),
$4.25 or more/hour; mechanic helper (with basic knowledge of automotive
repair), $6 or more/hour; recreation director and bus driver (willing to learn
and narrate about area and McKinley Park, plus work split shift and help in
store and campground), $4.50 or more/hour. "We have some on-site housing,
but most workers have to provide their own. Applicant must be able to enjoy a
rural area and be willing to keep working hours and social hours separate."
Send resume by May 1 to Corrine Colrud, Dept. SED, Box 34, Healy AK
99743; tel. 907/683-2379.

Rainbow King Lodge, Inc., Located in Alaska on Iliamna Lake.
Luxury sport fishing lodge for families, upper class business persons, major
corporations. Openings from June 1 to October 1; employees must stay
complete season. Needs 6 lodge helpers for serving, cleaning, room make up,
kitchen help, etc.; and 6 fishing guides, should be experienced fishermen and
boatmen with congenial personalities. Salaries are $650/month, including tips.
Room and board provided. No transportation to lodge provided; served by
scheduled airlines. Wants applicants who are "refined, with high morals; we
have strict rules and regulations." Apply by April to Ray Loesche, Owner/
Manager, Rainbow King Lodge, Inc., Box 3446, Spokane WA 99220.

Arizona

1,119 jobs available

National Parks

Grand Canyon National Park Lodges, Located on South Rim
Grand Canyon National Park in northwest Arizona (7,000 foot elevation).
National park with resort hotels, restaurants, and curio shops. Equal
opportunity employer. Openings year round with peak season being Easter
through September. Summer staff of 1,000, winter staff of 550. All personnel
must be able to work for at least 90 days; have opportunity to become full-
time/permanent. Interested in active retirees. No beards or goatees; men
required to have conventional tapered haircuts not to exceed collar length.
Needs hotel/restaurant personnel for various lodges, coffee shops, cafeterias,
curio shops, all positions front and back of the house, minibus drivers
(minimum age 21), and others. Entry-level jobs start at federal minimum wage;
room deduction automatic. Meals available at cost in employee cafeterias; no
cooking in rooms. All dorm rooms double occupancy (some summer triples);
no single rooms available. Housing available for couples (no children allowed).

Minimum number of trailer spaces available to rent. Apply to Grand Canyon National Park Lodges, Personnel Dept. SED, Grand Canyon AZ 86023.

Resorts, Ranches, Restaurants, Lodging

Canyon Squire Inn, Located at Grand Canyon. Motel and restaurant. Openings from April through October. Needs clerks for gift shop and front desk, waiters/waitresses, maids and housemen, recreation attendants, bus people, porters, and kitchen help. Salary open, includes room and board. "Call us." Apply by February or early March to General Office, Canyon Squire Inn, Box 130, Highway 64, Grand Canyon AZ 86023; tel. 602/638-2681, ext. 150.

Summer Camps

Maripai
Shadow Rim Ranch
Willow Springs Program Center, Camp Maripai, located in the Bradshaw Mountains, and Shadow Rim Ranch, located in Mogollon Rim country, are Girl Scout residential camps; Willow Springs, located in the Bradshaw Mountains, is a troop camping facility. Openings for college students, teachers, foreign students, local applicants from June 5 to August 15. Needs 3 assistant camp directors to direct, supervise and coordinate with unit staff and program specialists, $1,100-1,200/season; 3 nurses to supervise health and safety and operate camp infirmaries, $1,100-1,200/season; 9 unit leaders to direct, coordinate and supervise program for 30 girls and unit staff, $850-1,000/season; 27 unit counselors to assist unit leaders, $600-800/season; 5 program specialists to assume full responsibility for teaching a skill such as riding, nature, etc., $600-800/season; 2 business managers to assist camp director, $900-1,000/season; 3 maintenance persons/assistant rangers, $800-1,000/season. Room and board provided. Would hire handicapped as unit counselors, program specialists and maintenance persons. Send for application. Apply by March 1 to Margaret Stewart, Program Director, 1515 E. Osborn Rd., Phoenix AZ 85014.
Fringe Benefits: "Good learning experience and learning situations, good working conditions, scenic locale, wide variety of people, interesting work." **College credit** possible.

The Salvation Army Camp, Located in Oracle. Summer camp. Openings from June through the first part of September. Needs 14 counselors, male and female, $60-70/week, college students preferred; 1 lifeguard, $95/week, college student preferred; 1 nurse (RN), $125/week; 3 cooks, $50-175/week; 3 dishwashers, $30/week, high school seniors preferred; 2 maintenance workers, $35/week, high school seniors preferred; 1 secretary, $80/week, college student preferred; 1 crafts director and 1 wilderness director, $70/week, college students preferred. Room and board provided. Apply before February 28 to Captain Ray Peacock, Divisional Youth Secretary, The Salvation Army, Dept. SED, Box 13307, Phoenix AZ 85002; tel. 602/258-8085.
Fringe Benefits: "Camp is located in beautiful valley of ancient 400-year-old sycamores—an oasis in the desert." **College credit** possible.

Sky-Y, Located in the Bradshaw Mountains at Prescott. YMCA coed camp for children ages 8-13. Openings for college students and teachers from June 14 to August 16. Needs 18 general counselors, nurse, WSI. Salaries are $420-$540/season plus room and board. Apply before April to Cecil Miller, Camp Director, 350 N. 1st Ave., Phoenix AZ 85003.

Arkansas

35 jobs available

Summer Camps

Cahinnio, Located near Booneville. Girl Scout camp for girls ages 9-15. Openings from June 8 to July 26 (7-week season). Needs 3 unit leaders and 1 small-craft instructor, $300-400/season, college students or teachers preferred; 10 unit counselors, $200-300/season, college students or high school seniors preferred; 1 waterfront director, $350-450/season, college students or teachers preferred; and 1 nurse, $400-500/season, college students or teachers preferred. Room and board included at nominal cost. Apply by March 30, 1981 to Mt. Magazine Girl Scout Council, Dept. SED, Box 3274, Fort Smith AR 72913; tel. 501/452-1290.
Fringe Benefits: Development of outdoor skills; experience in Girl Scout camping. **College credit** possible.

Noark, Located on 1,039 acres at Huntsville in the Ozark Mountains. Primitive Girl Scout camp for girls ages 7-17. Openings for college students and teachers from June 8 to July 18. Needs 6 unit leaders (minimum age 21), who are mature, able to work with children and supervise unit staff, $55-75/week; 11 unit counselors, minimum age 18, $35-50/week; waterfront director (minimum age 21), WSI or equivalent plus ability to teach children, supervise teaching process, keep records and organize large groups, $55-75/week; and business manager (minimum age 21), experience in business methods, record keeping, buying and inventory control, $55-75/week. Food and lodging provided. "We want people who are imaginative, creative, responsible, and enjoy primitive outdoor life." Send for application and return by May 30 to Elizabeth A. Hastings, Camp Director, Dept. SED, Girl Scout Service Center, Rt. 1, Box 43, Fayetteville AR 72701; tel. 501/442-4507.

California

4,481+ jobs available

Business and Industry

Bentley Personnel Services, Located in San Francisco. Needs secretaries, typists, dictaphone operators, receptionists, convention aides, messengers, switchboard and all office positions. Considers college students, teachers, high school seniors and foreign students (*must* have valid, authorized work permit)."Brush up on typing, filing and office skills as the rate paid per hour depends upon your office skills and experience. We try to place our summer workers in the kind of office and industry they prefer. We deal with all types of industries and the experience is invaluable." Apply to Brenda Foster, Manager, Bentley Personnel Services, 625 Market St., San Francisco CA 94105.

Remedy Temporary Services, Located in San Juan Capistrano. Unlimited openings for college students, teachers, high school seniors and foreign students. Needs workers with all skills anywhere in Southern California. Salaries vary, based on skills. Top pay and vacation pay plan. Apply to Remedy Temporary Services, 32122 Camino Capistrano, San Juan Capistrano CA 92675.

TemPositions, Inc., Located in San Francisco. Temporary employment service. Openings from June 1 to September 15. Needs 20 word processors, $7-10/hour; 125 secretaries, $5-7/hour; 100 typists, $4-6/hour; and 75 clerk/typists and 25 receptionists, $3.50-4.50/hour. College students, teachers, high school seniors or local applicants preferred. "Be flexible. Attitude and willingness to work are as important as skills. Because of US immigration laws, we cannot accept applications from England or Europe." Apply to Patience Talcott, Vice President, 690 Market St., San Francisco CA 94104; tel. 415/392-5856.

Commercial Attractions

Disneyland, Located in Anaheim. Hires about 4,000 people (minimum age 18)/year for seasonal positions. Summer is biggest season, but open year round. Gives preference to persons available through Labor Day. "Orientation and training average 24 hours so it's very important to be available and train before our peak season begins." Needs ticket sellers/takers; merchandise markers; office and clerical workers; and hosts/hostesses for: culinary, custodial, attraction, warehouse, merchandising and wardrobe positions. Starting salary generally $3.50/hour (somewhat less for tipping positions). "It is necessary when you are cast as a part of 'The Disney Show' you display 'The Disney Look,' a neat and natural look with no extremes. You could expect to work a minimum of 25-30 hours/week during summer, Christmas and Easter holidays." Provides wardrobe for most positions. Living quarters, rentals, meals and transportation are not furnished, and "rentals are high in this area during the holidays and the summer season." Applications may be requested by mail, but requires personal interview at Disneyland Casting Office. For summer work, apply by the end of May. Equal opportunity employer. Apply to Disneyland Casting Office #J.S.P., Dept. SED, 1313 Harbor Blvd., Anaheim CA 92803.
Fringe Benefits: "Disneyland offers seasonal and part-time work that can be organized around school schedules. Working here provides a good opportunity to meet people from around the world."

Santa Cruz Beach Boardwalk, Located in Santa Cruz. Seashore amusement park. Openings from third week in May thru Labor Day. Needs employees, minimum age 18, for ride operations; cashiering, games, gifts, food service; grounds quality; parking lots; and more. Salaries competitive. Work 6-8 hours, 6 days/week. Discounts at most restaurants in park. Apply by mid-May; write or call Santa Cruz Beach Boardwalk, Dept. SED, Box 625, Santa Cruz CA 95061; tel. 408/423-5590.

Fringe Benefits: Opportunity to meet people from all over the world, free city transit to and from work.

Government

Department of Energy
Naval Petroleum Reserve, Jobs available at the regional office, Box 11, Tupman CA 93276. Applications must be made to Washington DC office. See Washington DC office (District of Columbia section) for complete descriptions of jobs available and how to apply information.

Department of Labor, Jobs available at this regional office, Federal Office Building, Room 10028, 450 Golden Gate Ave., San Francisco CA 94102. Office serves Arizona, California, Hawaii and Nevada. Applications must be made to Washington DC office. See Washington DC office (District of Columbia section) for complete descriptions of jobs available and how to apply information.

Environmental Intern Program/California, Located in San Francisco. Openings all year—mostly summer. Needs 120 college students for over 30 different positions/disciplines per year; field research and office research positions, 3 years college minimum, $140-250. Will hire physically handicapped depending on academic training. Send for application by March 2 (for summer employment) to Mr. Rob Lawrence, Regional Director, EIP/ California, Dept SED, 681 Market Street, San Francisco CA 94105.

Fringe Benefits: "Excellent learning experiences with creative professionals; opportunity to attend workshops and meetings relating to career training as part of participation." **College credit** possible.

National Transportation Safety Board, Jobs available at the regional office in Los Angeles. Applications must be made to Washington DC office. See Washington DC office (District of Columbia section) for descriptions of jobs available and how to apply information.

Nuclear Regulatory Commission, Jobs available at the regional office in San Francisco. Applications must be made to Washington DC office. See Washington DC office (District of Columbia section) for descriptions of jobs available and how to apply information.

Resorts, Ranches, Restaurants, Lodging

Boulder Lodge Inc., Located at June Lake. Motel and housekeeping apartments. Openings for college students and teachers, minimum age 19, for any three-month period, year round. BUNAC full-time students with social security number are most welcome to apply. Needs 6 maids for cleaning. Salaries to start at $3.25/hour; room with kitchen at $15/week rent. Bonus for full term through September 9. Enclose SASE for application. Apply by June 1 to D.M. Oldfield, Boulder Lodge Inc., Dept. SED, Box 68, June Lake CA 93529.

Summer Camps

Bearskin Meadow, Located in Kings Canyon National Park. Coed camp for children, ages 6-18, full program with diabetes care and education. Openings for college students and teachers from July to August, four 2-week sessions. Needs 10 specialty counselors for music, drama, woodwork, field sports, ceramics, leather craft; 5 cabin counselors. Some types of medical and nursing experience accredited. Apply by April to Diabetic Youth Foundation, 1128 Irving St., San Francisco CA 94122.

Big Bear, Located near Big Bear Lake. Youth co-ed camp. Openings from June 15 to September 5. Needs 4 waterfront staff (college students, teachers, local applicants preferred), WSI, First Aid required, $100-$150/week; 3 kitchen personnel, (college students, teachers, local applicants preferred), experience with group food preparation, $80-$250/week; and 2 maintenance personnel (college students, teachers, local applicants preferred), $75-125/week. Hires physically handicapped students. Send for application by March to Gary McCord, Camp Director, PO Box 1516, Dept. SED, Big Bear Lake CA 92315.
Fringe Benefits: College credit possible.

Bloomfield, Located in Malibu. Camp for blind, deaf and partially sighted children. Foundation for the Junior Blind. Openings for 60 to 70 college students and teachers from mid-June to August 31. Needs counselors, $350; nurse (RN), $750-850; office-programmer-secretary, $650; food service manager, $600. Apply to Dr. Norman Kaplan, Executive Director, Foundation for the Junior Blind, 5300 Angeles Vista Blvd., Los Angeles CA 90043.

Boys' Club of Hollywood—Camp 365, Located at Running Springs. Camp and conference center. Openings for college students and teachers from June 15 to August 30. Needs 12 counselors, $500-600; 2 crafts directors, 2 aquatics directors, $500-600; 2 naturalists, $500-600; registered nurse, salary open. Room and board provided. Apply by May 1 to John Yingling, Boys' Club of Hollywood, Dept. SED., Box 751, Running Springs CA 92382.
Fringe Benefits: Free postage and laundry. This is a modern camp (not primitive) with a "great climate and environment (altitude 6,500 ft.), situated in a National Forest." **College credit** possible.

Calamigos Star C Ranch, Summer Camp, Located in Malibu. Resident summer camp with major emphasis on horseback riding and water activities (pool and ocean). Openings for college students, teachers and local

applicants from June 22 to September 4. Salary range: $90-125/week. Needs 4 swimming instructors (Red Cross Program, WSI); 6 horseback riding instructors (CHA certificate preferred); 2 arts and crafts instructors. Room and board provided. Send for application. Apply before April 30 to Darrow Milgrim, Director, Calamigos Star C Ranch, Dept. SED, 327 So. Latigo Canyon Rd., Malibu CA 90265.
Fringe Benefits: College credit or internship programs available.

Cielo, Located at San Marcos Pass, Santa Barbara. Camp Fire resident camp for children ages 6-18. Openings from July to mid-August. Needs assistant camp director/program director, minimum age 21, (SLS, CPR, and First Aid preferred); unit director, minimum age 21; general counselor, minimum age 18; leadership training director, waterfront director, (must have CPR, First Aid, and WSI); waterfront assistant (WSI, CPR and First Aid required); handcraft specialist; archery specialist; outdoor specialist; horseback riding specialist; business manager (Class II license required); nurse (licensed in California); head cook; assistant cook; kitchen assistants; foods and equipment supervisor. Salaries $250-800/season, depending on position and experience. Room and board provided. Apply by June 30 to Judy S. Hoskins, Executive Director, Camp Fire, Inc., Dept. SED, Box 5363, Oxnard CA 93031; tel. 805/485-3417 or 659-2642.
Fringe Benefits: "Beautiful facility"; short working season (5-6 weeks). **College credit** possible.

Harmon Easter Seal, Located near Boulder Creek. Camp for physically and mentally handicapped children and adults, ages 8-60, in separate sessions. ACA accreditation. Openings for college students and teachers from June 17 to August 23, orientation June 13 to June 15. Needs unit directors (minimum age 21, 3 years college), program directors (minimum age 21, 3 years college): pool/water safety, arts and crafts, lodge/special and evening programs, nature/waterfront/boating and fishing, animal farm, campfire/drama; counselors (minimum age 19, 1 year college), head cook (minimum age 25), assistant cook (minimum age 21), supplementary staff (minimum age 19), kitchen aides, kitchen maintenance, maintenance, laundress. Room and board provided. Apply by April to Kathryn Parodi, Executive Director, Easter Seal Society of Santa Cruz County, Box 626, Santa Cruz CA 95061.
Fringe Benefits: Travel expenses paid in part to foreign counselors. **College credit** possible.

Mariastella, Located at Wrightwood, in the San Gabriel Mountains. Camp for girls, ages 8-16; coed deaf, ages 7-14; coed EMR, ages 10-40. Openings for college students, teachers and high school seniors from mid-June to end of August. Needs 25 cabin counselors, $225-475/season; 4 program specialists: arts and crafts, waterfront, nature, $400-500/season; nurse (RN), $100/week. "All applicants are personally contacted." Apply by mid-April to Sister Patricia McGowan, Director, Camp Mariastella, 1120 Westchester Pl., Los Angeles CA 90019.
Fringe Benefits: "A creative, Christian experience in cooperative, outdoor living." **College credit** available.

May-Mac, Located in Tahoma on Lake Tahoe. Camp for underprivileged children ages 9-14 from the San Jose area. Openings for college students from June 10 to August 31. Needs 12 counselors (minimum 1 year of college), waterfront director (minimum 1 year college), 3 arts and craft counselors (teaching pottery, leather, other craft projects); voluntary, no payment. Also needs 2 food service directors (minimum 1 year experience); tips only. Room and board provided. Send resume or application request. Apply by March 31 to Harry Brown, Program Director, Dept. SED, Box 143, San Jose CA 95103; tel. 408/998-7400.

Mendocino, Located in Fort Bragg. San Francisco Boys' Club; resident camp for boys and girls ages 6-14; approximately 250 campers every two weeks. Openings from June 13 to August 27. Needs 24 cabin leaders, college students, teachers, foreign students, $600/season; 1 chef, $1,200/season; 1 first cook,$800/season; 1 second cook, $600/season, must know how to cook for 400; 1 horse corral manager, college student or teacher preferred, $1,000/season; 1 lifeguard (WSI), $800/season; 1 RN, $1,000/season. Room and board provided. Apply to Les Andersen, Executive Director, San Francisco Boys' Club Camp Mendocino, 1950 Page St., San Francisco CA 94117; tel. 415/221-0790.
Fringe Benefits: Four days off during the summer; medical insurance provided. **College credit** possible.

Murrieta for Girls
Del Mar for Boys, Located in Washington, California, Texas, Wisconsin, Pennsylvania, Virginia and New England. Weight loss, nutrition education, and sports fitness camps for people ages 8-21. Needs college-age counselors, $500 and up; nutritionist, $1,000 and up; sports specialists; administrative personnel. *Qualified applicants must be able to interview in state where camp is located.* Send for application c/o Dave Kempton, Camp Murrieta/Camp Del Mar, Dept. SED, 8245 Ronson Rd., Suite D, San Diego CA 92111.

Nawakwa, Located in the San Bernardino Mountains of Southern California. Camp Fire summer resident camp for girls ages 6-17 and boys ages 6-14. (Camp Fire is a not-for-profit United Way youth agency.) Program emphasis: hiking, campcraft, singing, swimming, canoeing, crafts, informal sports, some horseback riding and advanced backpacking. Needs 35 staff from mid-June to end of August. Positions available: 6 unit directors, minimum age 21, need counseling experience, $800/season; 18 counselors, age 19, $600-750/season; program specialists in arts/crafts, waterfront, nature, and campcraft, $600-800/season; driver, $600-750/season; cooks with institutional experience, $1,000-1,800/season. Room and board provided. "We hire experienced, patient counselors looking for a challenging, rewarding, and tough summer." Write for an application and reference forms, more job details, and description of camp. Three written references required. Apply by March 31 for best chance of being hired. Interview at office in Claremont if at all possible; otherwise telephone interview. Apply to: Jan Matson, Camp Director, Mt. San Antonio Council of Camp Fire, 951 W. Foothill Blvd., Claremont CA 91711.

Okizu, Located in Nevada City. Coed Camp Fire camp for children ages 6-17. Openings for college students and teachers from mid-June to August. Needs assistant camp director, 6 waterfront/boating (WSI, ARC, small craft), program director; 5 program specialists: nature, campcraft, archery, crafts, backpacking; 22 unit counselors, 6 unit directors, male and female. Room and board provided. Apply by June 30 to Camp Okizu, Dept. SED, 2745 Downer, Richmond CA 94804; tel. 415/232-8765.

Fringe Benefits: Good working conditions; "experience for those who will be working with children or in social work after graduation"; a "feeling of self-worth."

Colorado

1,620+ jobs available

Commercial Attractions

Santa's Workshop, Located in North Pole. Openings for 55 college students, teachers and high school seniors from mid-May to December 25, but mostly during summer. Needs salesclerks, cashiers, office help, ride operators, parking lot attendants, warehouse workers. Salary is $2.60/hour plus bonus to those on contract; some higher without bonus. Apartments available in Colorado Springs. Apply by April 15 to Personnel Manager, Santa's Workshop, North Pole CO 80809.

Government

Department of Energy
Grand Junction Office, Jobs available in this regional office, Box 2567, Grand Junction CO 81501. Applications must be made to Washington DC office. See Washington DC office (District of Columbia section) for complete descriptions of jobs available and how to apply information.

Department of Energy
Western Area Power Administration, Jobs available in this regional office, ATTN: A1200, Golden CO 80401. Applications must be made to Washington DC office. See Washington DC office (District of Columbia section) for complete descriptions of jobs available and how to apply information.

Department of Labor, Jobs available at the regional office, Federal Office Building, Room 15412, 1961 Stout St., Denver CO 80294. Office serves Colorado, Montana, North Dakota, South Dakota, Utah and Wyoming. Applications must be made to Washington DC office. See Washington DC office (District of Columbia section) for complete descriptions of jobs available and how to apply information.

National Transportation Safety Board, Jobs available at the regional office in Denver. Applications must be made to Washington DC office. See Washington DC office (District of Columbia section) for descriptions of jobs available and how to apply information.

National Parks

Rocky Mountain Park Company, Located in Estes Park. National park concessioner. Openings for college students from Memorial Day to October 15. Needs 25 food service, 5 stockkeeping, 50 sales. Salaries are $400/month less room and board. Bonus and/or merit pay awarded. Apply by May 1 to Rocky Mountain Park Company, Box 1020, Estes Park CO. 80517.

Resorts, Ranches, Restaurants, Lodging

Aspen Lodge & Guest Ranch, Located in Estes Park. Guest ranch. Openings from June 1 to September 1 for US high school and college students to 21 years of age. Needs 19 young men as waiters, cabin attendants, dishwashers, kitchen helpers, lifeguard and wranglers; also needs 2 young ladies as baker and babysitter. Salaries are $175/month; also equal-split tips amounting to about $1,000 for entire summer. Room and board provided. Apply before June 1 to Mrs. Peggy Adams, Aspen Lodge & Guest Ranch, Long's Peak Rte., Estes Park CO 80517; tel. 303/586-4241.
Fringe Benefits: "Each employee during the summer shares equally in the tips." **College credit** possible.

Bar Lazy J Guest Ranch, Located in Parshall. Openings for college students and high school seniors from May 1 to September 30. Needs waitresses, counselors, cabin maids, relief employee, laundress, dishwashers, yard worker, wranglers, cook's helpers. Salaries dependent on age and experience. Room, board, tips and bonus provided. Laundry done weekly for free; towels and linens furnished. Attitude and willingness to work and learn are more important than experience. Room and board provided. Apply by June 30 to Chuck Broady, Bar Lazy J Guest Ranch, Box NDS, Parshall CO 80468.
Fringe Benefits: College credit possible.

Coffee Bar Restaurant, Located in Estes Park, near Rocky Mountain National Park. Restaurant. Openings for 36 college students, teachers, high school seniors and foreign students, minimum age 18, from May 1 to October 15. Must be able to stay through Labor Day. Needs waitresses, hostesses, bus boys, kitchen helpers, dishwashers, fry cooks. Wages are hourly. "Can arrange for housing at a cost of $23/week." Write for additional information; enclose large SASE. Apply by May 15 to Manager, Coffee Bar Restaurant, Dept. SED, Box 2210, Estes Park CO 80517.

Daven Haven Lodge, Located at Grand Lake Resort. Lodging, restaurant, lounge. Openings for college students, teachers and high school seniors from mid-May to mid-October. Needs 15 waitresses/waiters, 2 cocktail waitresses, $150-200; 8 bus boys, 10 maids, $125-350; 2 bartenders, $325-475;

10 kitchen help, $250-375, 2 maintenance, $125-350; entertainer (piano), salary open. Room and board provided. Enclose SASE when writing for application. Apply by April 15 to Daven Haven Lodge, Box 528, Grand Lake CO 80447.
Fringe Benefits: Resort atmosphere; staff parties. **College credit** possible.

Drowsy Water Guest Ranch, Located in Granby. Openings from May 15 to September 14. Needs 3 maids, 3 waitresses, 2 yard-maintenance, 1 children's counselor, 2 dishwashers, college students and high school seniors preferred, $150/month; 4 wranglers, college students preferred; 1 cook, college student or teacher preferred. Room, board plus tips provided. Apply to Randy Sue Fosha, Owner, Drowsy Water Ranch, Box 147 J, Granby CO 80446; tel. 303/725-3456.
Fringe Benefits: "A great summer experience meeting and entertaining people from all over the world."

Imperial Hotel and Imperial Players, Located in Cripple Creek. Hotel, restaurant, theater. Openings for 45 college students, teachers and high school seniors, minimum age 18, from mid-May through mid-September. Needs actors, actresses, $100/week; young pianist, $150/week and up; hotel maids, pantry personnel, kitchen personnel, desk clerks, salary; busboys, bartenders, waiters, waitresses, salary and excellent tip opportunity for competent personnel. Room and board provided. Enclose SASE when writing for application. Apply by May 15 to Wayne S. Mackin, Imperial Hotel and Imperial Players, 123 3rd St., Cripple Creek CO 80813.
Fringe Benefits: End-of-season bonus. **College credit** possible. "Excellent rapport with 70 young people, theater atmosphere, music, arts, etc. Professional experience in bartending, cooking, cashiering, etc. Excellent source of work references for the future."

Lazy H Ranch, Located in Allenspark. Guest ranch. Openings from May 1 to September 30. Needs 5 wranglers, $200-250/month; 2 cooks, $250/month; 2 waiters/waitresses, 2 housekeepers, 2 dishwashers, 1-2 counselors, 1-2 maintenance persons, $175/month. Room, board and $200 per month tips provided. "Applicants should be prepared to work hard, long hours, live with those they work with, be outgoing, enjoy meeting and being with people, plan to stay as long as they stipulate." Apply to Bill Halligan, Manager, Lazy H Ranch, Box 2489, Allenspark CO 80510; tel. 303/747-2532.
Fringe Benefits: Fringe benefits are "the friendships formed over the summer season between members of the staff—not only amongst themselves, but with guests; also, the hard work and the strength of character that goes with it." **College credit** possible.

Longs Peak Inn and Guest Ranch, Located at Estes Park. Dude ranch. Openings for 40 college students, teachers, high school seniors and foreign students, minimum age 18, from late May to October 1. Must be able to stay at least through Labor Day. Needs waitresses/waiters, hostess, desk clerk/secretary, maintenance workers, dishwashers, cooks, kitchen helpers, maids, children's counselor, bartender, entertainer, wrangler. Room and board

provided. Write for additional information and application form; enclose large SASE. Apply by May 15 to Bob Akins, Dept. SED, Longs Peak Inn, Longs Peak Route, Estes Park CO 80517.
Fringe Benefits: "Beautiful location;" bonuses provided. **College credit** possible.

Peaceful Valley Lodge and Guest Ranch, Located in Lyons.

Openings for 45 college students, teachers and high school seniors from mid-May through September. Needs waitresses, office assistants, secretary, counselors, driver-mechanics, wranglers, stable hands, general ranch hand-maintenance, housekeepers, gardener, cooks, cook's helpers, dishwashers. Salaries open. During the winter season, needs persons capable of and certified in instructing cross-country ski touring; person or persons to man snow-making equipment. Room and board provided. Apply before April 1 to Karl E. Boehm, Peaceful Valley Lodge and Guest Ranch, Dept. SED, Star Route, Lyons CO 80540.
Fringe Benefits: End-of-season bonus. **College credit** possible. "A learning and growing experience; Christian fellowship. Good working conditions. Participation in the ranch activities with guests (i.e., horseback riding; four-wheel drive trips; BBQs; breakfast rides; pack trips, for an extra charge; skiing; swimming and square dancing)."

Snow Mountain Ranch, Located in Granby. YMCA conference and

family vacation center. Openings from Memorial Day to Labor Day. Needs 25 housekeepers, 30 foodservice personnel, 6 office workers (secretarial skills), 15 maintenance, 20 counselors. Salaries are $240/month. Room and board provided. Offers some year-round employment. Hires physically handicapped students or teachers but "terrain is a problem with wheelchair persons." Send for application form. Apply by May 15 to Richard Engle, Managing Director, Box 558, Dept. SED, Granby CO 80446.
Fringe Benefits: Good working conditions, opportunity to meet interesting people, end-of-the-season bonus. **College credit** available.

Sun Valley Guest Ranch, Located at Grand Lake. Openings from

May 15 to October 1. Needs 3 kitchen helpers, cabin maids, laundry worker, wranglers, general ranch hand-maintenance, hay hands. Salaries are dependent on age and experience. Room, board and tips provided. Apply to Ken Bruton, Sun Valley Guest Ranch, Box 470, Grand Lake CO 80447.

Tamarron Inn and Golf Club, Located 18 miles north of Durango.

Resort hotel, condominiums and convention center. Openings from April 1 to October 30, November 1 to March 30. Needs personnel in the following areas: housekeeping (training program); kitchen crew (clean up); kitchen staff (chefs, cooks, sauciers, broilermen, pastry chefs, pantry workers, and stewards), must have previous experience in large kitchen, restaurant or hotel; desk clerks (light typing and some computer knowledge helpful); cashiers (typing and 10-key adding machine knowledge, previous background experience in handling money); general office (secretaries, clerk-typists, file clerks, payroll clerks, accounting clerks, stenographers, all require previous experience and skills); hostess and waitress (must be 21, 1 year previous experience); waiters (must be

21, 1 year previous experience); bus persons (must be over 16, 1 year previous experience); maintenance (assist plumbers, electricians, carpenters, etc., knowledge essential); grounds and golf course maintenance (driver's license, minimum age 18, previous experience). Other positions available: recreation leaders and assistants, auditors, mail clerks, activity desk clerks, babysitters, convention setup crew, banquet waiters and waitresses, bartenders, PBX operators, security guards, bellmen, drivers, spa attendants, golf and tennis clerks, stable wranglers, shipping and receiving clerks. No housing provided; housing lists are available in personnel department. Pay varies with position and experience. Write for application form to Adelle Anderson, Director of Personnel, Drawer 3131, Durango CO 81301; tel. 303/247-8801.

Tumbling River Ranch, Located in Grant. Guest ranch serving families. Openings for 30 college students (minimum age 19) and teachers from mid-May through September. Needs waitresses, cabin girls, cooks, assistant cooks, secretary, children's counselors, drivers, mechanics, wranglers, general maintenance persons, groundskeepers. Payment is monthly (plus tips). Also needs winter help (October through March or mid-April), and year-round help. In winter, needs 10-12 persons as cooks, cabin girls, waitresses, mechanics, general maintenance. Room and board provided. Applications must be in by March 15 for summer, by September 1 for winter; "state season you are applying for." Apply to Jim and Mary Dale Gordon, Tumbling River Ranch, Grant CO 80448; tel. 303/838-5981.
Fringe Benefits: Can room in bunk houses, individual buildings or in main ranch houses (2 persons/room; 4/bath). **College credit** possible. This guest ranch offers a "family atmosphere with close-knit staff and owners," and the opportunity to learn lots of jobs.

Vail Associates, Located in Vail. Ski mountain and summer resort serving young adults and middle-aged persons, including many Latin Americans and Europeans. Openings for college students and local applicants from November 15 to April 15 or June 1 to September 15; seasonal openings may lead to year-round employment. Needs for winter: cashiers, cooks, waiters/ waitresses, dishwashers, buspersons, food handlers, snow removal, parking attendants, bus drivers, janitors, ticket sellers, nursery attendants, ski rental/ repair persons, lift operators and ticket checkers. Limited summer positions; needs laborers, general and grounds maintenance, and conventional help. "Local housing situation consists of condominiums, mobile homes, duplex and home rentals. Monthly rentals start at $200/person for shared housing (utilities included) and run to over $1,200/month for 3-4 bedroom places. As we have limited summer openings, our main employment emphasis is on winter seasonal employees. Candidates interested in winter employment should secure local housing early in September. Vail has more than 50 restaurants ranging from fast food to gourmet." Apply to Vail Associates, Inc., Box 7, Dept. SED, Vail CO 81657; tel. 303/476-5601.
Fringe Benefits: "Both Vail and Beaver Creek are world class ski resorts catering to international clientele; they are located in the Colorado Rockies—a 2-hour drive from Denver. Employees can enjoy the resort atmosphere, skiing on some of the finest terrain in the world, and the fine Colorado climate." **College credit** possible.

Wilderness Trails Ranch, Located in Bayfield. Guest ranch.
Openings from May 20 to September 12; can start as late as June 1 and leave as early as September 4. Needs 6 wrangler-trail guides and 2 youth wranglers, college students preferred; 10 kitchen and cabin maids, 1 babysitter and 1 laundry person, high school seniors or college students preferred; 1 kitchen supervisor, college students preferred; 1 foreman, college students or teachers preferred; and 1 girl's supervisor, college students or teachers preferred. "Our main objective is the well-being and happiness of our guests." Apply by March 1 to Gene and Jan Roberts, 776 County Rd. 300, Durango CO 81301; tel. 303/247-0722.

YMCA of The Rockies, Located at Estes Park Center and Snow Mountain Ranch. Family and conference center. Openings for college students, teachers, retired teachers and foreign students from June 1 to Labor Day. Earlier and later if possible; camps open year round. Needs 60 business office, shops, fountain persons; 80 program; 80 housekeeping; 40 buildings and grounds maintenance; 90 food service workers. Salaries are $240/month. Room and board provided. Apply by May to E. Eugene Garris, Managing Director, YMCA of the Rockies, Estes Park Center, Association Camp CO 80511.
Fringe Benefits: "Next to Rocky Mountain National Park. Christian atmosphere."

Summer Camps

Anderson "Western Colorado", Located in Gypsum. Private boys and girls-separate, ages 8-17. Needs 30 general counselors. Pay is $550/season; college students and teachers preferred. Also needs nurses and cooks. Work from first part of June to latter part of August. "Counselors must have at least two years of college and a sincere interest in working with children." Apply by April to Anderson Camps Ltd., Gypsum CO 81637; telephone (303)524-7766.
Fringe Benefits: "Travel allowance up to $50. Opportunity to go on numerous outcamp trips." **College credit** possible.

Bear Pole Ranch, Located in Steamboat Springs. Coed camp. Openings for college students and high school seniors from June 5 to August 15. Separate programs by age: discovery, 9-13; expedition, 13-15; adventure bound, 15-18. Needs 15 senior counselors, 10 assistant counselors, cook, assistant cooks, nurse, wrangler, assistant wranglers, secretary, ranch hand. Apply to Dr. and Mrs. Glenn N. Poulter, Bear Pole Ranch Camp, Steamboat Springs CO 80477.

Cheley Colorado Camps, Inc., Located in Estes Park. Four boys' camps, 4 girls' camps. Openings for 100 college students (minimum age 19 and completed sophomore college year) and teachers, from June 10 to August 10. Needs nurses (RN), secretaries, cooks and kitchen helpers; instructors for archery, fencing, tennis, Western riding and horsemanship, mountain hiking, out camping, backpacking, woodcraft, nature lore, riflery (NRA), handcrafts, group

singing, land sports (no water sports offered); bus drivers, property maintenance. Salaries are $575 and up for season, based on experience. Room and board provided. Prefers applicants from Colorado, Texas, Arkansas, Oklahoma, Nebraska, Iowa, Illinois, Indiana, Missouri and Kansas. Staff employed only with personal interviews which are conducted during January and February in Midwest and South Central states; California interviews in December; interviews in Denver office until May 30. "We do most all of our hiring during the months of January, February, and March for the upcoming summer." Apply to D.S. Cheley, Dept. SED, Box 6525, Denver CO 80206.
Fringe Benefits: Insurance and travel allowance are provided. **College credit** available.

Colorado Outward Bound School, Located in Denver. Experiential education school. College students (over 21) and teachers preferred. Employment June, July, August (limited). Needs 16 assistant instructors (to start), $475/month plus food check and basecamp; 32 instructors (after one season as assistant), $575-750/month. "Applicants must meet some mountaineering skills criteria, plus have first aid card, experience at lead rock climbing, teaching experience in some capacity. Looking for qualified women especially." Apply by February 15 to Program Director, Dept. SED, Colorado Outward Bound School, 945 Pennsylvania St., Denver CO 80203; tel. 303/837-0880.
Fringe Benefits: College credit possible.

Colvig Silver Camps, Located near Durango. Coed camps. Openings for college students, teachers, high school seniors and foreign students for 10 weeks from mid-June to mid-August. Needs 45 head counselors, $500 up; 15 assistant counselors, $450; wrangler, salary open; nurse (RN), $750; 3 cooks, $750 up. Expedition trips to four states require special emphasis on outdoor living skills: woodsmanship, mountaineering, nature, archaeology and geology, crafts, horsemanship, backpacking, river rafting, riflery (NRA), swimming (WSI), archery, land sports. Room and board provided. Apply by March 1 to Craig Colvig, 9665 Florida Rd., CCD, Durango CO 81301.
Fringe Benefits: Health insurance provided. **College credit** available.

Easter Seal, Camp for physically and mentally handicapped children and young adults. Openings for college students, teachers and high school seniors from early June through late August. Need counselors, cooks, kitchen help, maintenance and maintenance helpers, nurse and specialty counselors for riding, swimming, crafts. Room and board provided. Apply by May 15 to Easter Seal Society of Colorado, Dept. SED, 609 W. Littleton Blvd., Room 300, Littleton CO 80120.
Fringe Benefits: "Easter Seal offers a good opportunity for growth through experiences, and a fantastic physical setting." **College credit** available.

Elephant Rock, Located on Palmer Lake, 50 miles south of Denver. Coed camp for youth, ages 8-12 and seniors. Openings for college students from June 20 to August 30. Needs program director; cook, up to $750; lifeguard, up to $500; 8 counselors, up to $450; maintenance, up to $350;

nurse, up to $750; assistant cook, up to $600. Room and board provided. Apply before March 15 to Divisional Youth Director, The Salvation Army, Box 2369, Denver CO 80201.

Flying G Ranch
Tomahawk Ranch, Located in central Colorado mountains, southwest of Denver. Girl Scout camps for girls ages 7-17. Openings from June to August. Needs troop leaders, $585-810/season; counselors, $360-540/season; riding staff, $360-850/season; nurses, $675-1,014/season; kitchen staff, $360-1,250/season; program specialists, $400-675/season; administrators, $500-1,350/season; maintenance, $675-900/season. Salaries subject to change. Request application January through May, from Girl Scouts, Mile Hi Council, 2727 Bryant St., Denver CO 80211.
Fringe Benefits: "A rewarding learning experience for resourceful individuals who enjoy working with children and living outdoors in a semi-primitive setting."

Geneva Glen Camps, Inc., Located at Indian Hills, 20 miles
southwest of Denver. Coed camp for children ages 8-16. ACA accredited; 48th year of operation. Openings for 60 college students from June 9 to August 9. Needs counselors with experience working with children; skills in counseling and leading children and a love of children essential. Skills in swimming, archery, horsemanship, music, crafts and riflery are helpful but not required. Counselors earn $450-550/season. Room and board provided. "Leadership and personal growth of the staff are a part of the camp philosophy." Other staff needs are nurse, $700/summer; 6 cooks, $500-700, based on experience; 5 maintenance crew persons, $300 and up; director of maintenance, salary based on experience and skills. Apply by April 1 to Robert and Carol Duvall, Directors, Geneva Glen Camps, Inc., Dept. SED, Box 248, Indian Hills CO 80454.
Fringe Benefits: Health and accident insurance provided; travel allowance for out-of-state employees provided. **College credit** available. Also, the camps offer "a tremendous leadership program for staff," a "supportive environment" and a close-knit staff. "We encourage all to get to know and understand each other."

Holy Cross, Located in Canon City. "A summer camp in the San Isabel National Forest for boys ages 9-14 from upper-middle-class families who come from all over America but mostly Texas, Oklahoma, Colorado, Kansas, New Mexico, Arizona and California. Teaches "the appreciation of the outdoors and the adventures of horsepacking and backpacking" Facilities include a large cookhouse with craft rooms and 10 cabins for 50 campers plus the lodge house and stables with 30 horses, a fishing pond, riflery and archery. Openings for college students from June 19 to August 4. Needs 6 counselors for groups of 15 boys each (WSI, first-aid); 3 backpack counselors to direct backpack trips in the Sangre de Cristo Mountains (first-aid); 1 full time nurse (to also teach crafts); 2 arts and crafts teachers to also work in sports. Salary range: $400-600/season. Room and board provided. "Applicants should be interested in young boys and able to take on any type of jobs in the mountains. Have good leadership with young men." Send for application form. Apply by March

31 to Brother Mark Cumrine, O.S.B., Director, Camp Holy Cross, Box 351, Dept. SED, Canon City CO 81212; tel. 303/275-8631.

Kotami, Located at Foxton in the Rocky Mountains. Resident coed camp for children ages 8-17. Openings for both males and females from June 7 to August 10. Needs assistant director, $90-100/week; nurse (LPN, RN, or GN), $80-90/week; cook and assistant cook, $75-100/week; 5 wranglers, specialists in archery, rock climbing, nature, arts & crafts, 10 unit counselors, $50/week; 7-10 junior counselor/kitchen aides, $30/week. "Applicants do not necessarily have to be college students or teachers; however, they are preferred. I am most impressed by a good healthy attitude toward children, the out-of-doors and new learning experiences. A strongly independent, co-operative (team oriented), positive, enthusiastic person has a better chance at the job than one with much experience and a blase attitude. Sell yourself!" Room and board provided. Send for application or send resume. Apply by April 15 (foreign applicants, by March 15, because of slow mail) to Nevada Brown, Associate Executive Director, Camp Fire, Inc., Dept. SED, 2901 W. 19th Ave., Denver CO 80204.
Fringe Benefits: "Kotami is located on a beautiful piece of mountain country (376 acres). Working here provides excellent experience for future resume material, dynamite co-workers and end-of-season bonus for remaining on the staff full term—it's *loads* of fun and a *real growing experience!*"
College credit possible.

Lazy Acres, Located in Rye. Girl Scout camp. Openings for college students and teachers from mid-June to early August. Needs camp director, 4 unit leaders, 7 counselors, assistant camp director, CIT director (minimum age 21), program specialist, handyman, kitchen personnel, nurse (RN). Room and board provided. Apply to Camp Lazy Acres, Columbine Girl Scout Council, 21 Montebello, Pueblo CO 81001.
Fringe Benefits: College credit possible. "This is a small camp so each staff member can get to know everyone on the staff. Available are lots of outdoor living possibilities, such as overnights and cookouts in the beautiful setting of the Colorado Rockies."

Sanborn Western Camps, Located 35 miles west of Colorado Springs. Two private western ranch camps, Big Spring Ranch for Boys and High Trails Ranch for Girls, ages 8-16. Openings available for qualified men and women from June 4 to August 21. Minimum requirements are 20 years of age and 2 years of college. Needs 2 nurses (RN); 4 cooks, $700; 60 counselors in backpacking, riding, nature, fishing, hiking, campcraft, all sports, crafts, geology, tennis, water sports, $500 and up. Room and board provided. Please state

---

Each summer the US government hires thousands of undergraduate and graduate students for jobs from clerk-typists to highly technical fields. See the District of Columbia listings and also US government listings in individual states.

qualifications and experience in inquiry. Apply by May to Roger A. Sanborn, Florissant CO 80816.
Fringe Benefits: Insurance and laundry are provided. **College credit** available. "Staff members have the opportunity for a rich and fulfilling summer. They learn a great deal about working with children, about the out-of-doors, and about themselves."

Shady Brook, Located in Sedalia. Resident, ages 8-15. Needs 16 counselors ($50-65/week), 1 cook ($200/week), 4 program specialists ($75/week), college students and teachers preferred; 1 nurse ($100/week); program director (for Catamount Ranch). Work June 11 to August 24. Apply to Dick Conrad, Director of Camping Services, Camp Shady Brook, Pikes Peak Y/USO, Box 1694, Colorado Springs CO 80901; telephone (303)471-9790.

Sky High Ranch, Located in Woodland Park. Girl Scout camp for girls ages 6-17. Openings for college students and teachers from June 14 to August 10. Needs riding director, 7 unit leaders, business manager, waterfront director, $93-120/week; 12 unit assistants, assistant cook, 2 riding assistants, trading post manager, $69-89/week. Apply to Gail H. Gurney, Wagon Wheel Girl Scouts, 518 N. Nevada, Colorado Springs CO 80903.

Trojan Ranch Summer Camp, Located in mountains west of Boulder. Camp for children ages 6-16. Openings for college students, teachers, high school graduates over 18 and local applicants. "Our major qualifications are that applicants be over 18 and have an honest interest in working with children, boundless enthusiasm and energy, and the ability to work well with both adults and children." Needs 4-6 cabin counselors to live in cabins with children; 8-12 day camp group counselors; 8-15 activities instructors in water safety, archery, riflery, handcrafts, nature crafts, nature lore, gardening, gymnastics, trampoline, games, sports, drama, horses, hiking, camping; kitchen help and bus drivers. Salaries $200-500 for summer depending on position and experience. Send for application by April 15 (out of state) or May 15 (local) to Lynn Walker, Program Director, Box 711, Boulder CO 80306; tel. 303/442-4557.
Fringe Benefits: "Trojan Ranch offers the opportunity to work in a warm, friendly community of children and adults in a beautiful mountain setting overlooking the Continental Divide." **College credit** possible.

Summer Theaters

Central City Opera House Association, Located in Denver. Summer theater involved in the production of opera, theater, dance and jazz, and in the historic preservation of 35 historical buildings. Needs 3 box office helpers for ticket sales and distribution including phone, mailings and walk-up, $125-175/week (May 15 to August 30); 12 ushers/maintenance workers for performance usherings, general maintenance, gardening, painting, plumbing, carpentry, $125/week; 7 tour guides/housekeepers for tours of historic museums, housekeeping for residences of artists, $125/week; 2 hotel assistants for clerk duty, switchboard, housekeeping, bookwork, $125/week; (all from May

25 to September 3). Housing provided. Kitchen available; food $5/day. Also possible year-round restoration work. Send for application. Apply by February 28 to Operations Manager, Central City Opera House Association, 910 16th St., Suite 636, Denver CO 80427; tel. 303/623-7167.
Fringe Benefits: "Picturesque Victorian town in the Colorado Rockies. On-site interaction with artists makes for interesting and educational summer."
College credit possible.

Connecticut

3,673+ jobs available

Business and Industry

Aubrey Thomas Inc., Located in Stamford. Temporary and permanent personnel agency. Works with over 100 major corporations in the lower Fairfield County area. Openings for full-time and part-time help from May 1 to September 15. Needs 250 typists, 250 secretaries, 200 gal/man Fridays, 100 receptionists, 100 clerk-typists, 100 accounting clerks and 100 word processors. Never a fee charged to applicants. Apply in person at 777 Summer St., Stamford CT 06902; tel. 203/357-0808; 167 East Ave., Norwalk CT; tel. 203/866-5556.

Electrolux Corporation, Located in Stamford. Unlimited openings in direct selling for college students, teachers and high school seniors during the summer and year round. Pays commission plus sales prizes and cash bonuses of $2,000, $1,250, $750 and $500 to qualified collegiate sales-makers. Apply to Norma Leitner, Electrolux College Program, 3003 Summer St., Stamford CT 06905.

Overseas Custom-Maid Agency, Inc., Located in Stamford. Employment agency. Places college students from April/May/June through September. Offers 500 openings for "Mother's Helpers" with families in metropolitan New York and New England—some with families traveling to resort areas. Duties are mainly child care and light housekeeping. Swimming and driving ability helpful. Salaries are $110-120/week; premium wage for cooks. Room and board provided. Employer pays airfare to the job. Employee responsible for own transportation home at end of assignment. There is no fee of any kind for any applicant to pay. Write in January or February enclosing SASE. Apply to Mrs. Henrietta E. Burnett, Overseas Custom-Maid Agency, Inc., 300 Bedford St., Stamford CT 06901; tel. 203/324-9575.

Summer Camps

Association of Independent Camps, Camps located in New England and Middle Atlantic States. Openings at 80 children's summer camps. Needs head counselors, group leaders, general and all specialty counselors.

Room and board provided. Apply by July to Association of Independent Camps, Dept. SED, 157 W. 57th St., New York NY 10019; tel. 212/582-3540.
Fringe Benefits: "Travel expenses paid in part or full; learning experiences, i.e., living and sharing with others; complete camp facilities in a healthy environment; time for socialization with peers." **College credit** "may be arranged by student at school."

Awosting for Boys
Chinqueka for Girls, Awosting is located at Bantam Lake; Chinqueka, Mt. Tom Lake. Independent camps for children ages 6-16. ACA, Connecticut accredited. Openings from June 22 to August 22. Needs counselors: 12 waterfront (WSI certified, includes instructors in sailing, synchronized swimming, rowing, canoeing, waterskiing, and scuba—must be qualified to teach swimming and 1 other specialty), 8 athletic, 2 riflery (NRA), 2 pioneering, 2 dramatic, 2 newspaper, 2 go-carting, 2 mini bike, 4 tennis, 1 modern dance, 2 archery (certified), 2 arts and crafts (fine arts), 2 shop work (woodwork, plastics), 2 gymnastics, 2 fencing, 1 music, 2 trampoline. College students (minimum age 19) and school teachers preferred. Salaries are $475-750/season plus tips. "If possible send resume, references, etc. We are seeking well-qualified counselors who like children and enjoy camp life. We welcome applicants from any place in the United States. We are also international camps. Knowledge of Spanish, German, French an added asset." Also needs 8 kitchen workers (college students, teachers and high school seniors preferred), $500/season; 2 assistant cooks, $1,800/season; 2 cooks, $2,500/season; 2 nurses (RN and LPN), $800/season. Room and board provided. "Preference given to experienced employees." For quick reply send SASE. Apply by April to Mr. and Mrs. Oscar Ebner, Directors, Awosting and Chinqueka, Dept. SED, Route 202, Bantam CT 06750; tel. 203/567-9678.
Fringe Benefits: Insurance and laundry provided. End-of-season bonus. **College credit** possible.

Birchwood, Located in West Goshen, Connecticut. Private, coed. Openings for college students and teachers for 8 weeks, starting about July 1. Needs 75 general counselors (minimum age 19), $150-300 plus tips; specialty counselors: 4 waterfront, $300-1,000; athletic, arts and crafts, ceramics, nature, etc. Room and board provided. Write for application. Apply to Laury Greenberg, Camp Birchwood, 140 Ash Dr., Roslyn NY 11576.
Fringe Benefits: Coed atmosphere. **College credit** available.

Buck's Rock, Located at New Milford, Connecticut. Creative work, coed, ages 12-16. Openings for graduate students, artists, teachers, craftsmen (minimum age 21), from late June to late August. Needs instructors for fine arts, crafts, commercial art, printing, performing arts, stage design and construction, folk music, folk dancing, science lab, sports, gymnastics, waterfront, electronics. Also needs kitchen, dining room, and maintenance staff (suitable for college students), and guidance counselors. Salaries are open. Room and board provided. Apply to Lou and Sybil Simon, Dept. SED, 140 Riverside Dr., New York NY 10024; tel. 212/362-2702.
Fringe Benefits: College credit possible. This camp offers "professional

studios and workshops, with an expert staff of artists, musicians, teachers and counselors."

Channel 3 Country Camp, Coed camp serving children ages 8-12 from families of low income, and others who pay according to family size and income. Openings for college students from June 21 to August 22. Counselors work with a group of six campers, $550-750; pool director (WSI, minimum age 21), $900; assistant pool director (WSI, minimum age 20), $750. Nonsmokers only. Room and board provided. Apply by May 1 to Edward F. Turn, Camp Director, Channel 3 Country Camp, RR1, Box 341, Andover CT 06232.
Fringe Benefits: Medical insurance provided. **College credit** available. This camp offers "experience working with children from families of low income—particularly helpful for those preparing for social work careers."

Connri, Located at Ashford. Salvation Army, coed, residential youth camp. Openings for college students, teachers and high school seniors from June to August. Needs junior and senior counselors, program director, specialty counselors (crafts, nature, waterfront, recreation), maintenance workers, kitchen help, laundry and housekeeping workers, nurse and relief nurse. Salaries are $250-750 and appropriate professional salaries. Room and board provided. Apply by June 1 to Divisional Youth Secretary, The Salvation Army, 855 Asylum Ave., Hartford CT 06101.
Fringe Benefits: Located in a "beautiful, wooded, natural camp setting."

Grand View Lodge, Located in Moodus. Summer camp offering "educational and recreational computing for all levels" for students ages 10-18. Openings from July 1 to August 20; can work for short duration of 2 weeks. Needs 5 counselors (college students preferred) to run sport-minded activities, $75/week. Room and board provided. Will hire physically handicapped students. Send resume by April 30 to Mike Flaks, Director, Box 22, Dept. SED, Moodus CT 06469.
Fringe Benefits: College credit possible.

Hadar, Located in Clinton. Private coed Jewish camp. Openings for 75 college students and teachers from June 26 to August 24. Needs counselors with specialties in sailing, canoeing, nature, archery, WSI, music, fencing, tennis; general counselors. Salaries are $300-1,000. Room and board provided. Apply by April 1 to Hal Watman, Camp Hadar, 435 Brooklawn Ave., Fairfield CT 06432.
Fringe Benefits: Laundry provided. **College credit** possible. "Hadar is just a highly-spirited, warm, *personal* kind of camp."

Ken-Mont for Boys
Ken-Wood for Girls, Brother-sister camps. Located in the Berkshire Mountains in New England on North Spectacle Lake, Kent, Connecticut. Openings for college seniors and teachers, minimum age 21, from approximately June 21 to August 20. Additional work available through August 31 for post-camp season. Needs counselors, group leaders, waterfront instructors (ARC or YMCA), specialty counselors, athletic counselors in all land

and water sports, bus drivers, secretaries, bookkeeping assistants, 2 physicians, 6 nurses (RN). Top salaries plus full maintenance; no tipping permitted. "Must have patience, positive feelings for children, and a love of the outdoors." Send resume to: Mr. and Mrs. Lloyd Albin, Ken-Mont and Ken-Wood Camps, 2 Spencer Place, Scarsdale NY 10583.

Laurelwood, Located in North Madison, 100 miles from New York City. Kosher (under Rabbinical supervision) coed camp for children ages 7-12 and teenagers ages 13-14. Needs counselors for a staff of 150. Apply to Norman J. Feitelson, Camp Laurelwood, 1156 Chapel St., New Haven CT 06511; tel. 203/624-2589.

Sloane YMCA, Located in Lakeville, Connecticut 06039. Coed; 500 children for nine-week season. Openings for college students, graduates and teachers, approximately June 22 to August 26. Staff of 160 people. Needs 40 general counselors with activity area skills, $575-625; 3-5 Section Heads and 4-6 Activity Heads (college graduates and teachers; couples OK) $900-1,200; WSI, RN, tripping, performing arts, riding, nature, crafts, sports, etc. Also needs clerks and maintenance help. Room and board provided. Apply early, as most of our positions are filled by returning staff members, and employees are hired for most remaining spots by Easter vacation. Apply no later than June 8, to Department SED, Camp Sloane YMCA, Inc., 344 Main Street, Mt. Kisco, New York 10549.
Fringe Benefits: College credit possible. "Excellent atmosphere; a chance to meet new friends. An outstanding reputation in camping built by an outstanding staff. 'We care and we listen.' "

United Cerebral Palsy Association of Greater Hartford,
Located on the Connecticut shore. Summer residential camp for physically disabled children, teenagers and adults. Openings for 8 weeks, June to August; college students, teachers, or local applicants preferred. Needs approximately 10 counselors, $80-100/week. Applicants "should be 18 years of age or older, mature and responsible and have a genuine interest in people. Experience in working with handicapped people is advisable but is not necessary. Counselors are first and foremost responsible for their campers. They are to see that campers are always comfortable, involved in the activities, and happy. They must also make sure that all the needs of all the campers are constantly met. This may include dressing, feeding, toilet needs, etc." Also needs 1 camp nurse, $1,200/season. "The camp nurse is responsible for the campers as well as the camp personnel. She must administer medication, keep records of illness or injury and assist staff in learning or receiving current first-aid methods. She must also evaluate the health and safety aspects of the camp and camp program." Also needs 1 assistant director, $1,100/season. College students or local applicants preferred. Must be presently attending or have already completed college with a future vocation in working with the physically disabled. "The assistant director is responsible for implementing and coordinating daily activities and for planning evening programs. He or she provides direct leadership to counselors and campers, maintains the program efficiency and insures the safety and happiness of each camper. Also must have a bus driver's

license." Also needs 1 director, $1,600/season. Must have a BS degree in recreation, physical education or special education with at least 2 years of experience working with the physically disabled, and 3 years in camp settings. "Responsibilities include developing and directing a summer camping program for physically disabled children, teenagers and adults afflicted with cerebral palsy and other multiple disabling conditions; and supervising a staff of 16 counselors, an assistant director and a nurse. Assisted by the Camp Coordinator and Recreation Director, hires seasonal staff." Additional advice: "We must always have at least 3 people who are able to drive a bus. In Connecticut a Public Service Operator's license is required. We must also have at least 2 people with their Water Safety Instructor's license." Room and board are provided with all positions. Apply by April 1 to Bev Jackson, Camp Coordinator, Dept. SED, 80 Whitney St., Hartford CT 06105; tel. 203/236-6201.

Fringe Benefits: College credit available. "We very often have students who are going into a field related to working with physically disabled individuals, and the 'hands on' experience of working with our campers proves to be an invaluable experience as does the social interaction."

Wangum, Located in Salisbury. Bristol Boys' Club. Openings for college students and teachers from late June to late August for 9 weeks. Needs general counselors, male and female (minimum age 19), first aid, swimming, fishing and canoeing (all SRL and WSI), riflery (NRA), archery, arts and crafts, nature, hiking, sports and games. Salaries are $750 minimum plus room and board, insurance. Apply to Norman J. Beland, Executive Director, Bristol Boys' Club, Box 374, Bristol CT 06010.

Yankee Trails, Located in Stafford Springs. Girl Scout camp, ages 7 to 17. Openings for college students and teachers from June 28 to August 16; includes pre-camp and closing. Needs Assistant Program Director, $550-750; 6 troop leaders, $475-675; 14 assistant troop leaders, $350-475, craft consultant, $350-500; waterfront director, $675-825; small-craft director, $450-650; waterfront assistants, $350-500; assistant cook, $450-650; nurse, $625-900; business manager, $500-750. Salaries are for season. Room and board provided. Apply by May 30 to Carmen Nielsen, Connecticut Yankee Girl Scout Council, Dept. SED, Box 504, 504 Main St., Farmington CT 06032.

Fringe Benefits: Modern, well-kept camp buildings; accreditation courses financed; accessible to ocean beaches, Boston, historic villages and seaports; staff house and laundry facilities; "excellent staff-administrative relationships." **College credit** available.

YMCA of Greater Bridgeport, Camp Mohawk (for girls) located in Cornwall, Connecticut; Camp Hi-Rock (for boys) located in Mt. Washington, Massachusetts, close to the Connecticut border in southwest Massachusetts. Camp for children ages 8-15. Openings for teachers and college students (minimum age 18), from June 22 to August 29. Needs cabin counselor/instructors in gymnastics, swimming (ARC or 'Y' SLS), sailing, canoeing, kayaking, birling, land sports (including tennis), riflery, archery, nature lore; specialists in waterfront management, arts and crafts, horseback riding

(English), photography, waterskiing, music; CIT director; unit directors; clerical workers; maintenance people; kitchen helpers; nurse (RN). Salaries are $600-$1,000. Additional salary is available for preseason maintenance beginning May 15. Room and board provided with all positions. Apply by May 1 to Tom Q. Moore, Executive Director, YMCA Camps, Dept. SED, Box 397, Litchfield CT 06759.

Fringe Benefits: Employees traveling more than 500 miles are given a travel allowance of 8¢/mile. **College credit** possible. This camp is a "fun place to work—staff and campers who like being at Mohawk and Hi-Rock make them enjoyable places to be."

Summer Theaters

Westport Country Playhouse/Connecticut Theatre

FDTN, Inc., Located in Westport. Openings for college students and theatre professionals from June 10 to September 10. Needs 12 apprentices, no salary; 8 box office staff, $125; box office treasurer, $175; house manager, $150; PR director, $250; and PR associate, $140. Salaries are weekly; room and board found in private homes for an average of $80/week. Apply by May 15 to Westport Country Playhouse, Box 629, Westport CT 06881.

Delaware

13 jobs available

Resorts, Ranches, Restaurants, Lodging

Nomad Village, Inc., Located at Tower Shores, Bethany Beach, Delaware 19930. Motel, apartments, bars, package store at a prime seashore resort. Openings for males only (no foreign students), 20-40 years of age, who are unprejudiced to homosexuals, from June 15 through Labor Day; some from May 15 through September 15. Family-type clientele—some gay (homophile) who are extremely discrete. No drag, hippie, S&M, militant or other offensive types tolerated—employees or clientele. Needs 2 lifeguards (pool only—must have SLS); 4 room stewards; 4 package store clerks, 3 bartenders, $120 up/week. "An apartment on the premises is available for single, male employees only at a nominal charge ($20/week). Employees sharing the apartment share the cost of food. There is no other charge for linens, utilities, etc." Apply by March 15 to Nomad Village, Inc., 2404 NE 13th St., Ft. Lauderdale FL 33304.

All employers listed in SED agreed to be in the book providing they would be contacted in exactly the way they specify. Read carefully all details in each listing on HOW TO APPLY.

District of Columbia

Business and Industry

Daughters of the American Revolution, National
Society, Located in Washington. Educational and patriotic organization. Openings from June to September. Needs 1 archivist's assistant, college student preferred, typing required to assist the archivist in the cataloging of historic documents, $306/biweekly; 1-2 librarians' assistants, college student preferred, typing a plus, history background preferred to assist the librarian in the care of volumes $306/biweekly; also need high school students for other jobs requiring typing. "Housing in Washington is expensive, but there are nearby YMCA's which are equipped to house persons in the area for a short while." Send for application by May to Miss Elizabeth Holland, Personnel Assistant, NSDAR 1776 D Street NW, Dept. SED, Washington DC 20006.
Fringe Benefits: "Washington is a great place to visit; it is scenic and historic. The DAR is a low-pressure place to work with a nice atmosphere. During the summer we have a 4-day work week." **College credit** possible.

Tele Sec Temporary Services, See telephone directory for suburban offices in Hyattsville and Rockville, Maryland; Falls Church, Virginia. Many openings year round and summers. Needs secretaries (60 wpm. typing, 80 shorthand), $5.25-7; typists (60 wpm), $4.25-6.25; typists (50 wpm), $4.25-5; keypunchers, input operators, accounting clerks and others. There is no fee to applicants. Apply to Tele Sec Temporary Personnel, Inc., Dept. SED, 1725 K St. NW, Room 1002, Washington DC 20006.
Fringe Benefits: "Washington, DC provides a chance for students to live and work in the capital of our country. The jobs allow employees to learn to adapt to all kinds of people, situations and environments. Employees have the opportunity to explore different fields before making a career choice." **College credit** possible.

Temporary Staffing, Inc., Temporary help service. Openings for college students and teachers. Needs 100 typists (60 w.p.m.), $5.00-6.00/hour; 3 secretaries (70 w.p.m. typing, 80 w.p.m. shorthand), $6.00-7.00/hour; 30 executive secretaries or word processors (80 w.p.m. typing, 110 w.p.m. shorthand), $7.00-7.50/hour. There is no fee to applicants. Apply to Temporary Staffing, Inc., 1900 M St. NW, Ste. 700, Washington DC 20036, tel. 202/659-3474.

Government

Those seeking jobs with the federal government must be US citizens and are required to submit either, or both, a form SF-171 or 1170/17 when applying.

Form 171 is a Personal Qualifications Statement of your experience and educational background.

Form 1170/71, a List of College Courses, may be used in place of or with your college transcript, depending on the office to which you are applying.

These forms may be obtained at most post offices and from Office of Personnel Management (OPM) area offices listed in government announcement 414.

Since the number of summer jobs available in government changes from year to year and budget to budget, we can not list a total number of jobs available in the District of Columbia.

For additional information see "Working for the Federal Government" in front of this book.

Civil Rights Commission, Jobs in Washington. Openings during summer for undergraduate and graduate students. Most positions are for graduate students whose research is more mission oriented. These people are required to have backgrounds in social science or education. Undergraduates are used for simple research, compiling Civil Rights data, working on forms. Send form 171 to Civil Rights Commission, Summer Personnel Coordinator, 1121 Vermont Ave. NW, Washington DC 20005.

Department of Energy, Jobs at main office in Washington and in regional offices: Tupman, California; Golden, Colorado; Grand Junction, Colorado; Idaho Falls, Idaho; Argonne, Illinois (Chicago operations); Aiken, South Carolina; Oak Ridge, Tennessee. Openings during summer for college students. Needs undergraduates as accounting aids (also in Oak Ridge Operations Office), physical science aids (also in Grand Junction, Chicago and regional offices), economics assistants, mathematics aids, engineering assistants (also in Naval Petroleum Reserve, California), engineering aids/technicians (in Western Area Power Administration—field work in Arizona, California, Colorado, Montana, Nevada, North Dakota, South Dakota, Utah, Wyoming), physical science technicians (Idaho), editorial assistants (Chicago and regional offices). Needs graduate students in fields of economics, statistics, computer science, engineering (electrical, mechanical, petroleum, chemical, nuclear), environmental science, business administration, public administration, liberal arts (few positions available), social science (few positions available), operations research, geology, law (first-year students in Western Area Power Administration, second-year students in Washington, DC), physical science (in Chicago operations and regional offices), geophysics (in Grand Junction office), industry economics (in Grand Junction office), mathematics (Savannah River operations). Apply with forms 171 and 1170/17 by March 1 (Law students by February 1). Department of Energy, Summer Employment Coordinator, 1000 Independence Ave. SW, Washington DC 20585.

Department of Housing and Urban Development, Jobs in Washington only. Openings for students with academic majors in business, public administration, English, sociology, urban studies and planning, accounting, economics, journalism, management systems and fields related to housing and community development. Applicants must have a bachelor's degree. Send forms 171 and 1170/17 and a list of extra-curricular activities to

Summer Employment Coordinator, Department of Housing and Urban Development, 451 7th St. SW, Washington DC 20410.

Department of Labor, Jobs at main office in Washington and in regional offices: Boston, Massachusetts; New York, New York; Philadelphia, Pennsylvania; Atlanta, Georgia; Chicago, Illinois; Dallas, Texas; Kansas City, Missouri; Denver, Colorado; Seattle, Washington; San Francisco, California. Openings for students during summer and possibly part-time during school year. Needs clerk-typists and students on technical and professional level in economics, engineering, accounting, law, physical and biological sciences, computer science, statistics and industrial hygiene. Applications must be made to Washington, DC office. Send form 171 and 1170/17 by April 1 to Summer Employment Coordinator, US Department of Labor, 200 Constitution Ave. NW, Washington DC 20210.

Environmental Protection Agency, Jobs are in Washington. Openings during summer and year-round for graduate students in computer science and engineering. Send form 171 from December 1 to April 15 to Environmental Protection Agency, Summer Employment Program, 401 M St. SW, Washington DC 20460.
Fringe Benefits: College credit available.

Federal Aviation Administration, Jobs are in Washington. Openings for college students during summer. The FAA belongs to the Federal Junior Fellowship Program which offers students employment during vacations and school breaks. Needs 275 clerk-typists, accounting clerks, clerk-stenographers, personnel clerks, staffing clerks, account technicians, computer aids, engineering aids, mathematics aids, law clerks, economic majors, and English majors (writers). Also needs people for trade labor jobs at the airport (landscaping and maintenance positions). Apply with form 171 and form 1170/17 (not necessary for clerks) to Johnny McLean, Summer Program Coordinator, Department of Transportation, Federal Aviation Administration, 800 Independence Ave. SW, Washington DC 20591; tel 202/426-3229.

Federal Home Loan Bank Board, Jobs are in Washington. Openings during summer for graduate students working on degrees in economics and finance. Also needs clerk-typists (40 wpm). Submit form 171 by April 15 to Marie Janios, Federal Home Loan Bank Board, Personnel Management Office, 2nd Floor, 1700 G St. NW, Washington DC 20552; tel. 202/377-6070.

Heritage Conservation and Recreation Service, Main office in Washington. Regional offices in Seattle, Washington; San Francisco, California; Albuquerque, New Mexico; Denver, Colorado; Atlanta, Georgia; Ann Arbor, Michigan; Philadelphia, Pennsylvania; Anchorage, Alaska. Openings for college students during summer. Needs clerk-typists, historians, architects, archaeologists, outdoor recreation planners, program assistants, social science technicians, architectural technicians. Applicants should have at least 2 years of college in a field related to the job for which they are applying. Applications should be made to Washington DC office. Send form 171 by May 15 to Heritage Conservation and Recreation Service, Department of Interior, 440 G St., Room 314, Washington DC, 20243.

Internal Revenue Service
Jobs are in Washington. Needs clerk-typists and clerk-stenographers during the summer. Apply with form 171 to Internal Revenue Service, Chief Employment Section, Attention: Summer Employment Coordinator, Room 1028 RM:N:PR, 1111 Constitution Ave., Washington DC 20224.

International Trade Administration, Jobs are in Washington.
Openings for college students during summer. Needs clerk-typists and graduate and undergraduate students with background in economics, computers, business administration, marketing, international trade, international relations. Send form 171 by January 15 to N. J. Smoke, Department of Commerce, International Trade Administration, Office of Personnel, Room 3515, Washington DC 20230.

Maritime Administration, Jobs are in Washington. Openings for
students and teachers during summer. Needs 20-25 clerk-typists (40 wpm); 10 people in GS-5 and above (college graduate through doctoral degree) in areas of economics, engineering, transportation, accounting and computer science; several law clerks. Send forms 171 and 1170/17 between February 1 and March 1 to Maritime Administration, Office of Personnel, Room 1099, Washington DC 20230.

National Transportation Safety Board, Jobs are at main
office in Washington and regional offices in Anchorage, Alaska; Atlanta, Georgia; Chicago, Illinois; Denver, Colorado; Ft. Worth, Texas; Los Angeles, California; Miami, Florida; Kansas City, Missouri; New York, New York; and Seattle, Washington. Openings for high school students as clerk-typists, college students as accounting clerks and law clerks. Applications must be made to Washington DC office. Send form 171 after mid-April to National Transportation Safety Board, 800 Independence Ave. SW, Washington DC 20594.

Nuclear Regulatory Commission, Jobs are at main office in
Washington and in regional offices: Atlanta, Georgia; Chicago, Illinois; Dallas, Texas; Philadelphia, Pennsylvania; San Francisco, California. Openings during summer for 50 college students in engineering (chemical, electrical, materials, mechanical, nuclear) and science (physics, health physics/radiation protection, computer science). Applicants should have completed sophomore year of college or 2 years of 5-year engineering curriculum, and must have reputable grade/point average. *US citizenship required.* Applications must be made to Washington DC office. Send form 171 and student resume or form 1170/17 before March 1 to Nuclear Regulatory Commission, Division of Personnel, PREP Branch, Washington DC 20555.
Fringe Benefits: Summer assignment may qualify student for participation in the cooperative education program.

Office of Surface Mining, Jobs are in Washington. Hires summer help. Apply between January 1 and April 15 to Personnel Office, Office of Surface Mining, Reclamation and Enforcement, Room 105, 1951 Constitution Ave., Washington DC; tel 202/343-4171.

US Air Force Headquarters, Jobs are in Washington. Openings for high school seniors and college students. Needs 200 clerk-typists. Send form 171 by April 15 to Headquarters, US Air Force, 1947 AS/DMPKS, Pentagon Room SE 871, Washington DC 20330; tel. 202/697-9335.

US Attorneys Office, Jobs are in Washington only. Openings for 12 undergraduates every summer. Needs pre-law students and students interested in public administration. This office is limited to filling positions with students eligible to be payed by their schools under a work-study program. Pay depends on funding of the school, but is roughly equivalent to $5-6/hour. Apply to Debra Markey, Personnel Officer, US Attorneys Office, US Court House, 3rd and Constitution Ave. NW, Washington DC 20001; 202/633-4943.

Florida

948+ jobs available

Business and Industry

Benjamin F. Bass, Located in Sanford. Openings for students and teachers starting in November to pick fruit in Florida. Needs 25 pickers. Work week 8 hours, 6 days/week. Send for application to Benjamin F. Bass, Box 3115 S.R.S., Sanford FL 32771.

Larene Field, Located in Frostproof. Openings for students and teachers from October to July 15 to pick citrus fruit in Florida. Needs 50 pickers able to handle ladders and carry bags of fruit, salary open. Free bus transportation to job sites. Living quarters nearby; rent averages $50/week, food $50/week. Send applications to Larene Field, Box 13, Rt. 2, Frostproof FL 33843.
Fringe Benefits: "We may pick oranges or other citrus at nearby lakes and other scenic locations. Lots of physical exercise climbing ladders all day and stretching to pick fruit or bending to pick it up from the ground." **College credit** possible.

Hartman Temporary Personnel, Located in Miami and Plantation, Florida; Austin and Dallas/Ft. Worth, Texas. Positions available year round, part-time and full-time for college students, teachers, high school seniors, local applicants. Needs 25 each: secretaries, typists, general office clerks, key punch operators, bookkeepers. Salaries range from minimum wage to $8/hour, depending on job requirements. Apply to office or telephone: Hartman Temporary Personnel, 3550 Biscayne Blvd., Suite 401, Miami FL 33137, tel. 305/573-4000; 8751 W. Broward Blvd., Plantation FL 33324, tel.

305/472-3950; 8705 Shoal Creek Blvd., Suite 207, Austin TX 78758, tel. 512/
458-3111; 6116 N. Central Expressway, Cowboy Building, Suite 404, Dallas TX
75206; tel. 214/691-7660.

Commercial Attractions

Walt Disney World Vacation Kingdom, Located 16 miles
southwest of Orlando. Openings from the first week of June through Labor Day
for 500 persons age 16 and older. Needs persons to work in shops, food
locations, custodial department and attractions. Also needs hosts and
hostesses. Shifts vary greatly and may change often during the season. All
applicants must provide their own transportation and their own housing;
housing not available on Walt Disney World property. Most employees average
30-35 hours/week. Personal interview is required at the Walt Disney World
Employment Center. Do not send resume or request application. Obtain
employment information by visiting the Employment Center Monday through
Friday throughout the year; appointments not scheduled in advance. Final
selection made within 1 month of the holiday season. EOE.

Expeditions, Guide Trips

Flint School Aboard Te Vega and Te Quest, Located in
Sarasota. Academic school ships in the Mediterranean and Europe. Openings
for college students, minimum age 19. Needs 6 persons for crew-in-training
program aboard 156 foot and 173 foot sailing schooners; should have ARC life
saving certificate, serve as working maintenance crew (painting, varnishing, sail
mending, rust removal, engine cleaning, laundry, galley and food service, ship
housekeeping) during travel program; teaching interns for academic or ship
staff career appointments. Shore leave schedule when in foreign ports. Only
those interested for a minimum of one full school year should apply. Write for
application forms to Captain Stoll, 4Rs Academic Method, Inc., Box 5809,
Sarasota FL 33579.

Government

National Transportation Safety Board, Jobs available at the
regional office in Miami. Applications must be made to Washington DC office.
See Washington DC office (District of Columbia section) for complete
descriptions of jobs available and how to apply information.

National Parks

Flamingo Resort, Located at Flamingo, in Everglades National Park,
overlooking Florida Bay. Resort serving national park visitors and families;
facilities include lodge, cottages, restaurant, cafeteria, lounge, gift shop, boat
cruises, tram trains, marina, service station and grocery store. Openings year
round, "with most positions available between November 1 and April 15. For
lodge, needs 5 desk clerks, $500-600/month; 3 clerical, $400-500/month; 2
housemen to handle hotel maintenance, $400-500/month. For restaurant,
needs 10 cooks, $500-600/month; 25 waiters/waitresses $160/month plus tips;

14 utility persons, $400-500/month; 4 bartenders, $250/month plus tips; 6 cashiers, $400-500/month; 3 supervisors, $500-600/month. For marina, needs 7 dock workers to handle boating activities, $400-500/month; 7 grocery store clerks, $400-500/month; 5 naturalists to lead sightseeing activities, $500-600. Room and board provided at cost of $15.60/week per person. Send for application and informational material to Personnel Manager, Dept. SED, Flamingo Resort, Flamingo FL 33030; tel. 305/253-2241.

Resorts, Ranches, Restaurants, Lodging

Lakeside Inn, Located in Mount Dora (Central Florida). Needs 6 waiters, 6 waitresses. Salaries $185/month plus tips; 6 housekeepers, $300/month plus tips. Work from Dec. 16 to April 20, 1982. Apply by Sept. 1, 1981 to R.W. Lee, Innkeeper, Lakeside Inn, Dept. SED, Mount Dora FL 32757; tel. winter (904)383-2151, summer (704)526-2171.
Fringe Benefits: Uniforms provided.

South Seas Plantation, Located at Captiva Island. Island resort hotel. Openings for college students, teachers and high school seniors on a seasonal or year 'round basis. Various positions available, mostly in the restaurant and housekeeping operations. Salaries average $500/month less inexpensive room and board. Three month *minimum* length of employment acceptable. Apply to Roy Collom, Personnel Manager, South Seas Plantation, Captiva Island FL 33924.

Summer Camps

Challenge, Located in Sorrento. Easter Seal camp for physically handicapped persons ages 6 to adult; one autistic children's session. Openings for college students, teachers and foreign students from June 7 to August 8. Needs 15 male counselors, 15 female counselors, 5 specialists (crafts, WSI, games), $45/week; 2 head counselors (1 male, 1 female), $55/week; and program director, $65/week; nurse (RN), $200/week. Salaries include room, board, and hospital and accident insurance. Apply to Jess Shumen, Camp Challenge, Rt. 1, Box 350, Sorrento FL 32776.

Circle F Dude Ranch, Located at Lake Wales. Private coed camp, ages 6-16. Openings for college students and teachers, minimum age 18, nonsmokers and nondrinkers, from mid-June to mid-August. Needs head counselors (minimum age 25); bunk and specialty counselors for riding, swimming, waterskiing, tripping, tennis, crafts, archery, nature lore, art; song leader; evening program director; nurse (RN). Salaries are $500 and up. Room, board and laundry provided. Apply by April to George F. Fischbach, Circle F Dude Ranch Camp, Lake Wales FL 33853.

Harder Hall Golf and Tennis Camp for Teens, Located in Sebring. Coed camp. Needs area representatives to recruit campers. Commission paid. "You can earn money all during the winter and spring." Also

needs general counselors, college golf and tennis team members preferred; experienced evening activity director to plan and carry out teenage socials, games, dramatics, etc; dining room supervisor; dramatic coach; nurse (RN); waterskiing and sailing instructors, lifeguards (WSI); and mature night security counselors. Considers mature couples in all areas. Write to Harder Hall Golf and Tennis Camp for Teens, Sebring FL 33870.
Fringe Benefits: Pays part tuition for camper-workers 16 or over.

Kadima, Located in St. Petersburg, Florida. Jewish oriented day camp for boys and girls ages 2-15. Camp dates: June 22 to August 15. Needs 10 counselors, local college students and teachers preferred, $350-650/season; 10 junior counselors, high school seniors, $300/season; aquatics director and assistant aquatics director, college students and teachers preferred, $600-800/season; 1 supervisor each for arts and crafts, music, tennis, college students and teachers preferred, $600-800/season. Housing should be worked out in area; expenses vary "from very low cost and exchange of services (babysitting) to motel/hotel accommodations." Apply by April to Fred Margolis, Director, Camp Kadima, Dept. SED, The Jewish Community Center of Pinellas County, 8167 Elbow Lane, St. Petersburg FL 33710; tel. 813/344-5795.
Fringe Benefits: This day camp provides learning situations, good working conditions, a social atmosphere, and "excellent training and evaluation on an ongoing basis." **College credit** possible.

Seacamp, Located in Big Pine Key. Private nonprofit camp for teenagers, ages 12-17; emphasis on marine science and scuba. ACA accredited. Openings for college students and teachers from June 1 to August 25. Needs 10 marine science staff/counselors preferably with degrees in related science; instructors; 2 sailing (ARC), outboard boating (ARC), first aid (ARC), 5 scuba (PADI, NAUI, YMCA), campcraft; 20 specialty counselors for arts and crafts, photography, journalism, music, WSI, fishing, canoeing; secretary; 2 assistant cooks; nurse (RN); dining hall manager. Apply by May 15 to Personnel Director, Seacamp, Dept. SED, Route 3, Box 170, Big Pine Key FL 33043.

Georgia

3,707+ jobs available

Commercial Attractions

Six Flags Over Georgia, Located in Atlanta. Theme amusement park. Openings for 2,600 college students, foreign students with work visas, high school seniors and local applicants to work weekends March-May, daily June-August, and weekends September-November. Positions available in rides, food service, games, grounds, parking lot, merchandise, warehouse, wardrobe, cash control, security and first aid. Wardrobe furnished and cleaned daily. Many special activities throughout the summer. Housing not provided to employees. All applicants must apply in person at Personnel Office located on Six Flags

Road. When applying, mention that you saw this notice in SED. Beginning in January, office will be open Monday through Friday, 9 a.m.-5 p.m. No appointment necessary. Must be at least 16 years old and have Social Security card to be employed. Equal opportunity employer. For more information write Jean H. Nolte, Personnel Staff Assistant, Six Flags Over Georgia, Box 43187, Atlanta GA 30336; tel. 404/948-9290.

Government

Department of Labor, Jobs available at the regional office, Room 110, 1371 Peachtree St. NE, Atlanta GA 30309. This office serves Alabama, Florida, Georgia, Mississippi, South Carolina, North Carolina, Tennessee and Kentucky. Applications must be made to Washington DC office. See Washington DC office (District of Columbia section) for complete description of jobs available and how to apply information.

National Transportation Safety Board, Jobs available at the regional office in Atlanta. Applications must be made to Washington DC office. See Washington DC office (District of Columbia section) for description of jobs available and how to apply information.

Nuclear Regulatory Commission, Jobs available at the regional office in Atlanta. Applications must be made to Washington DC office. See Washington DC office (District of Columbia section) for complete description of jobs available and how to apply information.

Summer Camps

Adahi, Located in Cloudland, Georgia. Camp for girls ages 8-17. Openings for college students and teachers from June 16 to August 8. Needs program director, min. $500; 4 unit leaders, min. $500; 4 waterfront instructors, min. $400; horseback riding director, min. $400; 4 unit counselors, min. $400; business manager, min. $400; assistant horseback riding instructor, min. $450; 4 assistant unit leaders, min. $450; nurse, $680; food manager, $680; 3 cooks, $600; handyboy, $300. Applicants must be high school graduates and at least 18 years of age. Should have experience working with groups of children, outdoor living experience, or camping experience. Each employee must purchase a staff shirt. Room and board provided. Send for application. Resume is "helpful but not necessary." Apply to Moccasin Bend Girl Scout Council, Inc., 301 W. 6th Street, Suite 101, Chattanooga TN 37402; tel. 615/267-3761.

Blue Ridge Camp, Located at Mountain City, Georgia, in the Blue Ridge Mountains. Coed residential camp for ages 6-16. "We are an athletic waterfront and cultural camp." Openings from June 18 to August 18 for college students, teachers and high school seniors. Needs 60 cabin counselors, specialists in instructing children in sports activities, waterfront activities, gymnastics, reading, math, riflery, archery, campcrafts, and arts and crafts. Salaries are $250-600/season. Provides room and board. Send for application to Camp Blue Ridge, Box 2888, Miami Beach FL 33140.

YMCA Camp Waco, Located near Atlanta. Camp operated by the YMCA in Atlanta for boys and girls. Openings from June 20 to August 22. Salary range: $45-85/week. Needs 1 aquatic director (WSI), 1 swimming instructor (SL), 1 lake instructor (SL), college students or teachers; 8 program counselors in baseball, archery, soccer, crafts, nature, drama, college students or teachers; 8 cabin leaders, high school students, minimum age 16; 1 office manager, 1 program director, college students or teachers. Room and board provided. Hires physically handicapped. Send for application. Apply by May 1 to Thomas S. Post, Director, Camping Services, YMCA Camp Waco, 145 Luckie St., NW, Atlanta GA 30303.
Fringe Benefits: "A chance to work in a camp environment under the YMCA philosophy, close to Atlanta, an exciting metropolitan area." **College credit** available.

Hawaii

42 jobs available

Summer Camps

Mokuleia, Located in Waialua, on the north shore of Oahu. Episcopal Church camp for children ages 8-14. Openings for 14 persons (minimum age 18) from June 15 to August 8. Needs 6 senior counselors, $600; 6 junior counselors, $400; truck driver, $500; nurse, $600. Prefers WSI certification for counselors. Salaries are for season. Room and board provided. Applications available December 1. Apply by February 1 to Camp Director, Camp Mokuleia, Dept. SED, 68-729 Farrington Hwy., Waialua HI 96791.
Fringe Benefits: One day and one night off a week with pay. **College credit** possible.

Paumalu, Located on Oahu, above Sunset Beach on the island's north shore. Girl Scout camp for girls ages 8-17. Openings for college students and teachers from June 20 to August 17. Needs assistant camp director, $600-800/season; waterfront director, $500-700/season; 8 unit counselors, $325-400/season; business manager, $400-600/season; 4 unit directors, $425-500/season; nurse (RN), $500-750/season; kitchen assistant, $400-500/season. Apply to Camp Paumalu Director, Girl Scout Council of the Pacific, Inc., 1717 Akahi St., Honolulu HI 96819.

YWCA, Located on Windward side of Oahu. Day camp for children ages 4-12. Openings for college students and teachers from June 1 to August 21. Needs 7 counselors and one coordinator. Salary $400-600, depending on experience and position. Possibility of additional money being earned after hours by teaching instructional classes. Certification and experience in outdoor activities, WST, sailing, canoeing, arts and crafts, drama, dance and sports. Lodging only provided. "Variety of food stores provided." Apply by April 1 to Donna D. Fouts, Kokokahi Branch YWCA, Dept. SED, 45-035 Kaneohe Bay Dr., Kaneohe HI 96744; tel. 808/247-2124.

Fringe Benefits: "Pleasant atmosphere—warm, sunny Hawaii. Pool, boats, tennis court, gym at your disposal." **College credit** possible.

Idaho

86+ jobs available

Business and Industry

Antonio M. Gomez, Located in Caldwell. Farm labor contractor. Openings for 16 local applicants from October until February to harvest apples. Salary depends on employees work. Applicants should be reliable. Apply to Antonio M. Gomez, 517 Kearney, Caldwell ID 83605; tel. 208/459-6949.

Government

Department of Energy
Idaho Operations Office, Jobs available in this regional office, 550 Section St., Idaho Falls ID 83401. Applications must be made to Washington DC office. See Washington DC office (District of Columbia section) for complete description of jobs available and how to apply information.

Summer Camps

Pine Creek Ranch
Alice Pittenger
Ta-Man-A-Wis, Located near Shoup, McCall, and Palisades. Girl Scout waterfront horse camp, for girls ages 6-17. Openings for college students and teachers from June to August. Needs 2 camp directors, $165-185/week; 2 assistant camp directors, $100-120/week; 30 counselors, $70-80/week; 7 waterfront and riding staffers, $70-80/week; 6 cooks and maintenance workers, $70-80/week; 2 nurses/first aiders, $70-80/week. Room and board included. Send for application by June 1. Apply to Silver Sage Girl Scout Council, Camp Staff, Dept. SED, 1410 Etheridge Lane, Boise ID 83704; tel. 208/377-2011.
Fringe Benefits: College credit possible.

Summer Theaters

Coeur d'Alene Summer Theatre, Located in Coeur d' Alene. Musical repertory summer stock. Openings for professional theater aspirants, college students, teachers and high school seniors from mid-June to Labor Day. Needs 32 actors and actresses, dancers, musicians, stage manager, lighting designer-operator, $40/week; 2 stage directors, $60/week; set designer,

---

Don't miss the "Late Arrivals" section at the back of this book for job listings that came late.

costumer. Room provided. Apply to Robert E. Moe, Coeur d' Alene Summer
Theatre, Box 622, Coeur d' Alene ID 83814.

Summer Theatre, Located at the University of Idaho, Moscow.
Openings for 10-15 college students as actors and technicians. Work from first
week in June to first week in August. Pays $350-$750. "Local apartments
available at fairly inexpensive rates." Apply by March 1 to Roy S. Fluhrer,
Chairman, Summer Theatre, Department of Theatre Arts, University of Idaho,
Moscow ID 83843.
Fringe Benefits: "Opportunity to work with professional directors/designers
and actors from MFA programs all over the United States." **College credit**
available.

Illinois

268+ jobs available

Business and Industry

Casey Services, Inc., Located in Mt. Prospect, Illinois. Temporary
help in accounting, clerical and data input. Almost all accounting, clerical and
data input positions available. Salary depends on experience; usually
$3.50-5.00/hour. Some knowledge of accounting, typing or data processing
desirable. Employment anytime. Apply to Helen Becker, Manager, Casey
Services, Inc., 247 E. Ontario, Chicago IL 60611; tel. 312/649-0755. Other
offices: Jill Meyerhardt, Manager, 314 N. Broadway, Suite 1163, St. Louis MO
63102, tel. 314/621-4880; Carl Vanhemelrk, Manager, 740 N. Plankinton,
Milwaukee WI 53203, tel. 414/276-6515; Stan Frost, Manager, 15 S. 5th St.,
Suite 1146, Minneapolis MN 55402, tel. 612/339-6923; Larry Braun, Manager,
Randhurst Shopping Center, Suite 56, Mt. Prospect IL 60056, tel.
312/392-2708; and Tom Kane, Manager, 110 Schiller, Elmhurst IL 60126, tel.
312/279-0113; Jene Munkirs, 1102 Grand Ave., Kansas City MO 64106, tel.
816/471-2867; Rosemary O'Meara, 910 16th St., Denver CO 80202, tel.
303/534-6163.

Debbie Temps, Inc., Located in Niles, Wheeling, Schaumburg and
Skokie. Temporary office services. Employment April to October or year-round
for secretaries; dictaphone secretaries, bookkeepers, clerks, typists, key punch.
"Please write or call as early as possible. We prefer people from northwest
suburban area of Chicago." Apply to Phyllis Galanter, Office Manager, Debbie
Temps, Inc., 7900 N. Milwaukee, Niles IL 60648; tel. 312/966-1400.

Commercial Attractions

Miller Amusements, Inc, Located in LaGrange. Needs 8-10 ride
erectors and operators, tent and booth erectors, $175/week and up. Day and
night help needed. "Any applicant can make much more if willing to work at
position." Work last week of May through Labor Day. Apply to N. A. Meyer or

Rich Wyatt, Miller Amusements, Inc., 9912 W. 55th St., Countryside (LaGrange) Il 60525; telephone (312)352-5870.

Government

Department of Energy
Chicago Operations, Jobs available in this regional office, 9800 S. Cass Ave., Argonne IL 60439. Applications must be made to Washington DC office. See Washington DC office (District of Columbia section) for complete description of jobs available and how to apply information.

Department of Labor, Jobs available at the regional office, 10th Floor, Federal Office Building, 230 S. Dearborn St., Chicago IL 60604. This office serves Illinois, Indiana, Michigan, Ohio and Wisconsin. Applications must be made to Washington DC office. See Washington DC office (District of Columbia section) for complete description of jobs available and how to apply information.

National Transportation Safety Board, Jobs available at the regional office in Chicago. Applications must be made to Washington DC office. See Washington DC office (District of Columbia section) for complete description of jobs available and how to apply information.

Nuclear Regulatory Commission, Jobs available at the regional office in Chicago. Applications must be made to Washington DC office. See Washington DC office (District of Columbia section) for complete description of jobs available and how to apply information.

Summer Camps

American Camping Association/Illinois Section, Located in Illinois and surrounding states including Wisconsin, Indiana, Michigan and Minnesota. The American Camping Association/Illinois Section is an association of persons involved with camps operated by social agencies, and private camp owners. More than 100 camps in Association. Openings for college students, teachers, foreign students and local applicants from late June to late August. Needs persons over 18 years of age who possess a variety of camp leadership skills for positions such as counselors, cooks, waterfront staff, camping and athletic skills teachers, nurses and program directors. Salaries are $500-1,000 for eight weeks or more. Room and board provided. Apply by writing the American Camping Association/Illinois Section, 19 S. LaSalle St., Room 1024, Chicago IL 60603; tel. 312/332-0833. A $2.00 fee must accompany application.

Butternut Springs, Located in Valparaiso. Girl Scout camp for ages 6 through 17. Openings for college students, graduates, teachers and foreign students from mid-June to mid-August. Needs director, assistant director, nurse, business manager/food service manager (minimum age 21, driver's license required), program consultants, waterfront director (ARC-WSI), waterfront assistants, group counselors, pack-out staff, maintenance assistant. Apply to Director of Camping and Properties/SED, Girl Scouts of Chicago, 14 E. Jackson Blvd., Chicago IL 60604.

Henry Horner, Located at Round Lake. Camp for children ages 9-15. Openings for college students and special education teachers from June 14 to August 14. Needs instructors: music-drama, archery, pioneer-survival, nature-ecology, $600-800; arts and crafts, waterfront instructors, WSI, $400-800; counselors, $350-600; maintenance, $500-800; driver (maintenance, minimum age 21), $600. Room and board provided. Apply by May 1 to Daniel Farinella, Director of Camping Services, Camp Henry Horner, Box 232, Dept. SED, Round Lake IL 60073; tel. 312/546-4435.
Fringe Benefits: Working with children from many different backgrounds.
College credit possible.

Mayer Kaplan Jewish Community Center, Located in Skokie. Day camp for children ages 3-13. Openings for college students, teachers and high school seniors from June 15 to August 13. Needs 100 counselors. Salaries are $608 and up for season. Apply by March to Mayor Kaplan Jewish Community Center, 5050 W. Church St., Skokie IL 60076.

Peacock Camp for Crippled Children, Located in Lake Villa. Camp for physically handicapped. Openings for college students, teachers and foreign students from mid-June to mid-August. Needs specialty counselors: 4 waterfront, arts and crafts, 4 land sports (recreation); waterfront director, assistant director; nurse (RN or graduate nurse), 2 cooks. Salaries for beginning counselors, $550-600; others open. Apply by May 15 to Dave Bogenschutz, Peacock Camp for Crippled Children, 509 Deep Lake Rd., Lake Villa IL 60046.

Pleasant Valley Outdoor Center, Located in Woodstock. Farm and environmental camp for preschool children to seniors. Openings for college students, teachers and foreign students from June 24 to August 31. Needs 4 lifeguards, 2 crafts persons, 2 naturalists, 15 tent camp counselors and 5 maintenance workers. Salaries average $560/season. Apply by April to Director, Pleasant Valley Outdoor Center, 13315 Pleasant Valley Rd., Woodstock IL 60098; tel. 815/338-5080.

Sherwood Youth Camp, Located in Dahinda. Resident camp for underprivileged boys ages 10-13. Openings for college students, teachers and high school seniors from first part of June to mid-August. Needs 13 senior counselors, craft-evening program director, $650-800; waterfront director (WSI), assistant director, $800-1,000; 2 junior counselors, $350-500; 2 kitchen helpers, $350-500. Room, board and laundry provided. Apply by May 1 to Mike Robson, 749 Maple Ave., Galesburg IL 61401.

Tapawingo, Located at Metamora. Girl Scout camp for girls ages 7-17. Openings for college students and teachers from June 4 to August 12. Needs C.I.T. and waterfront director, $810-1080/season; 6 unit leaders, $675-990/season; 12 unit counselors, $540-855/season. Room and board provided. Apply by June 1 to Jeanne Buysee, Kickapoo Council of Girl Scouts, 1103 W. Lake, Peoria IL 61614.

Waupaca For Boys, Inc., Located in Wisconsin. Recreational camp for boys ages 9-14. Openings for college students and teachers from June 20 to August 17. Needs 15 general counselors (to instruct in sports), 7 water instructors (WSI), crafts instructor, nurse (RN), caretaker (minor repairs and general maintenance), piano player, general sports. Salaries open. Room and board provided. Apply by April to M. Desnet, Director, 6850 N. Crawford Ave., Lincolnwood IL 60646; tel. 312/676-0911 (call collect, person-to-person).
Fringe Benefits: Laundry service, medical insurance, canteen, transportation; good time-off policy. **College credit** possible.

Indiana

182 jobs available

Summer Camps

Culver Summer School Camps, Located at Lake Maxinkuckee in Culver. Openings for 35 college students and teachers from June 16 to August 1. Needs male and female counselors for both junior high and elementary school age children, $600-1,000, depending on degree and experience. "Counselors should be skilled in some camp activity area. Certification desirable." Send for application and return by April 1 to Frederick D. Lane, Director, Dept. SED, Culver Summer Schools, Culver IN 46511; tel. 219/842-3311, ext. 207.

Dudley Gallahue Valley Camp, Located in Morgantown on 569 acres of wooded hills in Brown County. Girl Scout resident camp for girls ages 9-17. Openings for college students, teachers, high school seniors, foreign students and local applicants from June 8 to August 17. Needs director (experience and knowledge of Girl Scouts required, college degree preferred), $1,400-2,000/season; assistant director (college degree preferred), $1,200; business manager (typing, bookkeeping, office practice experience preferred), $650-$750/season; health supervisor (physician, physician's assistant, RN, LPN, paramedic, Camp Health Director, EMT, or state license required, also Red Cross Advanced First Aid and Emergency Care and/or Cardiopulmonary Resuscitation certificates preferred), $1,200/season; trip director (work experience with children as teacher or counselor required), $600-700/season; horseback director (work experience with children as teacher or counselor required), $650-750/season; food supervisor (minimum 2 years training in institutional management specializing in food service or experience); 4 cooks, $700-750/season; unit leaders: 1 waterfront, 2 general program, 3 horseback, 1 wrangler, 1 wilderness, 1 general barn (experienced as girl leader, camper or teacher, and supervision, first aid and lifesaving preferred), $600-700/season; assistant unit leaders: 2 waterfront, 6 general program, 2 horseback, 1 wrangler, 1 general barn, 1 wilderness (experience as camper or youth leader preferred),

$500-600/season; waterfront director, canoe/sailing trip leader, smallcraft instructor (WSI, ALS, and Cardiopulmonary Resuscitation, or YMCA Aquatic Leader Examiner, or Boy Scouts of America National Aquatic Instructor certificate, experience necessary), $650-750/season; waterfront assistant, canoe/sailing assistant (basic swimming instructor certificate from Red Cross, YMCA, or Boy Scouts of America, experience preferred), $500-600/season. Room and board provided. Send for application. Apply by March 1 to Deborah A. Smith, Director of Camping Services, Hoosier Capital Girl Scout Council, Dept. SED, 615 N. Alabama Street, Room 235, Indianapolis IN 46204.
Fringe Benefits: College credit possible.

Howe Military School Summer Camp, Located in Howe. Recreational and academic. Openings for college students from July 28 to August 8. Needs counselors, $600-900. Room and board provided. Apply to R. Kelly, Superintendent, Howe Military School, Howe IN 46746.

Henry F. Koch, Located in Cannelton. Girl Scout camp for girls ages 8-17. Openings for college students, teachers and foreign students from approximately mid-June to mid-August. Needs 15 assistant troop leaders, 5 troop leaders (minimum age 21), waterfront director, boating instructor, 4 waterfront staff, 3 cooks. Room and board provided. Apply by May 1 to Camp Director, Raintree Girl Scout Council, Box 3357, Dept. SED, Evansville IN 47732.

Ella J. Logan, Located in Syracuse, on Dewart Lake. Girl Scout camp for ages 6-17. Needs assistant camp director, $111-200; business manager $86-151; health supervisor (RN or LPN) $86-151; waterfront director (WSI, SCI) $101-191; assistant waterfront director, small craft instructor $81-133; waterfront assistants $61-81 (WSI preferred); unit leaders $73-98; unit assistants $61-81; head cook $81-101; kitchen help $61-93; waterskiing instructor (salary depending on qualifications and experience). Room and board provided. An equal opportunity employer. Apply by April 15 to Limberlost Girl Scout Council Inc., Camping Services Director, "C.E.J.L.," Dept. SED, 1820 N. Wells St., Fort Wayne IN 46808.
Fringe Benefits: "Free laundry facilities; use of waterfront on free time." **College credit** possible.

Wapi-Kamigi, Located in Hagerstown. Girl Scout camp. Openings for college students and teachers from early June to early August. Staff positions include 4 unit leaders, 7 unit counselors, waterfront director (WSI), 2 waterfront assistants, naturalists, nurse (RN), business manager and 2 cooks. Salaries are $400-700/7-week season; varies according to position and experience. Camp program includes canoe trips, bike trips, ACA Campcrafter, outdoor cooking, crafts, nature, tent living and international staff. Room and board provided. Apply after January 1 to Pat Mayer, Treaty Line Council of Girl Scouts, Dept. SED, 42 S. 9th St., Richmond IN 47374.
Fringe Benefits: "A staff shirt is provided. Soft drinks are sold at a minimal cost." **College Credit:** possible. "The atmosphere is pleasant, and the small size of the camp encourages much staff interaction. Skills learned are useable

throughout life. Experience working with girls is very helpful in future careers, particularly teaching."

YMCA Resident Youth Camp, Located at Blackman Lake, South Milford. Coed lakefront camp for children ages 8-15. Openings from June 1 to July 31, 8-week season. Needs 9 counselors (3 girls and 6 boys), age 21 or 1 year of college or 3 years as CIT for tennis, archery, riflery, canoeing, sailing, $500-650/season; waterfront director (WSI), $500-1,000/season; craft director, $500-650/season; kitchen manager, $100-175/week; cook, $100-175/week. Room and board provided. Send resume or write for application. Apply by May 15 to Topher Schlatter, Resident Camp Director, Dept. SED, 226 E. Washington Blvd., Fort Wayne IN 46802; tel. 219/422-6486.
Fringe Benefits: Health and accident insurance coverage. **College credit** possible.

Summer Theaters

Purdue Summer Theatre, Located in West Lafayette, Indiana. 184-seat theater with flexible staging. Openings for college students from May 30 to August 7. Needs 4-6 actors, $50-100/week; and 6-8 technicians, $50-100/week. Works with Equity artists. Submit resume indicating experience, qualifications and special talents by March 1 to Dr. Dale Miller, Director of Theatre, Purdue Summer Theatre, Purdue University, West Lafayette IN 47907; tel. 317/749-2695.

Iowa

368 jobs available

Summer Camps

Arrowhead, Agency, Iowa. YMCA resident, ages 6-17. Needs 1 program director, $70-90/week, college students and teachers preferred; 2 horseback riding instructors, $60-75/week, college students over 21 preferred; 3 waterfront directors, $60-75/week, college students preferred; 1 trip camp leader, $70-95/week, college student or teacher over 21 preferred; 6 general counselors, $45-60/week, college students, foreign students, high school seniors all acceptable. All salaries include room and board. Work from June 14 to August 15. Apply to Scott Brosman, Director, Camp Arrowhead, Route 1, Agency IA 52530; telephone (515)937-6614.

Foster, Located on East Lake Okoboji, Spirit Lake. YMCA coed camp for children ages 8-16. Openings for college students and teachers (some high school students) from approximately June 1 to August 17. All staff must have minimum one year of college except for junior staff who must be leaving grades 10, 11 or 12 depending on position. Needs about 18 general counselors, approximately $525 base/season; 1 waterfront director (WSI, age 21), $650 base/season; 2 pool directors (WSI, age 19 and 21), $525-625 base/season; 3 waterski instructors, $550 base/season; 6 cooks, $550-650/season; 2 ranch directors, $525 plus/season; 1 camp nurse (RN), $850 plus/season; tripping director (experienced), $625 plus/season; 7 Youth Conservation Corps (YCC) staff, for 8 weeks, good salaries. Room and board provided. Also seeking office, store, maintenance, day camp and campground staff; 20 junior staff, junior counselors and dish/support staff. A staff growth experience results, staff role models are of utmost importance." Apply early to Ken Lockard or Mike "Chief" Olson, Directors, Camp Foster YMCA, Dept. SED, Box 296, Spirit Lake IA 51360; tel. 712/336-3272.

Fringe Benefits: "A very positive, self-enhancing, supportive, open, caring, ego-nourishing, reinforcing work environment; caliber of staff members of highest fiber; excellent experience in working with children; and superb 7-day, pre-camp staff training program." **College credit** available.

Hantesa, Located in Boone. Camp Fire camp for boys and girls ages 6-18. Openings from June to August (8 weeks of camp and 1 week of training) for college students, teachers and local applicants. Needs 8 unit directors with interest in children, supervising counselors and programs, $440-600/season; 4 water safety instructors to supervise and instruct pool, canoe, sail, row boats, $400-600/season; 6 food service staff to prepare for 150-225 people/meal, $400-600/season; 1 nurse (RN), $400-600/season; 18 general counselors, $400-600/season. "Write for application before the end of March, prefer during the months of January and February." Apply to Susan Welch, Director, Camp Hantesa, Dept. SED, RR 1, Boone IA 50036; tel. 515/432-6325.

Hitaga, Located 20 miles north of Cedar Rapids. Camp Fire camp for girls ages 7-17. Openings for college students, teachers and foreign students from June to August. Needs 40 counselors for riding, swimming, canoeing, nature, campcraft, hand crafts, archery, photography, $450-800/season; 3 cooks, $500-800/season. Room and board provided. Apply by May 10 to Linda Johnson, Dept. SED, Camp Hitaga, 712 3rd Ave. SE, Cedar Rapids IA 52401.
Fringe Benefits: Social atmosphere, pre-camp training. Recreational facilities are available to the staff. **College credit** possible.

Little Cloud, Located in Epworth. Girl Scout camp. Openings for college students, teachers and high school seniors for 7-week season. Needs specialists: 6 unit leaders, 2 horseback riding, 6 WSI waterfront, nurse, naturalist, canoe instructor, arts and crafts, dancing and folklore, photography, $400-900; 30 riding counselors, $400-850; cooks, $200/week. Salaries are commensurate with qualifications and experience. Room, board and training for job provided. Send for application. Enclose SASE. Apply by May 1 to Joan Geisler, Executive Director, Dept. SED, 3250 Dodge St., Box 26, Dubuque IA 52001; tel 319/583-0081.
Fringe Benefits: College credit available.

Mississippi Valley Girl Scout Council, Located in Bettendorf. Two summer camps in Iowa, one in Illinois, for girls ages 7-17. Openings for 45 college students, teachers and foreign students from early June through mid-August. Needs 7 unit leaders, 15 unit assistants, 2 pool directors (WSI), 5 pool

assistants, 6 canoeing instructors (WSI, SCI), 6 specialized program staff including primitive, backpacking, and canoe tripping, 3 horseback riding staff, 2 nurses (RN, LPN), 3 cooks, 1 handyperson. Salaries are $700-1,100. Room and board provided. Apply by June 1 to Mississippi Valley Girl Scout Council, Dept. SED, 2388 Cumberland Sq., Box 1051, Bettendorf IA 52722.
Fringe Benefits: Insurance coverage and laundry provided. **College credit** possible. This ACA-accredited camp offers a "progressive, open atmosphere; all aspects of the camp are good."

Moingona Girl Scout Council Resident Camps, Sacajawea, Strother, Located in southern and central Iowa. Ages 6

to 17. Openings for college students, teachers, high school seniors and foreign students from early June to mid-August. Needs 40 counselors for sports, arts, campcraft, $60-75/week; 6 waterfront and small-craft instructors, $60-85/week; 2 nurses (RN, EMT or LPN), $110-170/week; head cook, 7 kitchen assistants, $90-175/week. Room and board provided. Apply to Camping Services Director, Moingona Girl Scout Council Resident Camps, 10715 Hickman Rd., Des Moines IA 50322.
Fringe Benefits: This is a "beautiful, modern facility with good working conditions and a social atmosphere. The work provides employees with a growing experience." **College credit** possible.

Sunnyside, Located in Des Moines. Easter Seal Society residential camp for physically handicapped children and adults. Openings for college graduates, college students, high school seniors from the beginning of June to August, 12 weeks. Needs 12 unit leaders, $95-105/week; 24 cabin counselors, $75-85/week; 12 counselors in training, $55-65/week; arts and crafts leader, $95-105/week; waterfront leader (WSI required), $95-105/week; sports and games leader, $95-105/week; woodlore and/or nature leader, $95-105/week; 10 activity specialists experienced in arts, crafts, music, drama, swimming (WSI required), nature, boating, sports, games, riflery, or archery, $75-85/week; 3 program directors, $125-135/week; 3 assistant nurses (RN, LPN with pharmacology course, or graduate nurse), $120-200/week; 3 assistant cooks, $110-140/week. Challenge Camping Program personnel experienced in outdoor camping, camp craft skills, nature, canoeing, swimming (current WSI or SLS required), sports, or music; must be willing to work with variety of clientele (i.e. blind, mentally retarded, autistic, physically disabled, etc.); program coordinator, $120-135/week; 5 counselor-program staff, $80-105/week. Room and board provided. Apply by March 31 (may accept applications as late as May 22 depending upon qualifications) to Ed Stracke, Camp Sunnyside, Dept. SED, Box 4002, Des Moines IA 50333.
Fringe Benefits: Linens, free laundry, accident and sickness insurance and "excellent experience in learning to work with disabled individuals." **College credit** available.

Summer Theaters

Strayer-Wood Theatre, Located in Cedar Falls. Educational theater facility on the campus of University of Northern Iowa. Flexible 500-600-seat theater (proscenium, thrust, arena). Opened in 1978. Openings for college students, teachers, high school students, foreign students and local applicants from June 1 to August 1. Needs 6-8 actors, approximately $650/season; 5 scene shop assistants, approximately $800/season; 3 costume shop assistants, approximately $650/season; 1 assistant director/stage manager, approximately $800/season. "Will assist in securing room and board for company members." Hires physically handicapped persons for front of house, management duties and in costume shop. "Tuition must be paid from salaries and all must be enrolled in summer school." During academic year employment available for enrolled students in tech, costume, and front office work. Send for application. "Applicants must audition if an actor or send video tape of same by March 13, 1981." Apply to Dr. D. Terry Williams, Director of Theatre, Theatre UNI, Cedar Falls IA 50614.

Fringe Benefits: Excellent learning situation (3 shows, 6 performances each in eight weeks; excellent staff)." **College credit** available.

Kentucky

20 jobs available

Summer Camps

Midway-Longview Riding Camp, Located at Midway, near Lexington. Private coed camp, formerly called Longview Riding Camp. For children ages 8-17. Openings for 20 male and female college students from June 7 to August 15. Needs specialty counselors for tennis, swimming (WSI), archery, arts and crafts, campcrafts, drama, general sports, horseback riding and jumping. Salaries are $600-900 depending on experience. Room and board provided. Submit resume and photo. Apply to John Kiewit, Midway-Longview Riding Camp, Dept. SED, Midway College, Midway KY 40347; tel. 606/846-4421.

Maine

2,601 jobs available

Commercial Attractions

Funorama, Located at York Beach. Arcade. Openings from May to mid-September. Needs cashiers (college students or teachers with some experience); floor or ticket people (college students or teachers); electronic engineer (electronic and mechanical machine experience necessary). Pays wage commensurate with ability. "There is plenty of housing nearby." Housing information available at time of interview. Write or call for personal interview at business address. Apply by June 15 to Mr. Dugrenier, Box 306, York Beach ME 03910; tel. 207/363-4421.

National Parks

Acadia Corporation, Located in Bar Harbor, in Acadia National Park. Concessionaire. Openings for college students, teachers, foreign students and nonstudents, minimum age 18, from May 15 to October 15; August 1 to 31 minimum. Needs 15 shop clerks, $134-$146/40 hour week. Applicants should enjoy meeting people. Employees must find own housing. Apply by March 15 to Acadia Corporation, Dept. SED, 85 Main St., Bar Harbor ME 04609.
Fringe Benefits: "Jobs provide the unique combination of business experience and a rustic environment."

Resorts, Ranches, Restaurants, Lodging

Oakland House, Located in Sargentville. Resort. Openings from June 16 to September 10. Needs secretary-receptionist ($80-125/week); hostess ($45/week plus tips), college student or teacher preferred; 6 waitresses ($35-40/week plus tips); 4 kitchen helpers and assistant cooks ($70-125/week); 2-3 maintenance workers and groundskeepers ($80-125/week), college students, foreign students both acceptable; 3 housekeepers ($35-45/week plus tips), college students, teachers, foreign students all acceptable. Room and board provided. Apply to James Littlefield, Manager, Dept. SED, Oakland House, Sargentville ME 04673.

Quisisana Lodge, Located in Center Lovell, Maine, on Lake Kezar. Resort hotel. Openings for college students from early June to August 30. Needs 16 dining room waitresses and busboys, $1,000 plus tips averaging $400 additional; 5 bellhops, $1,000 plus tips averaging $300 additional; 8 chambermaids, $875 plus tips averaging $300 additional; 6 groundsmen, $900 plus tips averaging $250 additional; 8 kitchen helpers, $1,000. Staff participates in some musical evenings, both classical and popular. Room and board provided. No application forms will be sent unless a large SASE is enclosed with inquiry. Apply to Quisisana Lodge, Box 25068, Fort Lauderdale FL 33320.

Summer Camps

Alford Lake, Located in Union. Private camp for girls, ages 8-15. Openings for college students and teachers from about June 16 to August 16. Needs about 5 specialists in tennis, art, swimming, nature, dramatics, riding, sailing, canoeing, campcraft or dance. Salaries are $425-700/season. Room, board and laundry provided. Apply by April 15 to Mrs. Andrew N. McMullan, 17 Pilot Point Rd., Cape Elizabeth ME 04107.

Androscoggin Jr.-Sr., Located in Wayne, Maine. Boys' camp. Openings for college students and teachers from end of June through end of August (8½ weeks). Needs specialty counselors: archery, arts and crafts, pottery, dramatics, bicycling, tripping, 5 canoe, 2 waterskiing, 3 baseball, 10 tennis, 10 swimming (WSI), 2 riflery, 3 sailing; 2 trip leaders, 2 radio broadcasters. Salaries are $400 and up, depending on age and experience. Room and board

provided. Apply to Stanley L. Hirsch, 733 West St., Harrison NY 10528.
Fringe Benefits: Laundry service and travel allowance provided. "We have an extensive wilderness tripping program. If you like kids, teaching your particular activity, and the outdoors, you should have a great time at our camp. Both our staff and campers have a high return rate."

Association of Independent Camps, Openings at 80 children's (ages 6-16) summer camps located in New England and Middle Atlantic States. Needs head counselors, group leaders, general and all specialty counselors. Room and board provided. Apply by July to Association of Independent Camps, Dept. SED, 157 West 57th St., New York NY 10019; tel. 212/582-3540.
Fringe Benefits: "Travel expenses paid in part or in full; learning experiences, i.e., living and sharing with others; complete facilities in a healthy environment; time for socialization with peers." **College credit** "may be arranged by student at school."

Cedar, Located in Casco, Maine. Camp for boys, ages 8-15. Openings for 57 counselors, minimum age 18, from approximately June 21 to August 22. "We are looking for people who like to work with boys, have teaching skills and are willing to work hard. Specialists needed in all camp activities, including: swimming (WSI), boating, sailing, waterskiing and boat drivers, scuba, arts and crafts, soccer, tennis, baseball, football, lacrosse, riflery, archery, photography, golf, campcraft, backpacking, judo, ham radio, music, drama, wrestling, track, and other skills. We also need RNs and kitchen workers. Salaries are from $500-1,000. Salary based on age, experience and teaching ability. We have a significant return of campers and staff each year, have superior facilities and want to hire people who recognize that camp counseling is a professional responsibility." Room and board provided. Apply by May or early June to Henry M. Hacker, Dept. SED, 1758 Beacon St., Brookline MA 02146; tel. 617/277-8080.
Fringe Benefits: Some travel expenses provided. "Working conditions are outstanding—time off on a regular basis, most evenings free. Our philosophy is that if our staff is happy, our campers will be the same." **College credit** possible.

Chewonki Foundation, Located in Wiscasset. Summer camp for boys age 9-17 and girls age 13-17, emphasizing wilderness trips. Employment begins June 17. Needs 10 cabin counselors (sensitivity to young people and to the process of community building); and 10 activity counselors (nature, wilderness trips and sailing stressed; also art, woodworking, photography, tennis, archery, gardening, swimming, kayaking). Salaries are $300-650/season. Hires physically handicapped for some jobs. Room and board provided. "Be ready for hard work. The process of counseling is important and challenging and requires a great deal of patience and understanding. It is a happy and growing experience for the staff as well as campers." Send resume and letter requesting application for Tim Ellis, Director, Camp Chewonki Foundation, RFD 3, Wiscasset, ME 04578.
Fringe Benefits: "We stress personal growth, community development and

sensitivity to the natural world in a relaxed atmosphere. Our program is challenging to a wide cross-section of young people." **College credit** possible.

Chickawah, Located in Harrison, Maine. Camp for boys, ages 7-16. Member ACA. Openings for college students, teachers and high school seniors, beginning July 1 for 8 weeks. Needs specialists for golf, baseball, basketball, soccer, tennis, riflery, canoeing and sailing (SCI), waterskiing, general swim instructors (WSI); counselors with tripping and pioneering experience, science and nature, dramatics, ham radio, photography, gymnastics; chef, waiters, dishwashers, kitchen helpers, baker, licensed drivers, groundsman, porter, nurse (RN). Salaries are $600 and up. Room and board provided. Nonsmokers only. Apply to Maurice Steinberg, Box 178, Dept. SED, Carle Place NY 11514.
Fringe Benefits: Travel allowance, laundry. **College credit** possible.

Cobbossee, Located at Lake Cobbosseecontee, Winthrop. Camp for boys ages 6-16. Openings for college juniors and seniors, college graduates and teachers. Needs counselors for athletics (baseball, basketball, soccer, softball, football), archery, boating, canoeing, crafts, golf, general group, ham radio, photography, riflery, sailing, scuba, swimming, tennis, trampoline, trap and skeet shooting, tripping, waterskiing, wrestling; secretary, nurse (RN). Salaries are $550-800 plus transportation allowance, laundry, basic camp uniform, and increment for each year counseling experience. Sister camp, Camp Somerset; see Somerset listing for address. Apply by May 31 to Camp Cobbossee, Dept. SED, Mianus Dr., Bedford NY 10506; tel. 212/823-7210.
Fringe Benefits: "We believe in Cobbossee and realize our positive attitude and ability to work with the staff are the 'hidden assets' of working here. We make employees feel they are more than employees."

Diocesan Camping Center, Located in Poland Spring. Coed agency camp, with Catholic affiliation, for socially integrated children ages 6-13. Openings for college students and teachers from June 26 to August 28. Needs specialized program directors such as waterfront director (WSI), boating director, arts & crafts, land sports etc, general cabin counselors, nurse (RN), and other administrative persons. Apply to Diocesan Camping Center, 87 High St., Portland ME 04101.

Fernwood, Located at Thompson Lake, Poland. Camp for girls ages 8-16. Openings for college students and teachers, minimum age 19, from June 19 to August 20. Needs male and female counselors for tennis, swimming (WSI), jewelry-metal crafts, woodworking, ceramics, canoeing, riflery, archery, sailing, English riding, gymnastics, field sports, piano accompanist (pop, by ear), waterskiing, dramatics (experienced); 2 nurses (RN). Salaries are $450-800/season, based on experience. Room and board provided. Apply by May 15 to Maxine B. King, 40 Elm St., Topsham ME 04086.
Fringe Benefits: Laundry provided. Travel allowance provided for those outside Maine and Massachusetts. "Coed staff; social opportunities provided." **College credit** possible.

Hiawatha, Located at Trafton and Stanley Lakes, Kezar Falls, Maine.

Camp for girls ages 6-16. Openings for college students, graduates and teachers who demonstrate a strong desire to become a member of a community of young people dedicated to innovation, individualized programing and excellence in teaching. Season runs June 22 to August 24. Campers come from all over the world. Needs counselors for wilderness program, tripping, gymnastics, archery, creative arts, ceramics, dance, scuba, water skiing, equestrian, and all field sports. Salaries are $450 and up. Room and board provided. Send for application; apply by June 1 to: Camp Hiawatha for Girls, Dept. SED, 84 School St., Manchester, MA 01944.
Fringe Benefits: Transportation allowance, linen and laundry service. Brother camp, Camp Robin Hood, is minutes away; many coed events for campers and staff. **College credit** possible.

Kamp Kohut, Located in Oxford, Maine, on Lake Thompson. Camp for boys ages 6-16. Openings for 80, minimum age 21, from June 21 to August 25. Needs specialty counselors for archery, athletics, baseball, basketball, canoeing, crafts, dramatics, golf, radio, music, nature, photography, riflery, sailing, scuba, soccer, pioneering, waterskiing, softball, swimming (WSI), tennis, tripping, adventure; art, ceramics, hockey, Indian lore, kayaking, outdoor living skills, track/field and woodworking; nurse (RN); group counselors; folksinger. Salaries are good. Increment is added to base salary for each year of previous acceptable experience. Room and board provided. Apply to Malcolm J. Itkin, Kamp Kohut, 451 Buckminster Dr., Norwood MA 02062; tel. 617/769-4685.
Fringe Benefits: Transportation allowance, laundry. **College credit** possible.

Kennebec Camps, Located at Salmon Lake in North Belgrade, Oakland, Maine. Private camp for boys ages 9-15. Employs college students, administrators and teachers from June 15 to August 19. Accommodations for married applicants. Needs nurses (RN); specialty counselors in archery, baseball, basketball, campcraft, canoeing, ceramics, crafts (wood/metal), cycling, dramatics/entertainment, nature, outward bound, photography, piano, sailing, soccer, swimming, riflery, tennis, track, trip leaders, waterskiing, white water rafting and wrestling. Salaries are $400-1,200/season, depending on specialty and experience. Room, board and laundry services provided. British applicants must apply through BUNACAMP. Others should apply by March 31 to Mr. Bernard Lemonick, Dept. SED, 405 Westview Rd., Elkins Park PA 19117.

Kippewa for Girls, Located at Lake Cobbosseecontee, Winthrop. Openings for college students from sophomore year on, and for teachers from June 22 to August 24. Needs specialty counselors for drama, arts and crafts, nature, canoeing, waterskiing, sailing, field sports, tennis, campcraft, tripping, archery, gymnastics; food service coordinator; 2 nurses (RN). Salaries are $500-750. Room and board provided. Apply by February 1 to Martin or Sylvia Silverman, 60 Mill St., Box 307, Westwood MA 02090.
Fringe Benefits: Some travel allotment, laundry. **College credit** available. "This camp offers a large staff with excellent staff supervision"; it is located in a "lovely area near all assets of Maine."

Laurel, Located 17 miles from Augusta, Maine, in the Central Lakes

Region. Coed camp for children ages 8-15. Openings for male and female college students, teachers, and graduate students, from June 22 to August 22. Needs specialty counselors for tennis, swimming, sailing, waterskiing, soccer, field sports, dramatics, riding, arts and crafts, ceramics, woodworking, sewing, cooking, archery, gymnastics, piano, photography, AM radio, nature, canoe and mountain trips, early childhood. Salaries are $550 and up. Room and board provided. Apply by April 15 to Ron Scott, Camp Laurel, Dept. SED, Box 848, New Paltz NY 12561.

Fringe Benefits: Good working conditions; warm, friendly atmosphere, good social life (coed camp); laundry provided. **College credit** available.

Matoaka for Girls, Located in Oakland, Maine. Openings for college students and teachers from June 22 to August 22. Needs specialty counselors: 6 WSI, 5 tennis, 5 arts and crafts, 4 waterskiing, 2 drama-music, 2 sewing, 2 gymnastics, 3 photography, 3 land sports, 4 riding, 2 tripping, 4 small-craft, $550 and up; computer operator; video and communication; secretary; 2 nurses (RN); kitchen supervisor. Apply to Camp Matoaka for Girls, Dept. SED, 6 Taylor Rd., Sudbury MA 01776; tel. 617/443-4226.

Fringe Benefits: Travel allotment. **College credit** possible. "This camp offers a chance to work in a beautiful setting in central Maine with warm, friendly people filled with a lot of traditional camp spirit."

Modin, Located in Canaan on a private lake and surrounded with 500 unspoiled acres. Established in 1922; serving its third generation of campers in a thoughtful Jewish cultural environment. ACA and AIC accredited. 110 boys/105 girls ages 7-17. Openings for college students and teachers with genuine interest in teaching and living with children from June 26 to August 14. Needs counselors and instructors in photography, canoeing, sailing, waterskiing, archery, tennis, softball, basketball, soccer, football, volleyball, arts and crafts, theater, music, self-defense; outdoor trip leaders; two nurses. Salaries $400-1,200. Room and board provided. Send resume or send for application by April 1 to Amy and David Adler, Directors, Camp Modin, Dept. SED, 47 E North Central Ave., Hartsdale NY 10530; tel. 914/997-7449.

Fringe Benefits: Transportation allowance, laundry, medical insurance. **College credit** possible.

Naomi, Located at Crescent Lake in Raymond, Maine. Coed camp for children ages 8-16. Openings for college students, teachers and foreign students from June 25 to August 26. Needs 30 counselors, $400-650/season; 4 unit heads, $750-1,400/season; 10 aquatics (WSI); director, $900-1,200/season; assistant directors: sailing, waterfront assistants, boating, waterskiing, canoeing, $450-1,000/season; 10 program specialists for tennis, arts and crafts, photography, nature, riflery, archery, campcraft, tripping, music, drama, land sports, $500-1,000/season; 2 nurses (RN), $800-1,200/season; kitchen and laundry workers. Apply by March to Leonard M. Katowitz, Executive Director, Dept. SED, Jewish Center Camps, 50 Hunt St., Watertown MA 02172; tel. 617/924-2030.

Pinecliffe, Located in Harrison, Maine. Camp for girls ages 8-16. Openings for college students, teachers and foreign students from June 20 to

CAMP RAPPUTAK

Established 1930

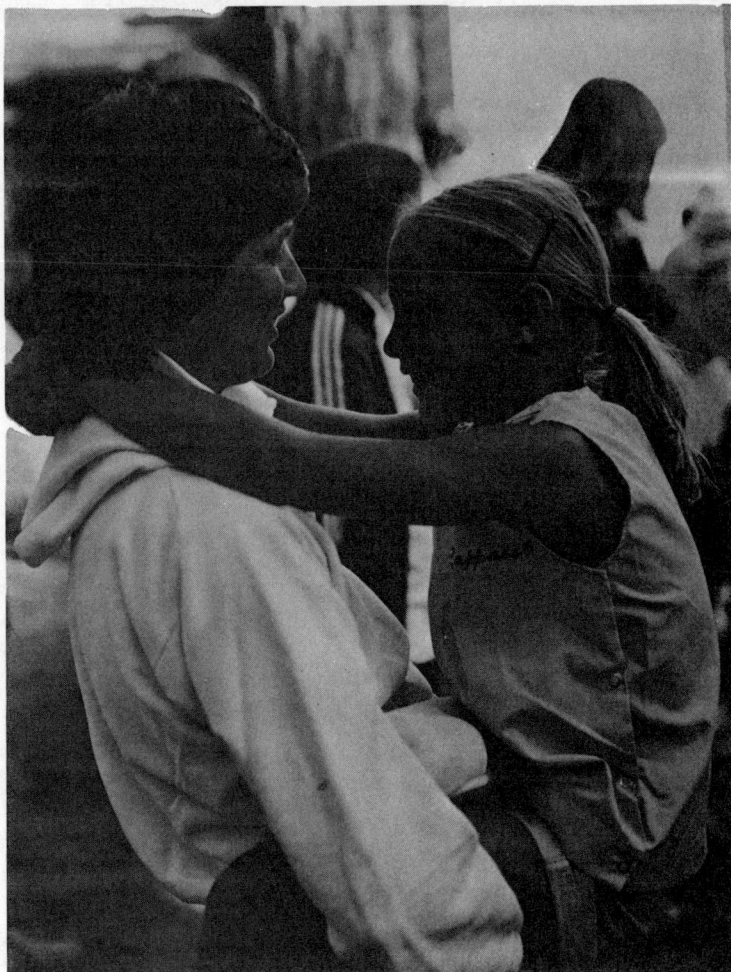

Members

American Camping Association * New England Camping Association

Maine Camp Director's Association * Association of Independent Camps

	Directors	
Summer		**Winter**
Fryeburg, Maine 04037	Mr. & Mrs. Howard J. Rymland	Stevenson, Maryland 21153

August 23. Needs program director; 2 unit leaders; specialty counselors: 5 waterfront, 3 tennis, 2 performing arts, 3 crafts, $500-900/season; nurse, $1,000/season. Apply by spring to Camp Pinecliffe, 200 E. 71st St., New York NY 10021.

Rapputak, Located on Lovewell Lake in the foothills of the White Mountains (in Fryeburg, Maine). Private camp for 170 girls ages 8-15. Openings for college women, graduates, and teachers, from June 15 to August 22. Needs camp doctor; nurse (RN); secretary; instructors in archery, arts and crafts, canoeing, choral singing, dramatics, field sports, gymnastics, piano accompaniment, riding, sailing, swimming (WSI), tennis, trampoline, tripping and waterskiing. Salaries are $500-1,200/season. Room and board provided. Apply by March 1 to Mr. and Mrs. Howard J. Rymland, Stevenson MD 21153.
Fringe Benefits: Transportation allowance and camp clothes provided. Free laundry, linen, and medical service.

Samoset II, Located in Casco, Maine. Camp for boys ages 7-16. "Samoset II is a sports oriented camp dedicated to teaching boys sports skills and providing an opportunity for competitive play." Openings for college students, teachers and high school seniors from June 23 to August 21. Needs 4 general counselors familiar with all sports; instructors for soccer, volleyball, baseball, basketball, tennis, archery, lacrosse, riflery, photography, wrestling, nature, universal weight training, drama, canoeing, karate, WSI, scuba, sailing, waterskiing, bicycling; directors for hiking and assistant, crafts and assistant. Salaries are $500-1,000. Room and board provided. Apply immediately to Stephen Feinstein, Director, 140 Waterman St., Providence RI 02906; tel. 401/421-5675.
Fringe Benefits: Laundry and insurance. **College credit** possible. "There are over 100 camps in the area which attract young people and tourists from all over the world. All recreational facilities are available for staff use during off-duty hours. Staff recreation with other camps is arranged. There is a liberal time-off policy."

Somerset For Girls, Located in Oakland, Maine. Openings for college students and teachers. Needs counselors for archery, athletics, canoeing, crafts, dramatics, fencing, golf, riding, riflery, skeet shooting, sailing, scuba, swimming, synchronized swimming, tennis, tripping, waterskiing, general group; nurse (RN); secretaries; dining room supervisor. Salaries are $550-850. Room and board provided. Brother camp, Camp Cobbossee. Apply by June 1 to Camp Somerset, 444 E. 86th St, New York NY 10028.
Fringe Benefits: Transportation, clothing allowance, laundry. **College credit** available. "We attempt to create a mature, interesting staff that works in a circular administration rather than in a pyramid. All staff members participate on various committees, formulating mechanics whereby the program goals are fulfilled. There is a ratio of 2-campers per staff member. We are concerned with the staff members' growth as we are with their performance. A liberal time-off policy, evening snacks and other fringe benefits combine to create good morale in a wholesome working condition."

Takajo, Located in Naples, Maine. Boys camp. Staff openings for teachers, upper college level students and graduate students (age 20 and up). Vacancies are in athletics, tripping, swimming (WSI), canoeing, sailing, waterskiing, dramatics, music, photography, radio and electronics, nature study, crafts, ceramics, woodworking, fine arts, riflery, archery and general counseling for younger boys. Would prefer high school coaching level applicants for head baseball, basketball, soccer, street hockey, and tennis. Salaries are $450-750. Room and board provided. Apply from November 1980 to June 20, 1981 to Morton J. Goldman, 3 Puritan Court, Princeton NJ 08540.
Fringe Benefits: Laundry service, linen service, transportation assistance. **College credit** possible.

Tapawingo, Located in Sweden, Maine, in the foothills of the New Hampshire White Mountains. ACA accredited camp established 1919. (The "Tap" family consists of 190 girls, ages 8-16; 75 counselors). Over 1,000 acres on private lake. Openings for college juniors, seniors, graduate students, teachers with genuine interest in teaching and living with children from June 22 to August 25. Needs counselor staff in arts and crafts, backpacking, canoeing, dramatics, gymnastics, land sports (including hockey and soccer), riding, sailing, swimming (including diving, competition and synchronized, WSI only), pianist (accompanist and transposer), tennis, waterskiing; nurses (RN). Limited accommodations for older women, men and married couple counselors. Excellent salary, commensurate with age, experience and skill. Room and board provided. Send for application, brochure and detailed information. Apply by early May to Mr. and Mrs. M. H. Rogers, Directors, 1890 S. Ocean Dr., Box 1225, Hallandale FL 33009.
Fringe Benefits: Transportation allowance, laundry. "Tapawingo has a reputation as one of New England's most dedicated camps with excellent facilities and equipment." **College credit** possible. "Our staff, the Tap family, is chosen for its good physical and emotional health. All the head counselors are professional. The counselors who work with and under the head in each activity are skilled and have the opportunity to become professional. We ask for dedication and for givers, not takers, for the 8 weeks the counselors are working and playing with the campers. The Tap spirit is contagious and the counselors leave feeling happy, with a wealth of new friendships."

Vega for Girls, Located on Echo Lake at Kents Hill. Private camp for girls ages 8-15. Openings for college students and coaches who enjoy working and living with children. Needs instructors for swimming (WSI), sailing, waterskiing, canoeing, pioneering, tripping, English riding, tennis, drama, landsports, arts and crafts. Salaries are $500-1000/season. Room and board provided. Apply by April to Richard Courtiss, Camp Vega for Girls, Dept. SED, Kents Hill ME 04349.
Fringe Benefits: Laundry and uniforms, **College credit** available.

Wild Goose, Located at Great Moose Lake in Harmony, Maine. Top rated private camp for 70 boys ages 8-14; includes all land and water sports and wilderness tripping. Openings from June 22 to August 23. Needs nurse (RN or LPN), $800-900/season; secretary/typist with car, $800-900/season; kitchen workers, salary open depending on age and experience; counselors with sports background, $400-800/season depending on age and experience. Apply by April 30 to William E. Trauth, Dept. SED, 328 Summit Ave., Leonia NJ 07605; tel. 201/944-6271.

Wyonegonic Camps, Located in Denmark, Maine, near the White Mountains of New Hampshire. Three small private girls camps adjacent to one another with separate facilities, program and staff. Openings for college students, teachers, graduate students and married couples, from late June to mid-August. Needs specialty counselors (minimum age 21) for waterfront, canoeing and mountain trips, sailing, tennis, riflery, gymnastics, piano, archery, waterskiing, riding, arts and crafts. Salaries are $500-700 depending on age, experience and responsibility. Room and board provided. Apply by May to Mr. and Mrs. George N. Sudduth, 30 Hancock Rd., Hingham MA 02043; tel. 617/749-5515.
Fringe Benefits: College credit possible.

Summer Theaters

Brunswick Music Theater & Coastal Theatre Workshop, Located in Brunswick. "Only remaining all professional equity music theater in the country." Openings from June 1 to August 30. Needs director of apprentice and intern program (intelligent, organized, leader interested in professional artistic training), $200/week; assistant general manager (bookkeeping background, organized, pleasant personality), $150/week; 3 technicians (carpenters, assistant technical director, etc.), salary negotiable; prop master or mistress (artistic, able to build, organized), salary negotiable; professional costume designer and assistant costume designer, salaries negotiable. Free housing for apprentices/interns. For non-apprentices: rooms and apartments, $35-70/week; reasonably priced restaurants. Also needs professional cast for appearances with the Portland Symphony in February. Send resume, request application or interview. Apply by March 1st to Victoria Crandall, Executive and Artistic Director, Dept. SED, Clark's Point, Wiscasset ME 04578.
Fringe Benefits: Coastal Theatre Workshop for apprentices and interns. 5 scholarships and **college credit** available.

Maryland

338+ jobs available

Business and Industry

Temp Force, Temporary office personnel contractor. Openings for college students, teachers, high school seniors during vacations and holidays. Needs secretaries, typists, stenographers, clericals and accountants. Salaries based upon experience. Apply to Temp Force, 1 Investment Place, Towson MD 21204; tel. 301/828-0778.

Fringe Benefits: "Tempforce employees are all entitled to participate in our vacation bonus program and compete for our employee of the month award. They also gain valuable work experience while earning money to further their education."

Government

National Security Agency, Jobs are at Ft. George G. Meade. Openings for 25-50 college juniors for the summer of 1982. Needs students in scientific fields: engineering, electrical engineering, computer science and mathematics. Also uses some language majors. Student must be a US citizen and have 3 point or better grade average. Applicants should apply in 1981 for jobs in 1982—it takes 6 months to obtain the top-secret security clearance required for jobs with the National Security Agency. Send form 171 to National Security Agency, Attention: M 32, Summer Employment Coordinator, Ft. George G. Meade MD 20755.

Summer Camps

Airy, Louise, Hebrew camp for boys and girls. Openings for college students, teachers and foreign students from June 22 to August 22. Needs 70 counselors with skills in WSI, riflery, crafts, music and outdoor living. Salaries are $300-500 with annual increments, travel and laundry allowance plus room and board; program specialists and unit leaders are paid differentials for additional skill and responsibility. Apply by May 10 to Sidney N. Chernak, 5750 Park Heights Ave., Baltimore MD 21215.

Children's Fresh Air Society, Inc., Located in rural setting 40 miles northeast of Baltimore. Challenging, rewarding positions for college students and teachers working in resident summer camp for boys and girls from lower income families. Many openings—general counselors, swimming instruction, canoeing, arts and crafts, music. Genuine desire to teach children a must. Also needs capable people for positions in kitchen personnel and maintenance. Interested should send resume before May 21st to Executive Director, Dept. SED, 615 Cherry Hill Rd., Street MD 21154.
Fringe Benefits: Bonuses for counselors who work the entire summer. **College credit** possible. "Counselors at the Fresh Air Camp live and work together at the very challenging job of teaching children. Few other jobs offer so much experience in human relations and getting along/working with others."

Conowingo Camps, Located in Conowingo. 700-acre girls' resident camp including cabins, tents and 100-year-old mansion; for girls 6-17. Openings

---

COLLEGE CREDIT is offered for completion of many jobs in this book. Check the "Fringe Benefits" section of listings for employers who offer this bonus.

for college students, teachers, foreign students, high school students and local applicants from June 8 to August 23. Needs 2 assistant directors $1,000-1,500/season; 2 program directors, $700-1,000/season; 1 administrative aide, $700-1,000/season; 1 director and 3 assistants for waterfront (WSI, ALS, CPR, first aid), $500-1,000/season; 35 counselors, $500-up/season. Room and board provided. Would consider hiring physically handicapped. Send for application. Apply by February to Joan W. Fincutter, Director of Camping Services, Girl Scouts of Central Maryland, Dept. SED, 730 W. 40th St., Baltimore MD 212ll.

Fringe Benefits: Uniforms provided. Located 3 hours from New York City; near Baltimore, Philadelphia and Washington DC. **College credit** possible.

Elk's Camp Barrett, Located in Annapolis. Summer camp for boys and girls ages 9-14. Openings for college students and teachers from early June to late August. Local residents may apply for position as cook. Needs 2 lifeguards/counselors (with WSI and CPR certification), 5 counselors (camping experience and skills in sports, archery, campcraft or nature), and 5 junior counselors with similar skills, $1,000/season; cook, $2,000/season. Room and board provided. EOE. Send resume by March 2 to Robert Destelhorst, Executive Director, Elk's Camp Barrett, 1001 Chesterfield Rd., Annapolis MD 21401; tel. 301/224-2945.

Greentop, Located at Lanz. Camp for physically disabled children (ages 6-18) and adults (18 and up). Needs 14 cabin program leaders and 26 counselors. "Counselors work with cabin groups and in activity areas; water safety instructor required for swimming; crafts and sports require experience with children. Room and board provided. Experience working with children and adults desired." Also needs clerical, business and kitchen personnel and nurses/LPNs. Needs counselors for adult camp session from mid- to late August, usually 2 weeks. For children's camp, work from late June to mid-August. Apply to Chad M. Casserly, Director, Camping Recreation, The League for the Handicapped, Inc., 1111 E. Cold Spring Lane, Baltimore MD 21239; tel. 301/323-0500.

Fringe Benefits: Transportation from Baltimore to camp.

King's Landing, Located 6 miles north of Prince Frederick on the Patuxent River. YMCA resident coed camp for children ages 7-15; day camp for ages 6-12. Openings for college students, teachers, high school seniors, minimum age 18, from approximately June 20 through August 25. Needs 25 counselors, $630-810 season; 8 junior counselors (minimum age 17 with counseling experience), $300-350/season. Salary depends on experience. Room and board provided. Apply by April to YMCA King's Landing Camp, Box 88, RR1, Dept. SED, Huntingtown MD 20639.

Letts, Located in Edgewater. Coed YMCA camp. Openings for college students, teachers and high school seniors from mid-June to mid-August. Needs 30 counselors, $350 up; 3 assistant waterfront-pool directors, $350-600; 7 unit leaders, $500 up; 2 waterfront-pool directors, $650 up; land activities director, $550 up; program director, $750 up. Room and board provided. Application deadline: March, but may accept applications until June. Apply early to YMCA Camp Letts, Box 208, Dept. SED, Edgewater MD 21037.

Tockwogh, Located on the Chesapeake Bay near Worton, Maryland. Coed YMCA camp for children ages 8-15. Openings for college students, teachers, and graduating high school seniors from June 17 to August 29. Needs counselor/activity instructor, $550 and up; counselor/activity director, $625 and up; activity specialists, $700 and up; administrative staff, $900 and up; instructors and directors needed for sailing, skiing, boating, canoeing, swimming, WSI, archery, riflery, tennis, arts and crafts, photography, riding, bay studies, dramatics, dancing, puppetry, campcraft, tripping, athletics and soccer; nurse (RN); grad and student nurses; office secretary. Room and board provided. Application suggested before March 1, but may accept applications until June. Apply early to YMCA Camp Tockwogh, 11th and Washington Sts., Wilmington DE 19801.

Camp Waredaca Inc., Located in Gaithersburg. Resident 5-day week summer camp for children ages 7-15 with year-round recreational activities. Openings from mid-June to mid-August. Needs 1 cook (college student, teacher, high school student, foreign student or local applicant) to prepare 3 meals a day, Monday through Friday for 150 people, $200/week; 1 nurse (college graduate, RN) for general health care of about 120 children, emergency first aid, $110/week; 2 WSIs (college students, teachers) to organize waterfront program on lake, $90/week; 8 counselors (college students, teachers, high school students, foreign students, local applicants), $40-85/week. Also needs horseback riding instructor and hay ride driver year round. Room and board provided. Send resume, phone, or send for application. Apply by Easter break to Susanne Marfak, Director, Dept. SED, Camp Waredaca, Inc., 4015 Damascus Rd., Gaithersburg MD 20760; telephone 301/924-4991. **Fringe Benefits:** Weekends off. Free time to horseback ride and swim. **College credit** available.

Summer Theaters

Old Bay Playhouse, Located in Lexington Park. Openings from June 10 to August 10. Needs 12 actors (professional), $150/week. Send resume by March to David Davis, Artistic Director, Charles Hewitt St. Mary's Summer Festival, 272 Three Notch Rd., Lexington Park MD 20653. **Fringe Benefits: College credit** available.

Massachusetts

2,592+ jobs available

Business and Industry

Brook Street Bureau of Mayfair Ltd., Permanent and

temporary personnel agency. Openings for unlimited number. Needs permanent and temporary secretaries, "Fridays," and typists. All fees paid. Office: 8 Winter St., Boston MA 02108. Apply to Administration Office, Brook Street Bureau of Mayfair Ltd., 136 E. 57th St., New York NY 10022; tel. 212/688-3910.

Dot DeMayo School of Charm and Modeling, Located in Attleboro. Modeling school. Opening during June and July for maintenance person to take care of large in-ground pool and the school grounds. Person should have experience in caring for pools. Room and board provided. Apply by phone before June 30 to D. E. DeMayo, Directress, Dot DeMayo School of Charm and Modeling, 42 Prairie Ave., Attleboro MA 02703; tel. 617/222-7246.

Environmental Intern Program/Northeast, Located in Lincoln. Intern program. Places upper-level undergraduates and graduate students in short-term (3-month) professional positions for career experience. Openings for 120 students all year, but mostly summer. Needs students for over 30 different positions/disciplines used annually: field research and office research positions; 3 years college minimum. Salaries are $140-$250. Would consider hiring physically handicapped students. Send for application. Apply by March 2 to Ms. Margot Iwanchuk, Regional Director, EIP/Northeast, Dept. SED, Box 277, Lincoln MA 01773.
Fringe Benefits: "Excellent learning experiences with creative professionals; opportunity to attend workshops and meetings relating to career training." **College credit** possible.

Olsten Temporary Services, Located in Boston. Office and industrial employment service. Positions available for loaders-unloaders, packers, warehouse workers, kitchen help, typists, secretaries, clerks, key punchers, switchboard operators and demonstrators. Positions are daily, long- and short-term assignments. Paid weekly on Fridays. Top hourly rates. Apply in person to Olsten Temporary Services, 8 Winter Street, 2nd floor, Boston MA 02108; tel. 617/426-3910 (office); 617-423-7426 (industrial).
Fringe Benefits: Attendance bonuses and vacation with pay.

Government

Department of Labor, Jobs available at the regional office, Room 1001, JFK Federal Building, Government Center, Boston MA 02203. This office serves Connecticut, Maine, Massachusetts, New Hampshire, Vermont and Rhode Island. Applications must be made to Washington DC office. See Washington DC office (District of Columbia section) for complete description of jobs available and how to apply information.

Summer Camps

Association of Independent Camps, Openings at 80 children's (ages 6-16) summer camps located in New England and Middle Atlantic States. Needs head counselors, group leaders, general and all specialty counselors.

Room and board provided. Apply by July to Association of Independent Camps, Dept. SED, 157 W. 57th St., New York NY 10019; tel 212/582-3540.
Fringe Benefits: "Travel expenses paid in part or in full; learning experiences, i.e., living and sharing with others; complete camp facilities in a healthy environment; time for socialization with peers." **College credit** may be arranged by student at school.

Avalon, Located at Cape Cod. Girls' camp. Openings for college students for 9 weeks during the summer. Needs instructors for sailing, tennis, swimming (WSI), gymnastics, trampoline, crafts, archery; program aide, nurse (RN). Salaries are $500 and up. Room and board provided. Apply to Mr. and Mrs. George N. Laffey, Jr., Camp Avalon, Chatham MA 02633.

Clara Barton, Located in North Oxford. Camp for diabetic girls ages 7-17. Openings for college students and teachers from approximately June 22 to August 22. Needs 20 specialty counselors for arts and crafts, canoeing, boating, sailing, swimming (WSI), campcraft, nature, gymnastics, bicycling, team and individual sports, dance, apparatus, Indian lore, $450-600; waterfront director, $750-800; assistant waterfront director, $650-700; 5 unit directors, $650-1,000; program director and assistant camp director, $1,200-1,500; 3 nurses (RN or graduate nurse), $800-1,000; head dietitian, $1,000; assistant dietitian, $700-900; 3 nurse's aides, 3 lab technicians, $500-800; head cook, $1,200-1,500; assistant cook, $700-900; 3 kitchen aides, 2 maintenance aides, $350-550. Apply by March 1 to Elizabeth Kruczek, Camps Complex Administrator, UUWF, Dept. SED, 6 Betty St., Auburn MA 01501.
Fringe Benefits: College credit can be arranged through respective colleges if program is available.

Belvoir Terrace, Located in Lenox, Massachusetts. Fine arts summer school for "talented, motivated teenage women." Openings for college graduates from June 20 through August 20. Needs specialty counselors for art, music, theater, gymnastics, waterfront (WSI) and tennis. Salaries are commensurate with experience. Room and board provided. Apply to Nancy Goldberg, 145 Central Park West, New York NY 10023.
Fringe Benefits: "Fine working conditions; an opportunity to take classes with the campers." **College credit** possible.

Cape Cod Sea Camps/Monomoy-Wono, Located in Brewster. Private coed summer recreational camp for children ages 7-17. Openings for college students and teachers (minimum age 19) from end of June to middle of August. Salary range: $500-up/season. Needs 2-4 WSI's; 2-4 sailing instructors with first aid, CPR certificates; 2-4 experienced instructors each for tennis, archery, riflery, gymnastics, woodworking, art. Room and board provided. Send for application. Apply by June 1981 to Ms. Nancy Garran, Personnel Director, Dept. SED, Cape Cod Sea Camps, Brewster MA 02631.
Fringe Benefits: "Recreational facilities, coed working situation, scenic locale (Cape Cod), excellent growing and learning experience, social atmosphere, interesting work." **College credit** possible.

Crane Lake, Located in West Stockbridge, Massachusetts, 3 miles from

Tanglewood Music Festival in the Berkshire Mountains. Private coed camp. Openings for college students and teachers from late June to late August. Needs physical education majors and teachers to coach basketball, baseball, football, soccer, tennis; specialty counselors: 6 waterfront (WSI), small craft, hiking, gymnastics, drama, music, fine arts, painting, sculpturing, nature, riflery, arts and crafts, guitar, sailing, canoeing. Salaries are $500 and up depending on age and experience. Room and board provided. Apply by April 30 to Ed Ulanoff, Crane Lake Camp, Dept. SED, 4465 Douglas Ave., Riverdale NY 10471.

Fringe Benefits: Free laundry, trips into Boston and the Tanglewood Music Festival and other cultural performances. **College credit** possible.

Danbee, Located in Peru, Massachusetts. Girls camp. Openings from June 22 to August 22. Needs specialty instructors for swimming (WSI), sailing, canoeing, diving, competitive swimming, synchronized swimming, gymnastics, volleyball, basketball, archery, ceramics, sculpturing, painting, jewelry, weaving, dramatics, cooking, sewing, piano (accompanist), photography, typing, tennis, campcraft, waterskiing, soccer, bicycling, yearbook, recreational games, golf, dance, and field hockey. Salaries are $550 and up depending on age and experience. Apply to Ann B. Miller, Camp Danbee, 2031 Rittenhouse Square, Philadelphia PA 19103.

Farley, Located in Mashpee. Coed 4-H summer camp for 4-H and non-4-H members ages 8-13. Program includes environmental studies, recreation, swimming, boating, arts and crafts, archery and horses. Openings for college students, teachers and high school seniors from April 1 or July 1 to September 1. Needs maintenance person; specialists: 2 recreation/sports, 1 archery, 2 arts and crafts, 2 smallcraft boating, 2 swimming (WSI), 2 horseback riding, 2 environmental studies and 1 theater arts. Salary negotiable. Room and board provided. "We are interested in creative individuals who are flexible enough to try new things to make the program work. Previous camp experience is a must whether that means as a camper or counselor. Recreation majors and active people interested in getting other people active in all facets of camping life will be highly regarded. Anyone accepting a position with us should bring any resource materials (books, notes) that might help them here to develop their area." Send resume, request application or call. Apply by July 10 to Peter Mackiewicz, Executive Director, Dept. SED, Box 97, Forestdale MA 02644; tel. 617/477-0181.

Fringe Benefits: "In the case of the program director and in a limited number of other staff members, we provide space for the families of these individuals as well as provide the benefit of allowing the children of such staff members to attend the program free of charge." **College credit** possible.

Good News, Located at Forestdale, on Cape Cod. Christian, coed camp. Openings for college students and teachers from June 23 to August 18. Needs 40 counselors, kitchen staff, laundry workers, store help, office worker, maintenance, nurse. Salaries are $450-600. Room and board provided. Apply to Faith Willard, Dept. SED, Box 74, Forestdale MA 02644.

Fringe Benefits: College credit possible. "Great atmosphere—95 percent of staff call this work the most beneficial growing experience of their lives!"

Greylock for Boys, Romaca for Girls, Located in Becket and Hinsdale, Massachusetts. Brother-sister camps, founded 1915. Openings from June 19 to August 19 for university and college students and teachers, minimum age 20. Needs 4 group leaders/department heads, $800-1,200; 24 waterfront (ARC, WSI, SCI), $600-900; 60 specialists for all land and water sports, popular/jazz/rock/folk music, art, drama, handcrafts, carpentry, hiking, radio, electronics, nature, kitchen and maintenance, top salaries; 2 doctors, 4 nurses (RN). Room and board provided. Apply by June 15 to Bert Margolis, Camps Greylock for Boys, Romaca for Girls, Dept. SED, 25 E. 83rd St., New York NY 10028; tel. 212/861-2450.
Fringe Benefits: College credit available. "This camp offers excellent food in almost unlimited amounts. Employees work in a brother-sister, semi-coed situation; a fun job!"

Elliott P. Joslin, Located in Charlton. Private, nonprofit, specialty camp for diabetic boys ages 7-15+. Needs 1 assistant (WSI) waterfront director, $650-900; 2 waterfront specialists (e.g. canoeing, boating, sailing, kayaking), $600-850; 2 senior counselors, $600-800; 1 accountant/bookkeeper, $800-1,000; 2 campcraft specialists (to include some backpacking, canoe trips), $650-850; 2 arts and crafts specialists, $650-850; 2 nature specialists, $650-850. College students preferred. Also needs 2 junior counselors, $500-625, college students or high school seniors preferred. Work from June 21 to August 28. "Waterfront personnel must be certified by the American Red Cross in areas they are applying for. Applicants should be looking for a challenging and busy position." Salaries depend on previous experience and training. Room and board provided. Apply by May to Paul B. Madden, Camp Administrator/Director, Dept. SED, Elliott P. Joslin Camp, 1 Joslin Place, Boston MA 02215.
Fringe Benefits: "The camp is situated on approximately 300 acres with its own large pond and several recreation fields and courts. Our low staff-to-camper ratio (50 to 90) gives us an excellent opportunity to do close one-on-one work with the children." **College credit** "has been arranged frequently in the past."

Lenore-Owaissa for Girls, Located in Hinsdale, Massachusetts, in the Berkshires. Camp for girls ages 7-17. Openings for college seniors, graduate students and teachers from June 26 to August 22. Needs specialty counselors for tennis, arts and crafts, WSI, sailing, soccer, waterskiing, pioneering, archery, fencing, drama, dancing, gymnastics and music. Salary $600. Apply to Director, Camp Lenore-Owaissa, 851 E. 23rd St., Brooklyn NY 11210.

Lenox, Located in Lee, Massachusetts, in the Berkshires on Shaw Lake. Private boys' camp. Openings for college students (minimum age 20, sophomore and above), graduate students, for 8 weeks. Needs instructors for lacrosse, physical fitness, golf, basketball, baseball, tennis, photography, drama, radio, archery, swimming (WSI), waterskiing, small crafts, sailing, scuba, soccer; counselors for overnight camping, nature, arts and crafts; pianist, industrial arts

majors, typist, kitchen help. Salaries based on maturity, experience and training. Room and board provided. Personal interview can be arranged in the New York area. Apply by July 1 to Monroe Moss, Director, Camp Lenox, Dept. SED, 270-14R Grand Central Parkway, Floral Park NY 11005.
Fringe Benefits: Transportation assistance; laundry. **College credit** possible. "Recreational experiences in a beautiful setting; camaraderie."

Mah-Kee-Nac, Located in Lenox, Massachusetts. Private boys' camps; 53rd summer. Three small camp divisions. Staff of 90 graduate students, teachers, upper classmen. June 22 to August 24. Seeks warm, patient youth leaders. Needs counselor specialists in aquatics (WSI, swimming, canoeing, sailing, waterskiing), overnight camping, tennis (18 Har-Tru courts); also in nature, music, ceramics, woodworking, kayaks, ham radio, electronics, riflery, baseball, soccer, basketball. Attractive salaries. Room and board provided. Apply to Joseph Kruger, Dept. SED, 20 Allen Ct., South Orange NJ 07079.
Fringe Benefits: College credit possible. "This camp offers experience in leadership of campers in attendance 8 weeks; a chance to work with colleagues of high caliber, under a supportive director; and a social-and-professional milieu that fosters staff development."

Meadow Lark Camp, Inc., Located at Monterey in the Berkshire Hills. Coed private camp. 41st year. Total enrollment for 60 children. Camp open from June 21 to August 24. Needs specialists in arts and crafts, woodwork, nature, sports (non-competitive); nurse. Applicants must be over 21; graduates and teachers preferred. Also needs assistant counselors (minimum age 18½). Salary commensurate with training and experience. All counselors have cabin duties. A personal interview, if at all possible, is preferred. Applicants must love children and be interested in the children's development and in furthering their potential in all areas. Apply to Eric H. Craven, Meadow Lark Camp, Inc., Box 248, Monterey MA 01245.

Mohawk in the Berkshires, Located at Lanesboro, Massachusetts. Private coed camp for children ages 8-15. Openings for college students and teachers from June 28 to August 24. Needs counselors (ages 19 and older) for music (play piano and sight-reading), sailing, nature, canoeing, drama, dance, tennis, soccer, basketball, softball, ceramics, woodworking and skiing, 2 teenage trip leaders (skills in canoeing, campcraft, bike riding, minimum age 21), $450-900. Include SASE with correspondence. Room and board provided. Apply to Ralph Schulman, Mohawk in the Berkshires, Dept. SED, 107 Davis Ave., White Plains NY 10605.
Fringe Benefits: Travel expenses. "Supervision by an M.S.W. or M.Ed. in excellent working conditions." **College credit** possible.

New England Camping Association, Inc. (ACA), Staff referral service for overnight camp jobs throughout New England. Openings for college students and teachers, minimum age 19, for 8 weeks. Needs specialty counselors for advanced lifesaving, archery, arts and crafts, bicycling, boating, campcraft, canoeing, golf, drama, gymnastics, horseback riding, land sports, music, nature-ecology, photography, piano, radio-electronics, riflery, sailing (SCI), scuba, tennis, waterskiing, WSI; trip leader, unit leader, administrative personnel, chef, baker, kitchen workers, clerical, maintenance workers, doctors, nurses (RN). Salaries start at $450 and are commensurate with age, education, camp experience and type of position. Room and board provided. Apply by July 1; $2 application fee. Send SASE to New England Camping Association, Inc., Room 410, 29 Commonwealth Ave., Boston MA 02116.

Fringe Benefits: "Working in a summer camp offers excellent experience working with children; pre- and post-camp work possibilities; opportunities to meet foreign counselors and campers; and to make contacts for future jobs and references for future jobs; a chance to gain experience in teaching skills; and a chance to spend the summer out-of-doors." **College credit** possible.

Patriots' Trail Girl Scout Council Camps, Located on Cape Cod, Massachusetts and in the New Hampshire Lakes Region. Three Girl Scout camps for ages 7-17. Season (including precamp training) is for the nine weeks from the end of June to the end of August. Openings for teachers, college students, and high school graduates. Needs waterfront staff; sailing staff; unit leaders and assistants; specialists for backpacking, biking, drama, crafts; kitchen staff; administrative positions; nurses. Salaries from $500-1,000/season. Room and board provided. Write to the Director of Outdoor Programs, Patriots' Trail Girl Scout Council, Inc., 6 St. James Ave., Boston MA 02116.

Fringe Benefits: Insurance provided. **College credit** possible. "Camps are located in tourist areas; opportunities to visit New England. Camps are eligible for many work/study programs."

Romaca, Located in Hinsdale, Massachusetts. Camp for girls in grades 1-9. Openings for college students and teachers, minimum age 20, from approximately June 25 to August 26. Needs specialty counselors for tennis; waterfront: swimming (WSI), sailing, small craft (SCI), canoeing, waterskiing; performing arts: music (camp piano-other), show directors, modern dance; creative arts; land sports; individual sports: fencing, golf, archery, gymnastics, horseback riding (English); photography; radio; electronics; outdoor living skills: woodslore; hiking; overnights; nature; general counselors experienced in working with young children (grades 1-3); secretary-bookkeeper. Salaries are $350 and up. Room and board provided. Apply to Romaca for Girls, 87 Marlborough Court, Rockville Centre NY 11570.

Fringe Benefits: Laundry, medical insurance available at small cost to counselor."

Sandy Brook, Located at Norwich Lake, Huntington. Girl Scouts; resident tent camp for girls ages 7-17. Openings from June 21 to August 24. Needs 4 unit leaders, minimum age 21 (college students, teachers, foreign students and local applicants, experience in working with and leading groups, knowledge of girl scouting and camp counseling preferred), $100-125/week; 7 unit assistants, must be high school graduate (college students, foreign students, local applicants, experienced with group leadership, camp program skills), $76-103/week; waterfront director, minimum age 21 (WSI, college student, teacher, local applicant, experience teaching swimming and small crafts on organized waterfront), $110-135/week; 3 waterfront assistants, must be high school graduates (college students, foreign students, local applicants, WSI, Life

Saving), $80-103/week; head cook, minimum age 21 (college student, teacher, local applicant, training and experience in menu planning, food ordering and cooking for large numbers), $125-175/week; assistant cook, must be high school graduate (college student, teacher, local applicant, interested in quantity cooking, ability to take direction), $76-103/week; nurse (local applicant, RN in Massachusetts, first aid training, able to work with children), $110-135/week; riding instructor (college student, teacher, local applicant, Massachusetts license, ability to instruct Western riding and supervise riding program), $110-135/week; craft specialist, must be high school graduate (college student, teacher, foreign student, local applicant, ability to teach hand arts, especially nature crafts), $76-103/week; 3 riding assistants (college student, teacher, foreign student, local applicant, must be high school graduate), experienced in western riding and group leadership, $80-103/week. Salaries include room and board; tax deductions based on including value for room and board. "Applicant must like children and living outdoors in all kinds of weather." Send for application. Apply by April 1 to Priscilla Wahlen, Camp Director, Dept. SED, RFD 1, Peckvill Rd., Box 78, Shelburne MA 01370; tel 413/625-2303.

Viking, Located at South Orleans, Cape Cod. Summer sailing camp for boys. Needs 4 sailing counselors, 3 swimming counselors (WSI required), 2 shop counselors, 2 athletic counselors, 2 archery counselors, 2 tennis counselors, college students and teachers preferred, $450-700/8 weeks; 3 kitchen helpers, college students and high school seniors preferred, $65/week. Dates of employment, June 26 through August 21. "Although Viking has a number of sound activities, we specialize in teaching small boat sailing, and have for fifty years. A great deal revolves around the water, including overnight sailing expeditions, which almost everyone is involved in at one time or another. Applicants should be interested in camping and working with young boys." Write for application to Tom Lincoln, Director, Camp Viking, Box 405, South Orleans MA 02662; telephone (617)255-2739.

Wampatuck, Located in Hanson. Camp for girls. Openings for college students and foreign students for 9 summer weeks. Needs general counselors; specialty counselors for arts and crafts, riding, small crafts, campcraft, tripping, sports, swimming; nurse (RN or LPN). Salaries are $400-800. Apply early to Mrs. Bristol Crocker, 11 Fairway Lane, Foxboro MA 03025.

Watitoh, Located in Center Lake, Becket, Massachusetts. Private coed camp. Openings for college students and teachers from June 28 to August 24. Needs instructors: 6 WSI, 2 small craft, 3 tennis, waterskiing, all team and individual sports. Salaries are $500-1,000. Room and board provided. Apply to Sheldon Hoch, 28 Sammis Lane, White Plains NY 10605.
Fringe Benefits: This camp is located on Center Lake, in the Berkshires of western Massachusetts. Six days off/summer; transportation assistance. **College credit** possible.

Winadu, Located in Pittsfield, Massachusetts. Sports camp for boys ages 6-16. Openings from June 25 to August 22. Needs 14 head tennis counselors and 20 head waterfront counselors, $600-2,000/season; many basketball,

baseball, and soccer counselors, $600 plus/season; 1 karate and 1 ham radio counselor, $600 plus/season; and 4 arts and crafts counselors, $600 plus/season. Room and board provided. "Please send letter for an application or call." Apply to Mr. Shelley Weiner, Director, 5 Glen Lane, Mamaroneck NY 10543; tel. 914/381-5983.
Fringe Benefits: "Excellent location." **College credit** possible.

Wind-in-the-Pines, Located in Plymouth. Girl Scout resident camp for ages 6-17. Openings for high school graduates, college students and teachers from mid-June to mid-August. Needs waterfront director, water safety instructors, smallcraft director, canoeing and sailing instructors, unit leaders, unit assistants, business manager, cooks and nurse. Salaries are $520-1,800. Room and board provided. EOE. Apply to Plymouth Bay Girl Scout Council, Inc., Box 711, Taunton MA 02780.

Wonderland, Located in Sharon. Salvation Army, church, welfare camp; ages 7-12. Openings from late June to Labor Day. Needs 30 counselors, 5 waterfront, $550 and up; 7 program specialists for nature, crafts, athletics, pioneering, etc., $600; nurses, $900 and up. Room and board provided. Apply by March 31 to Salvation Army Camp Wonderland, Dept. SED, 147 Berkeley St., Boston MA 02116.
Fringe Benefits: College credit possible. "This camp offers a unique opportunity to work with underprivileged youngsters in a relaxed atmosphere—excellent for young people preparing for teaching or working with youth."

Summer Theaters

Berkshire Theatre Festival, Located in Stockbridge. A professional resident summer stock theater. Needs administrative, technical and production workers. Write for application and information about specific job openings; include resume outlining professional experience. Apply to Josephine R. Abady, Artistic Director, Berkshire Theatre Festival, Box 218, Stockbridge MA 01262; tel. 413/298-5536.
Fringe Benefits: College credit possible.

College Light Opera Company, The, Located in Highfield Theatre, Falmouth, Massachusetts. Music theater, light opera, Gilbert and Sullivan. Openings for college students and high school seniors from June 15 to September 1. Needs 10 staff members, all positions, salary available; 35 singers, 6 technical backstage workers, 6 costume shop, 2 piano accompanists, orchestra (all instruments), room and board, no salary. Deadline for applications: March 15, "but openings in some areas until May 1." Apply to Robert A. Haslun, The College Light Opera Company, 162 S. Cedar St., Oberlin OH 44074.

South Shore Music Circus, Located in Cohasset. Summer theater serving families, teenagers, senior citizens. Needs office, box office, press, management personnel, April 15 to September 15, salary open; technical personnel, May 15 to September 15, salary open; apprentices, June 1 to

September 15, $50/week. Local housing listings made available by theater. Send for application. Apply by April 1 to Ronald Rawson, Producer, South Shore Music Circus, Box 325, Cohasset MA 02021; tel. 617/383-9850.

Williamstown Theatre Festival, Located in Williamstown. Summer theater. Openings for college students, teachers, high school seniors and foreign students from approximately June 11 to September 1. Needs 10 staff members, salary open; 45-50 apprentices, tuition charged by contract; Equity and non-Equity actors. Apply by May 1 to Lynda Scofield, Williamstown Theatre Festival, Box 517, Williamstown MA 01267.

Michigan

2,773+ jobs available

Business and Industry

CDI Temporary Service, Located in Detroit. Office, Marketing, light industrial personnel. Offers college students, teachers, high school students and other qualified people interesting temporary work at a variety of companies in diversified industries during summer vacation, semester breaks and year round. Work 1 to 5 days, 2 weeks at a time, a month, or for entire summer. Top hourly pay, according to skills, on a weekly basis. Never a fee. Needs all office, marketing and light industrial skills, e.g., receptionists, typists, secretaries, transcribers, word processors, keypunch operators, figure clerks, bookkeepers, switchboard operators, sorters, stuffers, inventory workers, product demonstrators, market researchers, machine operators, factory workers, assemblers and many others. Suggest contacting office prior to availability. Apply to CDI Temporary Service, Renaissance Center, Bldg. 100, Detroit MI 48243.

Joann's Fudge Shop, Located on Mackinac Island. Openings for students from May to October. Peak season, July 1 to Labor Day. Needs clerks and fudgemaker's helpers. Enclose SASE with resume. Apply to Frank Nephew, 261 Altorf Strasse Rte. 4, Gaylord MI 49735.

Seabrook Foods, Inc., Located in Lake Odessa. Farm labor contractor: harvesting and processing. Openings for college students, teachers, high school students and local applicants: peas, June 25-July 25, fewer jobs available; beans, main season, August 1 to mid-September. Harvest crew may move around Lake Odessa once or twice a day; processing crew stays in the plant in Lake Odessa. Needs 150 general factory workers, $3.50/hour; drivers for harvesting machines (some experience with farm equipment), $3.50/hour; quality control (some foods science work), $4/hour; mechanics (some knowledge of machinery), $4/hour. Work 7 days/week, 10-12 hours/day; overtime pay for over 40 hours/week. Transportation to field job sites. Food plentiful; rooms at local cottages if reservations are made far in advance. Send

for application, write a letter giving qualifications and dates available for work or, if anything other than general labor, send a resume to Cenda Hoogerland, Personnel Manager, Seabrook Foods, Inc., Box 577, Lake Odessa MI 48849.
Fringe Benefits: Near Grand Rapids; 50 miles from Lake Michigan; large lake in Lake Odessa; many Spanish-speaking people in area. **College credit** available; "we have had internships with Michigan State University."

Resorts, Ranches, Restaurants, Lodging

Brocato's Knife and Fork, Located on Mackinac Island, Michigan. Resort restaurant. Openings for college students and high school seniors from June to Labor Day. Season ends Labor Day. Needs waitresses, bus boys, dishwashers and cooks who are reliable. Salaries plus sizeable tips. Housing provided, employee pays rent. "We are interested in students to apply who need money to further their education—not a vacation." Apply by April 1 to Samuel C. Brocato, Box 776, Scottsdale AZ 85251.

Chippewa Hotel, Located on Mackinac Island, Michigan. Openings for college students, teachers and high school seniors. Needs maids, cooks, salad makers, bellboys, dock porters, bartenders, bar help, housekeepers, bus boys, hostesses, waitresses, lifeguards, dishwashers, porters, etc. Give earliest arrival date in spring and latest departure date in fall. Enclose SASE. Apply by August 1 to Nathan Shayne, Box 325, Scottsdale AZ 85252.

El Rancho Stevens, Inc., Located in Gaylord. Western-style resort/ranch. Openings from May through Labor Day for 40 college students, teachers, high school seniors and local applicants. Needs waiters, waitresses, cooks, bus boys, kitchen helpers, maids, waterski instructor, riding instructors, trail guides, lifeguard, children's counselor, recreational directors, guitar and banjo players, musicians, bartender, typist, office help, gift shop clerk. Excellent salaries based upon applicant's maturity, experience and training. "The ranch is not a swinging night-life sort of place but offers a wholesome out-of-doors kind of summer. Staff all work together in their leisure time to produce little informal entertainments, skits, etc. Sound morality and character are essential." Send SASE for application. Apply to C. Stevens, Co-owner, El Rancho Stevens, Inc., Dept. SED, Box 366, Gaylord MI 49735; tel. 517/732-5090.

Flora-dale Resort, Located in Mears. American plan for families. Openings for 14 college students from June 9 through Labor Day. Needs 5 waitresses, 2 cottage cleaners, 2 office workers, recreation director, 2 handyman-dishwashers, cook's helper and all around girl. Salaries are $1,600-2,400/season after room and board charges. Prefers employees with some musical talent. All live in at moderate room and board charge. Send SASE for application and details to E. Bauer, Flora-dale Resort, Dept. SED, Mears MI 49436.
Fringe Benefits: Small, family operation, Christian atmosphere. Room and board furnished at a reasonable rate; staff menu same as guests'; use of resort facilities when not working; staff and guests on first-name basis and "enjoy each other's company." Unique setting with sand dunes across the lake (2 miles from

Lake Michigan), the approximately 100 guests are "families who like to have fun together. We have a 3½-day orientation before the season begins and weekly staff shows to entertain guests." **College credit** possible.

Michillinda Beach Lodge, Located on the shore of Lake Michigan in Whitehall. Summer resort. Openings from June 20 to Labor Day (Sept. 7). Needs 8 waitresses and dining room hostesses, college students preferred, $400/month; 4 kitchen staff, college students preferred, $350-400/month; and 6 maids, college students or high school seniors preferred, $350-400/month. A service charge is distributed throughout the season and as a bonus at the season's end. Most employees average more than $550/month when service charge is included. "Board and room at nominal charge. (1980 rate was $30/month for room and $45/month for board.) Applicants should write for employment application after January 1. Applications must be received prior to March 10 with notifications sent out April 15." Apply to Don Eilers, Manager, Dept. SED, Michillinda Beach Lodge, 5207 Scenic Dr., Whitehall MI 49461. **Fringe Benefits:** "Michillinda is a family oriented, friendly resort. Working conditions are pleasant; resort facilities are available to staff during off-duty time. Staff members are encouraged to take part in all activities planned for our guests." **College credit** possible.

Pennellwood Resort, Located at Berrien Springs. Openings for college students, minimum age 18, from Memorial Day to Labor Day. Needs 15 waitresses. Salary plus excellent tips. Dormitory lodging mandatory. Applications taken after January 1. Apply early to Jack Davis, Dept. SED, Pennellwood Resort, Route 2, Box 51, Berrien Springs MI 49103.

Sunny Brook Farm Resort, Located at South Haven. Openings from early June through Labor Day for 31 college students, teachers and high school seniors, minimum age 17 (refreshment stand only, minimum age 16). Needs waitresses, waiters, cooks, desk clerk, lifeguard-recreation director, kitchen helpers, chambermaids, children's counselors, maintenance helpers, yardman, musicians (part-time only, piano), night watchman, refreshment stand workers, assistant cook, assistant maintenance foreman. Seasonal earnings after room and board charges are met, $500-1,200. Apply by April 15. Send SASE for application form and salary scale to Mary C. Ott, Sunny Brook Farm Resort, South Haven MI 49090.

Ye Olde Pickle Barrel Restaurant (Cafeteria), Located on Mackinac Island. Openings for students from May to September. Peak season July 1 to Labor Day. Needs cooks, fry cooks, kitchen help and counter girls. Enclose SASE with resume. Apply to Frank Nephew, 261 Altorf Strasse, Rt. 4, Gaylord MI 49735 (winter address).

Summer Camps

American Camping Association/Illinois Section, Located in Illinois and surrounding states including Michigan, Indiana, Minnesota and Wisconsin. The American Camping Association/Illinois Section is an association of persons involved with camps operated by social agencies, and private camp owners. More than 100 camps in Association. Openings for college students, teachers, foreign students and local applicants from late June to late August. Needs persons over 18 years of age who possess a variety of camp leadership skills for positions such as counselors, cooks, waterfront staff, camping and athletic skills, teachers, nurses and program directors. Salaries are $500-1,000 for eight weeks or more. Room and board provided. Apply by writing the American Camping Association/Illinois Section, 19 S. LaSalle St., Room 1024, Chicago IL 60603; tel. 312/332-0833. A $2.00 fee must accompany application.

Camp O' The Hills, Located at Brooklyn. Girl Scout camp for girls ages 6-17. Openings for college students, teachers, high school seniors and foreign students from July to August. Needs program director, nurse, $650-700; CIT director, $500; 3 unit leaders and 5 unit assistants, $450-600; 3 waterfront assistants and waterfront directors, $450-600; cook, $660-800; assistant cook, $650-800; business manager, $450-600. Room and board provided. Apply to Camp Director, Dept. SED, Irish Hills Girl Scout Council, Box 1362, Jackson MI 49204.
Fringe Benefits: College credit possible. This camp offers employees "the learning experience of working with girls, adults and handicapped children."

Cavell YWCA, Located at Lexington on Lake Huron. YWCA camp for girls ages 7-15 offering general and specialized camping program. Openings from June 15 to August 16 for college students and teachers (in the field of Special Education and Related Studies). "Staff required to attend one week staff training." Needs 24 cabin counselors/instructors (minimum age 18), $425-700/season; instructors in archery, nature, arts and crafts, dance, sports, waterfront, tennis, gymnastics and campcraft, $425-700/season; directors of sports, nature, arts and crafts, campcraft, performing arts and waterfront (minimum age 21), $600-900/season; 3 unit directors (minimum age 21), $600-900/season; Head Director, $600-900/season. Room and board provided. Send resume or application request. Apply by May 30 to Carol Kubiak, Camp Administrator, YWCA, 2230 Witherell St., Detroit MI 48201; tel. 313/961-9220.

Chief Makisabee, Located in Eau Claire. Coed camp for inner city, interracial children ages 7-14; also special unit for mentally retarded. Total camper capacity is 286. Openings for college students and teachers from June 15 to August 25. Needs approximately 60 unit counselors, nature director, 8 unit leaders, waterfront director (minimum age 21, WSI), 6 lifeguards, boating instructor, canoe instructor; 3 craft instructors (emphasis on use of local materials, campcraft), 2 campcraft/archery instructors (minimum age 21), nurse, photography instructor, drama instructor, director of small games and activities. Will possibly hire handicapped persons. All salaries competitive in camping field. Room and board provided. Send for application. Apply by May 15 to Juanita L. Ryzner, Director, Camp Chief Makisabee, Chicago Youth Centers, Dept. SED, 8800 Black Lake Rd., Eau Claire MI 49111.

Fringe Benefits: This camp provides an "opportunity to live and work with people from a variety of backgrounds." Staff works with inner-city children from Chicago. **College credit** possible.

Chippewa Trail Camp, Located in Rapid City. Campers are girls ages 6-16. Needs 4 directors, minimum age 21, salaries negotiable, for waterfront (WSI), camping, horseback riding (English), food service; 3 waterfront instructors (WSI); gymnastics instructor (advanced skills); dance-modern jazz instructor (advanced skills); tennis instructor; arts and craft instructor (skilled in children's projects); horseback riding (English) instructor. Instructors serve as cabin counselors in non-activity hours. Salaries $55/week and up depending on age and experience. Room and board provided. Send for application to Susan M. Webb, Associate Director, Box 1927, Rt. 1, Rapid City MI 49676; tel. 616/322-4242.
Fringe Benefits: "Transportation allowance given to out-of-state staff."
College credit possible.

Crystalaire, Located in Frankfort. Private/independent camp for children ages 8-15. Openings from late June to mid-August. Needs 14 counselors (male and female), college students and teachers preferred, $50-90/week; waterfront director/sailing master, college student or teacher preferred, $100-plus/week; art instructor, teacher preferred, $75/week; barn and garden coordinator, college students preferred, $60-75/week; 2 cooks, college students and teachers preferred, $100-150/week; 2 ecology/trips program people, college students and teachers preferred, $60-90/week. "We are a loosely structured camp which demands that staff members be highly flexible and have skills or interests in a number of program areas—music, art, waterfront, etc." Apply as early as possible (including up to opening time) to David B. Reid, Director, Crystalaire, Frankfort MI 49635; tel. 616/352-7589.

Happy Hollow, Located in Mayville. Private camp for mentally and emotionally impaired persons ages 7-50. Openings from mid-June to the last week in August. Needs waterfront director, 3 program specialists, $750/season; 4 senior counselors, 12 counselors, $550-650/season. All salaries are for live-in positions and room and board is provided. "The earlier applicants apply the better, since positions are filled by early spring." Apply by March 1 to Vicki L. Blackburn, Executive Director, Camp Happy Hollow, Inc., Route 1, Box 105A, Harmon Lake Rd., Mayville MI 48744; tel. 517/673-3666.

Lake of the Woods, Greenwoods, Located in Decatur, Michigan. Private camp for boys and girls ages 8-15; separate but adjacent camps. Openings for college students and teachers, minimum age 19, from approximately mid-June to mid-August. Needs counselors for swimming (WSI or Life Saving), sailing, canoeing, rowing, English and Western riding, waterskiing and boat driver, tripping, guitar, arts and crafts, archery, campcraft, riflery, gymnastics, tennis, golf, land sports, nature, dramatics, cheerleading, storekeeper, secretary, kitchen help, dishwashers, groundskeepers, carpenter, maintenance, bus driver. Also, nurses (RN), program staff, waterfront director. Salaries are $600-1,500, depending on age, position and experience. Room

and board provided. Apply to Laurence Seeger, 1765 Maple St., Northfield IL 60093; tel. 312/256-2444. Summer phone 616/423-3091.
Fringe Benefits: "Staff T-shirts and yearbooks provided; extensive orientation program prior to campers' arrival." **College credit** possible. "Camp is only 3 hours from Chicago and from Detroit—nice for days off; ½ hour from Kalamazoo, a nice, friendly college town with lots of activities; and 1 hour from Lake Michigan beaches, Saugatuck, and Holland."

Maplehurst, Located in Kewadin. Coed camp, ages 7-17. Openings for college students, teachers and foreign students from mid-June to mid-August. Needs 30 general and specialty counselors for waterfront (WSI), riding (English and western), sailing, boating, canoeing, arts and crafts, photography, dramatics, tennis, waterskiing, scuba (NAUI), gymnastics, dance, archery, fencing. Salaries are $500-1,100. Room and board provided. Apply by June 15 to Camp Maplehurst, Dept. SED, 7366 Balsam Court, West Bloomfield MI 48033; tel. 313/661-0271.
Fringe Benefits: Maplehurst offers use of camp facilities, an excellent learning atmosphere and future job recommendations. **College credit** available; offers psychology courses through University of Michigan.

Miniwanca, Located in Shelby, Michigan, on Lake Michigan and Stony Lake. Christian oriented camp for girls and boys. Also operates Camp Merrowvista, Ossipee, New Hampshire. Male staff may serve at *either* or *both* camps. Openings for college students, graduates, teachers and high school seniors for varying periods from mid-June through August. Needs workstaff (high school seniors and above); counselors (minimum age 18) with skills in archery, bicycling, canoeing, crafts, photography, riflery, sailing, sports, swimming, tennis; directors (upper college and above) for waterfront, tripping, program, unit, workstaff; food service chef/manager; nurse (RN). Salaries are based on age and experience. Room and board provided. Apply to Ken Bryant, American Youth Foundation, 3460 Hampton Ave., St. Louis MO 63139.
Fringe Benefits: Travel allowance, laundry and insurance provided.

Newaygo, Located in Newaygo. YWCA camp for children ages 7-17. Openings for college students and teachers during July and August. Needs 12 general counselors, $400-550/season; waterfront director, $500-700/season; arts and crafts director, CIT, tripping director, nature director, $450-600/season; specialty counselors in backpacking/ecology, waterfront including sailing (WSI, SLS, SCI), and drama, $400-600/season. Room and board provided. Apply by April or May to Beverly Cassidy, YWCA Camp Newaygo, Dept. SED, 25 Sheldon Ave. SE, Grand Rapids MI 49337.

O'Fair Winds, The Timbers, Two separate camps for girls. Camp O'Fair Winds is located in Lapeer, serving girls 9-11 years. The Timbers is for junior and senior high school girls, located at Traverse City. Openings for college students and teachers from June 14 to August 16. Positions include: unit assistants, waterfront assistants, unit leaders, arts and crafts director, smallcraft director, business manager, nature specialist, cooks, nurses. Room and board provided. Apply by May 15 to Camp Director, Dept. SED, Fair Winds Girl Scout Council, 202 E. Boulevard Dr., Room 110, Flint MI 48503.

Fringe Benefits: College credit possible. This camp offers "excellent experience in developing teaching skills."

Douglas Smith, Located in Ludington, Michigan. Four-week session of girls' camp and 4-week session of boys' camp. Openings from June 12 to August 18 or September 1. Needs specialty counselors for archery, riflery, tennis, canoeing and tripping, waterskiing, waterfront (WSI), sailing, arts and crafts, and photography. Also needs female counselors from June 12 to July 14, and male counselors from July 19 to August 18. Salaries are $650 and up. Cooks, nurse (RN) and maintenance salaries arranged. Apply by May to Dick Martin, Camp Douglas Smith, Dept. SED, 620 Lincoln Ave., Winnetka IL 60093. **Fringe Benefits:** "Comfortable working conditions, room, excellent food and excellent recreational facilities are provided. Many staff members are from other parts of the world." **College credit** available.

Tocanja, Located at Twin Lake, Michigan. Girl Scout camp for girls ages 9-17. Openings for college students, teachers and high school graduates from mid-June to mid-August. Needs unit leaders, unit and waterfront assistants, waterfront director, business manager, program directors. Salaries are $450 and up. Apply by May 15 to Director, Camp Tocanja, Girl Scouts of the Calumet Council, 8417 Kennedy Ave., Highland IN 46322.

Walden, Located in Cheboygan. Private coed camp. Openings for college students, teachers and foreign students from mid-June to late August. Needs cabin counselors; specialty counselors for English riding, arts and crafts, tennis, golf, modern dance, ballet, folk dancing, drama, radio, computers, fencing, photography, waterfront, sailing, rowing crew, canoeing, kayaking, campcraft, tripping, land sports, gymnastics, music, puppetry; 2 nurses (RN), drivers, secretaries. Salaries are $600-1,500 including room and board. Cabins, tents and dorms provided for housing. Apply to Larry Stevens, 31070 Applewood Lane, Dept. SED, Farmington Hills MI 48018.

Summer Theaters

BoarsHead Theater, Located in Lansing. Equity professional year-round theater. Openings from early to mid-June through early September; but prefers qualified candidates available for full year. Needs scenic designer, $150/week; costumer, $150/week; 2 technical director/lighting designers, $150/week; properties master and seamstress, $140/week; Stage Manager, $190/week; carpenter, $140/week; master electrician/sound designer, $140/week. Also non-salaried summer apprentice program, **college credit** available. "Salaries negotiable based on experience. Send resume and two letters of reference from different sources if possible." Apply by May 1 to Dennis Sherman, BoarsHead Theater, Dept. SED, 425 S. Grand Ave., Lansing MI 48933; tel. 517/484-7800.

The Cherry County Playhouse, Located in Traverse City. Summer Equity Star stock theater presenting 6 plays and musicals in a 9-week season. Openings from June 1 or 5 to September 1, 3 or 7. Needs box office treasurer (prior box office experience *required*, college student or teacher preferred), $175/week; 2 box office assistants (prior box office experience required, college students preferred), $125-135/week; administrative secretary (good typing, bookkeeping and shorthand helpful, college student preferred), $150/week; 2 property/wardrobe (college students and teachers preferred), $150/week; assistant technical director (college student or teacher preferred), $150/week; director of apprentices (teacher preferred), $175-200/week; promotion/publicity director, $175/week; promotion assistant/house manager, $150/week; 16 apprentices (to learn and present 4 children's plays, no fees, college and high school students preferred), $30/week. "Rooming houses and some apartments for share; room about $30-40/week. Have a serious interest in theater and be willing to work long hours under considerable pressure. Must be punctual and responsible at all times." Send resume by April 15 to William J. Hooton, General Manager, Dept. SED, Box 661, Traverse City MI 49684; tel. 616/947-9560, winter tel. 707/894-5872.

Minnesota

933+ jobs available

Resorts, Ranches, Restaurants, Lodging

Grand View Lodge and Tennis Club, Located in Brainerd. Resort. Openings from May through late September for college students, teachers and foreign students with work permits. Needs 20 waitresses, 3 desk clerks, 10 maids, 5 clerks, 3 beach boys, 4 bus boys, 4 dishwashers, 3 cooks and 5 kitchen help. Salaries are open, depending upon job and experience. Room and board available for $150/month. Apply by April 1 to Timothy Moore, Grand View Lodge and Tennis Club, Dept. SED, RFD 6, Brainerd MN 56401.
Fringe Benefits: College credit possible.

Gunflint Lodge, Inc., Located in Grand Marais. Resort with family and fishermen clientele. Openings from May 15 to October 15 for college students, teachers, high school seniors and foreign students. Needs 2 maids; 3 waitresses; 4 kitchen helpers; first, second and third cooks; 3 dock attendants; 4 canoe trip guides for the Boundary Waters Canoe Area; 8 outfitters; 3 naturalists; handyman. Salaries are $325-600/month. Room and board provided. Enclose SASE. Apply by March 30 to Bruce Kerfoot, Gunflint Lodge, Inc., Box 100ND, Grand Marais MN 55604.
Fringe Benefits: Year-end bonus. **College credit** possible. This camp provides "a chance to work in the wilderness of northeastern Minnesota next to the Boundary Waters Canoe Area."

Island View Lodge, Located in Brainerd. Openings for college students, teachers, high school seniors from May 1 to October 15. Needs beach and boat attendant, kitchen help, dishwasher, 8 waitresses, 3 front desk personnel, bartender, 2 recreation directors, 4 maids, groundskeeper, entertainment person and/or group, $3.40-4.00/hour and bonus. Apply to

Island View Lodge, Route 6, Gull Lake, Brainerd MN 56401.
Fringe Benefits: "Year-end bonus; recreational facilities available; excellent working conditions." **College credit** available.

Izatys Lodge, Located in Onamia. Family resort. Openings for college students from May 1 to October 15. Needs 8 waitresses, 2 bus boys, 2 bartenders, 6 maids, 2 playground supervisors, 2 yard workers, 2 dishwashers, 4 kitchen helpers and office help. Salaries are $3.10/hour plus season bonus or bonus agreed upon in advance. Room and board provided for $4.95/day. Apply to J. L. Dubbs, Manager, Dept. SED, Izatys Lodge, Onamia MN 46359.

Lutsen Resorts, Inc., Located in Lutsen. Resort and Alpine slide. Openings for college students, teachers and foreign students from late May to mid-October, mid-December to April and some year-round. Needs 18 waiters/waitresses and 1 bellhop, minimum wage plus tips; 2 bartenders and 2 hostesses, $3/hour plus tips; 10 housekeeper/laundry workers; 2 stream guides (fly fishing), minimum wage; 12 Alpine slide operators, 2 secretaries, salad maker, baker's helper, first cook, 4 second cooks, salary open. Housing on premises or can be arranged nearby. Send resume to Lutsen Resort and Alpine Slide, Dept. SED, Lutsen MN 55612.

Madden Resorts, Located in Brainerd. Openings for college students, teachers and high school seniors from June 1 to September 15; some positions open late April to late October. No foreign applicants. Needs assistant managers, front desk clerks, waitresses, waiters, shop manager, bartenders, bus boys, service boys, store clerks, craft instructor, cabin maids, children's hostess, assistant caddy masters, cooks, cook's helpers, kitchen helpers, dishwashers, boat attendants and yard help. Salaries and applications available on request. Enclose stamped return envelope. Only those considered will be contacted further. Apply to Madden Resorts, Box 387, Brainerd MN 56401.

Nelson's Resort, Located at Crane Lake. Family resort with conventions in fall. Openings for college students, teachers and high school seniors from May 1 to October 15. Needs 6 waitresses, 2 bus boys, 2 dock attendants, 2 dishwashers, kitchen helper, store clerk, yard help and cook's helper. Salary is federal minimum wage plus tips, less room and board; 40-hour week. "Minnesota law states charges at $1.50/night board, $1.15/meal, deductible from wages." Apply by April 1 to Ms. G.N. Pohlman, Nelson's Resort, Dept. SED, Crane Lake MN 55725.
Fringe Benefits: "End-of-season bonus; social atmosphere; use of all equipment—boat, motor, beach, games—when not in use by guests."

Summer Camps

Birchwood, Located at Steamboat Lake, LaPorte. Resident girls' camp; wilderness boys' camp. Openings for college students and graduates, teachers and married couples from June 10 to August 18 and 30. Needs canoe wilderness guides, counselors for riding, tennis, archery, canoeing, riflery, swimming (WSI), crafts, ceramics, $450-700; activity directors (married couples),

$500-800 each. Send resume to James C. Bredemus, Camp Birchwood, Dept. SED, Steamboat Lake, LaPorte MN 56461.

Boys Club, Located in Mound, Minnesota. Residential camp for low-income boys and girls mostly from the inner city. Needs 5 camp counselors to coordinate daily schedule for 8 boys or girls, instruct in a variety of skill areas, group skills helpful, $800 and up/season; 1 cook for meal preparation and some clean-up, $900 and up/season; 3 program specialists (naturalist, riding instructor, waterfront director/WSI), $900 and up/season; 1 food service coordinator to supervise overall food service program (85 people/meal), supervise 3 staff and keep records, $1,300 and up/season. Room and board provided. Hires physically handicapped who can do a particular job. Send for application. Apply by May 15 to Jim Crotty, Director of Outdoor Life, 2410 Irving Ave. N., Minneapolis MN 55411.

Fringe Benefits: "Exceptional learning opportunity for child psychology or social work students." **College credit** possible.

Buckskin Inc., Located at Lakes MacDougal, 29 miles southeast of Ely. Coed camp for children ages 8-13. Openings for college students and teachers from June 8 to August 19. Needs program director; counselors for archery, camping and canoeing, swimming (WSI), reading, riflery, arts and crafts, ecology and campcraft, $650-850; assistant cook, camp secretary, salary open. Room and board provided. Send for application as early as possible to R.S. "Duffy" Bauer, Camp Buckskin, Dept. SED, Box 389, Ely MN 55731; in winter, 3811 West Broadway, Robbinsdale MN 55422; tel. 612/536-9749 (day); 612/533-9674 (evening).

Fringe Benefits: Travel assistance after first year. **College credit** available. "This is a coed camp with a wide age range of staff; it offers excellent experience."

Camp Fire—St. Paul Council, Located in St. Paul. Resident camps providing a summer extension of the Camp Fire program with emphasis on personal goal setting and accomplishment. Openings for college students and teachers from mid-June to mid-August. Needs 3-4 riding instructors (experienced), $350-650/season; 4 waterfront instructors (WSI or small craft safety instruction), $350-650/season; 20 counselors, $300-550/season; 1 nurse, $550-750/season. Room and board provided. Would possibly hire handicapped, must be able to walk on uneven ground for a distance. Application deadline May. Send resume to Camping Coordinator, Dept. SED, Camp Fire, 65 E. Kellogg Blvd., St. Paul MN 55101.

Perhaps you would like to spend this summer working in Britain or some other foreign country. See the back of this book for information on other valuable books published and/or distributed by Writer's Digest Books— Overseas Summer Jobs, Summer Jobs Britain and Kibbutz Volunteer.

Fringe Benefits: "Skill training available, near Twin Cities, optional post-season staff canoe trip." **College credit** possible.

Courage, Located at Maple Lake. Camp for physically handicapped, speech and hearing handicapped children and adults. Openings for college students, teachers and high school seniors from June 8 to August 28. Needs 42 counselors, $650; 25 program specialists, $675-1,200; 12 speech therapists, $1,600; 2 nurses (RN), $900; 8 kitchen staff, $550. Some counselor scholarships also available. Room and board provided. Apply by May 1 to Robert Polland, Courage Center, Dept. SED, 3915 Golden Valley Rd., Minneapolis MN 55422.
Fringe Benefits: College credit available. "Courage Center offers learning opportunities and association with professionals in the fields of physical handicaps, recreation, speech and hearing problems, and adapted physical education. There is also the opportunity to spend a summer outside in a camp environment."

Friendship, Located in Annandale. Residendial camp for mentally retarded of all ages. Openings for college students and teachers from June to September. Needs 2 nurses (LPN and RN graduates to live-in), $85-110/week; nutritionist to plan and serve special trays where/when needed, $55-70/week; 50 counselors to live with campers and plan daily activities, $55-70/week; 1 boat mechanic to keep all boats and motors in good repair, salary negotiable; 10 instructors in arts and crafts, music, recreation, nature, $55-70/week; lifeguards (WSI), $55-70/week; store clerk to handle camper money and run camp store, $55-70/week; receptionist for filing and phone duties, $55-70/week. Room and board provided. Also needs help for winter camp from right after Christmas until February 15. Hires physically handicapped as nutritionist, receptionist, camp store clerk. Send for application. Apply year round to Judi Morris, Program Director, Camp Friendship, Rt. 3, Annandale MN 55302.
Fringe Benefits: "Bonus of $15 bonus at summer's end for meeting terms of your contract. Valuable experience relative to working with and understanding people who are retarded." **College credit** possible.

Greenwood
Ruby Lake
Lockeslea Arts Camp, Three Girl Scout camps for girls ages 6-18. Openings from June 15 to August 15. Needs 3 directors, teachers preferred, $1,400-2,300; 3 assistant directors, teachers preferred, $900-1,500/season; 3 cooks, local applicants preferred, $800-1,200/season; 2 waterfront directors, college students or teachers preferred, $700-1,200/season; 2 nurses, degree required, $700-1,200/season; 6 general counselors, high school seniors, foreign students, local applicants and college students acceptable, $500-900/season; 9 program specialists, college students and teachers preferred, $500-1,100/season; 3 unit leaders, college students and teachers preferred, $600-1,200/season; 2 assistant cooks, college students, teachers, high school seniors or local applicants preferred, $500-900/season; CIT director, college students and teachers preferred, $850-1,100/season. Salaries include room

and board. Send letter of application to receive more information. Apply by June 15 to Colleen J. Edwards, Outdoor Program Director, Attention Dept. O.P.D., Greater Minneapolis Girl Scout Council, 200 Gorham Building, 127 N. 7th St., Dept. SED, Minneapolis MN 55403; tel. 612/338-0721. **Fringe Benefits: College credit** possible.

Kici Yapi, Located at Prior Lake. YMCA day camp for children ages 4-11. Openings for college students, teachers, foreign students and high school volunteers from June 8 to August 14. Needs counselors, $730-795; unit directors, $855; riding director and instructors, $575-950; bus drivers, plus camp salary, $540. No overnight facilities; counselors provide own housing. Free bus service from metropolitan area of Minneapolis. Personal interviews required. Apply by May 15 to Southdale YMCA, Attn: Bob Ecklund, 7355 York Ave. S., Edina MN 55435.

Lakamaga, Located 30 miles north of the Twin Cities near Forest Lake. Camp serving girls ages 6-14 from rural and urban areas; basic Girl Scout camping program of campcraft, swimming, boating, nature, plus special programs in biking and sailing. Openings for college students, teachers and high school seniors from mid-June to mid-August. Needs camp director (minimum age 25, must have car, camp experience, knowledge of Girl Scout program and valid driver's license), $1,400-2,200/season; assistant camp director (must have car, camp experience, knowledge of Girl Scout program and chauffeur's license), $880-1,200/season; 6 unit leaders (experienced in working with groups of children, and preferably in camp counseling or Girl Scouting, and Red Cross Lifesaving and/or First Aid), $720-1,040/season; 10 assistant unit leaders (experienced in working with groups of children, and preferably in camp counseling or Girl Scouting, and Red Cross Lifesaving and/or First Aid), $656-880/season; waterfront director (WSI, experienced in canoeing, and preferably camping), $760-1,240; 2 waterfront assistants (ALS, prefers camp experience), $656-920/season; health supervisor (RN, LPN, EMT, prefers First Aid training), $720-1,240/season; food supervisor (experienced in quantity cooking, prefers training in food management), $880-1,400/season; cook's assistant (prefers experience in cooking), $800-1,000/season; packout person (physical stamina and basic math skills required), $656-880/season. Room and board provided. Equal opportunity/affirmative action employer. Request application to Kay Kramer, Camping Services Director, Girl Scout Council of St. Croix Valley, Dept. SED, 400 S. Robert, St. Paul MN 55107; tel. 612/227-8835. **Fringe Benefits:** "Beautiful surroundings." **College credit** possible.

Lincoln/Lake Hubert, Located at Lake Hubert. Private resident camp serving children from around the world. Openings for college students and teachers. Needs 40 counselors to live and direct youth with guidance in recreational areas (June 6 to August 20, minimum age 19), $300 and up/month; 30 activity and administrative directors in charge of a specific program area for skill development in riding, sailing, swimming, archery, riflery, dance, crafts, camping skills (June 1 to August 25, minimum age 21), $350 and up/month; 20 maintenance, food service, office personnel and nurses (May 1 to September 1, minimum age 19), $300 and up/month. Room and board

provided. Also needs employees in May, September and October. Would possibly hire physically handicapped. Send for application. Apply by June 1 to Sam Cote or Bill Jones, Directors, Camp Lincoln/Lake Hubert, 3940 W. 49½ St., Edina MN 55424.
Fringe Benefits: "Travel allowance, opportunity to meet people from all over the world." **College credit** possible.

Manakiki, Located at Lake Waconia. Camp for children ages 8-14. Openings for college students, college graduates and teachers from mid-June to mid-August. Needs cabin counselors; specialty counselors for arts and crafts, nature study, WSI waterfront (swimming and small craft); nurse (RN); business manager; supervisors; and cooks. Salaries are $650-900/season, depending on qualifications and position. Room and board provided. Apply by June 1 to Camp Personnel Coordinator, Pillsbury-Waite Neighborhood Services, Inc., 720-22 E. 26th St., Dept. SED, Minneapolis MN 55404.
Fringe Benefits: Health insurance provided. **College credit** possible. "Tremendous learning experience for students planning teaching or social work careers."

Metropolitan Minneapolis YMCA Camps, Located near Minneapolis. Four YMCA resident camps. Openings for college students and teachers from June 7 to August 24 (dates vary within camps). Salary range: $55-70/week. Needs 80 counselors: nature, horseback riding, sailing, arts and crafts; nurse, trips director, wilderness canoe guides. Room and board provided. Send for application. Apply by April 15 to Rita DeBruyn, Camp Program Director, YMCA Camp Ihduhapi, Loretto MN 55357.
Fringe Benefits: "Scenic locale, yet near metropolitan Minneapolis area; staff from all over the country." **College credit** possible.

Mishawaka, Located at Grand Rapids, Minnesota. Private, ACA accredited, separate camps for children ages 8-16. Openings for college students and teachers, minimum age 20, from June 13 to August 11. Needs (boys' camp): 15 general counselors with skills in nature study, campcraft, Indian lore, sailing, dramatics, swimming, track, athletics, boating, ropes course, crafts, $500-750 according to skill and experience. Needs (girls' camp): 12 counselors with skills in swimming, canoeing, tennis, music, drama, dance, riding, archery, $500-750. Also needs driver (minimum age 21), $600-750; Food Service personnel: head cook, assistant cooks, head steward, trip outfitter, $1,000-1,500 for 10 weeks from June 4 to August 12; nurse (RN) needed for both camps, $750-900. Room and board provided. Apply by April 15 to Ernest S. Cockrell, Box 252, Marion MA 02738.
Fringe Benefits: "Cordial atmosphere, travel allowance, staff/camp continuity, all ages, international, beautiful location, interesting trips." **College credit** available; must be arranged in advance.

Sherwood Forest Camp, Located at Deer Lake, Deer River. Private camp for girls ages 7-17. Openings for college students and teachers from June 13 to August 13. Needs specialty counselors for English riding, swimming, lifesaving, diving, water ballet, waterskiing, sailing, canoeing, campcraft, archery, dramatics, dancing, tennis, arts and crafts, gymnastics, riflery; also program director, CIT director, secretary-driver, cooks, nurse (RN). Salaries include room and board and are based on skills and experience. Apply early to Maxine Gunsolly, 805 2nd Ave. NW, Grand Rapids MN 55744.

Thunderbird for Boys, Thunderbird for Girls, Located in Bemidji, Minnesota. Independently owned brother-sister camps for children ages 8-15. Openings for 140 college students, teachers and foreign students from mid-June to mid-August. Needs supervisory staff; swim director; riflery instructor (NRA); riding directors; counselors for backpacking, bicycling, riding, nature lore, Indian lore, sailing, arts and crafts, waterskiing, canoe tripping, cabin; laundry helpers, food service workers; kitchen helpers; and cooks. Salaries are commensurate with skills. Room and board provided. Send early in spring for application to Allen L. Sigoloff, Dept. SED, 10976 Chambray Court, St. Louis MO 63141.
Fringe Benefits: Travel allowance provided; campers from all over US.
College credit available.

Villa Maria, Located in Frontenac. Private camp for girls ages 9-16. Openings for college students from June 15 to August 8. Needs instructors for water safety, canoeing, tennis, dancing/gymnastics, riding, drama, art; also assistants for kitchen and maintenance. Salaries are commensurate with skills and experience. Room and board provided. Apply by March 1 to Directress, Camp Villa Maria, Dept. SED, Frontenac MN 55026; tel. 612/345-3455.

Missouri
282+ jobs available

Government

Department of Labor, Jobs available at the regional office, Room 100, 911 Walnut St., Kansas City MO 64106. This office serves Iowa, Kansas, Missouri and Nebraska. Applications must be made to Washington DC office. See Washington DC office (District of Columbia section) for complete descriptions of jobs available and how to apply information.

National Transportation Safety Board, Jobs available at the regional office in Kansas City. Applications must be made to Washington DC office. See Washington DC office (District of Columbia section) for complete descriptions of jobs available and how to apply information.

Summer Camps

Blue Sky, Located in St. Louis County. Resident and day camps for mentally retarded persons ages 3 and older. Openings for college students, teachers, high school seniors, and local applicants from June 6 to August 15.

Needs 75 counselors, WSIs, campcraft and outdoor education specialists. Salaries are $350-600/season. "Special education majors are given preference; experience in working with trainable and educable retarded citizens ideal. Call or write for camp brochure, application and personal interview date." Room and board provided in resident camp. Apply by March 30 to Mrs. Elizabeth Gilbert, Director of Camping, St. Louis Assoc. for Retarded Citizens, Camp Blue Sky, Dept. SED, 1240 Dantel Lane, St. Louis MO 63141; tel. 314/569-2211.

Fringe Benefits: "This work offers an excellent learning, hands-on experience for students of psychology, social services, recreation and therapeutic recreation, as well as students of mentally handicapped, disordered behavior, emotionally disturbed and learning disabled persons. We are accredited with some universities and colleges." **College credit** available.

Cedarledge, Located in Pevely. Resident Girl Scout camp for girls ages 7-17. Openings from June 7 to August 9. Needs 3 administrative persons, college students and teachers preferred, $1,000-2,500/season; 3 nurses, $1,100-1,400/season; 11 troop leaders, college students and teachers preferred, $1,000-1,200/season; 20 assistant troop leaders, college students, teachers and foreign students considered, $600-900/season; 3 specialists (in nature, crafts, canoeing), college students and teachers preferred, $600-900/season; 12 swimming, wranglers, college students, teachers and foreign students considered, $600-900; 2 maintenance workers, supply clerk, college students and high school seniors preferred, $300-500. Room and board provided. Apply by June 30 to Doris Winnemann, Camping Services Director, Camp Cedarledge, Girl Scout Council of Greater St. Louis, 915 Olive St., St. Louis MO 63101; tel. 314/241-1270.

Fringe Benefits: College credit possible. "Employees have the opportunity to take part in program facilities, i.e., swimming, canoeing, horseback riding, etc."

Cherokee Ridge, 1,100 acre resident Girl Scout camp located on the St. Francis River for girls ages 8-17. Needs college students, teachers for: 1 camp director (minimum age 25, camp administrative experience), May 31-July 26 plus one week flexible for hiring/evaluation, $850-1,100/season; 1 assistant camp director (minimum age 21, knowledge of business procedures), May 31-July 26, $540-640/season; 1 waterfront director (minimum age 21, WSI), June 7-July 26, $400-500/season; 1 canoeing instructor (minimum age 18, SL or WSI), June 7-July 26, $300-400/season; 2 waterfront assistants (minimum age 18 SL or WSI), June 7-July 26, $275-375/season; 1 wrangler (minimum age 21, experience with horses, must be willing to take 4-day Council Wrangler-in-Training Course or have had equivalent), June 7-July 26, $400-500/season; 1 assistant wrangler (minimum age 18, experience with horses, must be willing to take 4-day Council Wrangler-in-Training Course or have had equivalent), June 7-July 26, $275-375/season; 1 outpost unit director (minimum age 21, camp staff experience, thorough knowledge of advance campcraft skills) June 2-27 and July 19-25 (includes 1 week staff training), $250-350/season; 3 unit leaders (minimum age 21, training in the Girl Scout program, camp counseling and/or leadership techniques), June 7-July 26, $375-475/season; 5 assistant unit leaders (minimum age 18, leadership training and/or experience), June 7-July 26, $275-385/season; head cook (minimum age 21, must have experience preparing food in large quantities and supervising kitchen production. Also needs 1-2 kitchen helpers (college students, teachers, local applicants, minimum age 18, knowledge of food preparation in large quantities), June 7-July 26, $350-450/season; 1 kitchen aide (high school student or local applicant, minimum age 16, able to maneuver large kitchen equipment), June 7-July 26, $210-310/season; 1 nurse or EMT (college student, teacher, local applicant; minimum age 21; licensed RN, LPN or EMT), June 7-July 26; 1 handy person (college student teacher, local applicant, high school student, minimum age 17, current driver's license), June 7-July 26, $275-375/season. Room and board provided. Hires physically handicapped as assistant cooks, kitchen aide/camp helper (general kitchen and camp "gofer" duties, must be able to drive). Send for application. Apply by April 1 to Donna Hopper, Advisor to Resident Camp, Dept SED, Otahki Girl Scout Council, 108 N. Park, Cape Girardeau MO 63701. **Fringe Benefits: College credit** possible.

Derricotte, Located in Troy. 6-week (July-August) camp for disadvantaged girls ages 6-10 from metropolitan St. Louis. Needs 1 program director (leadership ability, teacher), $950/season; 16 counselors (college students, teachers, local applicants), $240-550/season; 7 activity leaders (college students, teachers, local applicants), $240-550/season; 4 waterfront personnel (college students, teachers, local applicants, WSI), $240-550/season. Applicants should be experienced in working with children. Room and board provided. Send for application or make appointment for interview if in town. Apply by May to Mary Pat Gillian, Camp Director, YWCA, 1015 Locust, Suite 310, St. Louis MO 63101.
Fringe Benefits: "Setting in Troy, Missouri, offers a lake, river and forest land. Working at camp provides a positive experience with low-income children." **College credit** possible.

Forty Legends/The Aud Homestead, Located in Franklin County. Private resident camps serving children ages 8-15. General camping activities include canoeing, backpacking, campcraft, archery, horsemanship, ecology, swimming (lake and pool), music, crafts, climbing, Indian lore and a special emphasis on homestead skills such as blacksmithing, broommaking, log construction, draft horses, spinning/weaving, animal husbandry, furniture making and gardening. Salary commmensurate with skills and experience with children. Openings for college students, teachers and independent adults from early June to mid-August (includes 1 full week of training). Spring "school camp" program (April and May) offers additional employment opportunities. Needs cabin counselors, skilled specialists, kitchen personnel, nurse, maintenance staff and junior staff (minimum age 17). Salaries are $300-1,500/season, commensurate with skills and experience with children. Room and board provided. "We do not hire persons who smoke or have a dependency on drugs or alcohol. We are inter-faith, inter-racial and coed." Apply to Joseph C. Soete Sr, Owner/Director, Forty Legends, Rt. 2, Box 836, Washington MO 63090; tel. 314/239-6087.

Latonka, Located on Lake Wappapello. Girl Scout camp for girls ages

8-17. Openings for college students, teachers and foreign students from mid-June to early August. Needs 7 unit counselors and 2 waterfront assistants, $300-500; 2 consultants, canoeing and waterskiing instructor, $300-500; 5 unit leaders and waterfront director, $350-600; wrangler, $400-600. Room and board provided. Apply by March to Ann Brown, Cotton Boll Girl Scout Council, Inc., Box 684, Sikeston MO 63801.

Sherwood Forest Camp, Inc., Located near St. Louis. Summer camp for children ages 12-16 from metropolitan St. Louis. Program for handicapped ages 9-14. Openings for college students, teachers and local (Missouri, Arkansas, Illinois) applicants from June 1 to August 15. Salary range: $250-500/month. Needs 12 cabin counselors, (college students, minimum age 19); 6 program specialists (skilled in crafts, archery, homesteading or photography); 5 waterfront directors (WSI, experience in teaching canoeing and swimming. Room and board provided. Also offers spring and fall employment. Send for application or phone. Apply by March 1 to Executive Director, Sherwood Forest Camp, Dept. SED, 7 N. 7th St., St. Louis MO 63101.
Fringe Benefits: "Scenic Ozark locale, transportation to and from St. Louis, every other week-end off and 1 week off between boys and girls programs." **College credit** possible.

Woodland, Located in Albany. Girl Scout camp for girls ages 7-17. Openings for college students, teachers, high school seniors and foreign students from mid-June to early August. Needs camp director, assistant camp director, 3 unit leaders, 9 assistant unit leaders, 3 riding counselors, dining hall hostess, 2 cooks, Water Safety Instructor. Room and board provided. Apply before April 30. Send for application to Barbara Braxdale, Camp Woodland, Midland Empire Girl Scouts, Dept. SED, 402 City Hall, St. Joseph MO 64501.
Fringe Benefits: Free laundry facilites. **College credit** possible.

Zoe, Located in Salem. Private, coed, ages 7 to 16, specializing in western riding and canoeing on the Current River. Openings for 20 college students and teachers from early June to mid-August. Needs 10 general counselors; 10 specialty counselors for western riding, canoeing, waterfront (WSI), arts and crafts, nature/campcrafts, tennis, archery, riflery, nurse. Salaries are $400-600 for the season. Apply to John R. Peters, Camp Zoe, Gladden Star Rt., Salem MO 65560.

Montana

1,272 jobs available

National Parks

Glacier Park, Inc., Located in Glacier National Park, Montana. Resort hotels, motor inns. Openings for 900 college students and teachers from June 1 (some May 1) to September 10-16 (some October 1). Also needs midseason replacements. Needs stenographers, chief room clerks, room clerks, night clerks, auditors, front office cashiers (including some N.C.R. posting machines No. 42), information clerks, switchboard operators, reservation office clerks, bellmen, porters, cabin porters/bellmen, housekeepers, assistant housekeepers, linen room attendants, housemen, maids, cleaners, dormitory matrons, chefs, first cooks, second cooks, cook's helpers, head bakers, baker's helpers, salad-pantry helpers, vegetable preparers, kitchen workers, assistant dish machine operators, cafeteria servers, grill cooks, fountain clerks, kitchen storekeepers, dining room managers, dining room cashiers, waiters, waitresses, bus boys, grill waiter/waitresses, head bartenders, bartender-waiters, gift shop senior and junior clerks, warehouse receiving clerks, accounting clerks, truck drivers, bus drivers (minimum age 21), service station attendants, night watchmen, deckhands, full time combos (3-piece), full time string trios, organists, laundry workers, washer extractors, seamstress, golf pro, assistant golf pro, undergardeners and lifeguards. "Talented students given additional consideration as are hotel and restaurant majors. Our guest entertainment programming is an important part of our schedule." Recruitment begins January 1. Salaries are all described and listed in Employment Circular, sent when applying. Apply by April or May to Ian B. Tippet, Assistant General Manager, Glacier Park, Inc., 1735 E. Ft. Lowell, Suite 7, Tucson AZ 85719.

Granite Park & Sperry Chalets, Located in Glacier National Park. "Hotel and dining rooms reached only by trails; serving backcountry hikers, horseriders, and active professional families." Openings for 19 college students and local applicants from June 21 through the day after Labor Day. Needs cooks, bakers, dishwashers, waitresses, laundry personnel, $2,200/season. "Must room and board on premises, $50/week. This is a work situation, 7 days a week, for 11 weeks in semi-primitive living conditions." Send for application by May 1 to L.R. Luding, Chalet Coordinator, Belton Chalets, Inc., Box 188, Dept SED, West Glacier MT 59936; tel. 406/888-5511.

Yellowstone Park Service Stations, Located in Yellowstone National Park. Concessionaire. Openings from May 1 to October 31 for college students and teachers, US citizens only (minimum age 18); minimum work period is June 10 to Labor Day. Needs 85 male or female gasoline service station attendants, 6 warehouse/office/clerical help, 8 journeyman automobile mechanics and 8 mechanic's helpers. Wages for all positions are based on hourly rates, with none being less than the federal minimum wage. Apply by May 1 to Employment Department, Box 11, Dept. WDB, Gardiner MT 59030.

Resorts, Ranches, Restaurants, Lodging

Flathead Lake Lodge, Located in Big Fork. Dude ranch. Openings for college students from May 1 to September 10. Needs 2 cooks, $300-600/month; 3 wranglers, $150-300/month; 10 cabin maids, 6 waitresses, hostess, 2 waterfront attendants, $150-200/month. Room and board provided. Enclose long, self-addressed, stamped envelope. Apply by May to Doug Averill, Flathead Lake Lodge, Box 248, Big Fork MT 59911.
Fringe Benefits: College credit possible.

Lazy K Bar Ranch, Located in Big Timber; isolated in a mountain canyon. Working Dude ranch, 100 years old, serving families (primarily Eastern). Openings for college students, teachers, and high school students from June 15 to Labor Day. Must stay through the season. Needs head cook, $300/month; second cook, $250/month; 4 male wranglers (with Western horse and riding experience, bonus for horseshoeing), $200/month; female wrangler (children's wrangler), $200/month; laundress, $175/month plus half of guests' laundry bills; chore man (able to milk, or learn to milk cows by hand), $175/month; 4 dining room and/or kitchen workers, $130-150/month; 3 cabin workers, $130-150/month. Room, board and tips are provided. "No drinking. Ability to work happily without complaining is necessary. We place great value on our employees' loyalty to us as an employer." Send for application; enclose long, stamped, self-addressed envelope. Apply by March 1 to Barbara K. Van Cleve, Dept. SED, Lazy K Bar Ranch, Big Timber MT 59011; tel. 406/537-4404.

Nine Quarter Circle Ranch, Located south of Gallatin Gateway. Family dude and livestock ranch. Openings for college students from June 5 to September 15. Needs 3 cabin maids, dishwasher, kitchen helper, laundry worker, $200-225; babysitter, second cook, $225-275. Room and board provided. Apply by April 1 to Mr. C.B. Kelsey, Nine Quarter Circle Ranch, Dept. SED, Gallatin Gateway MT 59730.
Fringe Benefits: End-of-season bonus. **College credit** possible. "Good social atmosphere."

St. Mary Lodge Motels, Located at the east entrance to Glacier National Park, St. Mary, Montana. Summer resort. Openings for 150 college students (minimum age 19) from May 1 to October 15. Needs waiters/waitresses/pantry/fry cooks, gas station attendants, maids, gift shop/supermarket/sporting goods store clerks, bartenders/cocktail waitresses, dishwashing/kitchen helpers, lodge desk/office personnel. Waiters/waitresses, $345/month plus $30/month bonus; others, $585/month plus $15/month bonus. Room and board provided. Preference given to hotel/restaurant management students. Apply by April 30 to (winter address): Roscoe Black, General Manager, St. Mary Enterprises, Box 1808, Sun Valley ID 83353.
Fringe Benefits: End-of-season bonus. **College credit** possible.

Sweet Grass Ranch, Located in Big Timber. An operating stock ranch. Emphasis on riding, working with stock and ranch life. Features moonlight rides, cook-outs and pack trips. Openings for college students, teachers, foreign students. Needs 1 housekeeper and 1 store clerk/laundress from first of June to end of August, $175/month; 1 girl friday from mid-June to mid-August, $150/month. Also needs 1 cook (college student, teacher) from mid-June to mid-August, $300/month. Room and board provided. Hires physically handicapped as store clerk/laundress or girl Friday. Send resume. Apply by April to William Carroccia, Owner, Sweet Grass Ranch, Melville Rt., Box 161, Dept. SED, Big Timber MT 59011.
Fringe Benefits: Riding one day a week when horses permit, family atmosphere, chance to experience ranch life, scenic mountain country, interesting people, good working conditions. **College credit** possible.

Summer Camps

Big Sky Girl Scout Council, Camp Scoutana, Located in
Augusta in the Bob Marshall Wilderness area. Openings from June 25 to
August 12. Needs unit leaders, $60-65; counselors, $50-55; handyman, $65;
cook, $90-100; assistant cook, $60-75; nurse, $65. Room and board provided.
Send for application. Apply early to Pat Phelps, Big Sky Girl Scout Council,
Suite 11, Holiday Village, Great Falls MT 59405.
Fringe Benefits: College credit possible.

Summer Theaters

Bigfork Summer Playhouse, Located in Bigfork. Openings for 25
people from early June to Labor Day. Needs directors, actors, instrumentalists,
technicians, designers, choreographers, costumers and box office personnel.
Salaries are $50-100/week. Housing provided. Apply by March 1 to Bigfork
Summer Playhouse, Bigfork MT 59911.
Fringe Benefits: "The theater is located on Flathead Lake, a resort area
with beautiful surroundings." **College credit** available.

Nebraska

40 jobs available

Summer Camps

Maranatha Bible Camp, Located near North Platte. Camp with
Christian atmosphere. Openings for college students and teachers from June 1
to August 3. Needs 20 maintenance workers, 5 recreation specialists, 10 kitchen
helpers, and 5 lawns and wood crew. Salaries are $300-500/season. Room and
board provided. "For a very rewarding summer in mid-America, consider
Maranatha Bible Camp. Nestled in a cedar forest near a 40-acre lake, many
recreational opportunities await you during your free time." Upon request, a
complete packet of information including application will be sent to you. Apply
by May 15 to George W. Cheek, Executive Director, Dept. SED, Box 549, North
Platte NE 69101; tel. 308/582-4512.
Fringe Benefits: Use of recreational facilities. **College credit** available.
"Maranatha is a great place to make quality friendships."

Nevada

67 jobs available

Resorts, Ranches, Restaurants, Lodging

Echo Bay Resort, Located 20 miles south of Overton. Hotel, restaurant, national park concessionaire. Openings for college students, teachers, high school students, foreign students and local applicants for all jobs from May or June to October (except no high school students as waiters, waitresses, bartender, cocktail waitress, cashiers, front desk personnel and auditors). Needs 5-8 waiters/waitresses; bartender, cocktail waitress (latter two should be experienced in basic and exotic drinks); 5-8 cooks and kitchen helpers; 5-8 motel and houseboat maids and laundry persons; 10-15 cashiers, front desk personnel, and auditors (cash handling experience necessary); 15-18 dockhands to pump gas and help boats in/out of marina (boat handling experience helpful); 4-6 maintenance persons for grounds, electricity, refrigeration, plumbing and carpentry (experience helpful); 4-6 mechanics for maintenance of outboards and inboard-outboards (mechanical experience necessary). "Most wages are hourly, none pay less than federal minimum wage. There are some salaried supervisory positions with additional benefits open. Housing is provided for a minimal rent charge or if one wants to bring their own camper, mobile home or travel trailer, space and utilities will be provided. Some housing units will have kitchenettes; otherwise meals are served in employees side hall at cost (approximately $2/meal)." Resort includes houseboat, ski boat, fishing boat and patio boat rentals. Customers consist of fishermen (older folks), skiers (young people), and houseboaters (families and young people); substantial group of young ski boaters and visitors from Las Vegas on weekends. "Be able to acclimate to hot, dry climate. Should enjoy lake and beach recreation. Resort is located in remote area but only 60 miles from Las Vegas." Send for application by April 1; include brief description of past experience. Apply to Don Wilson, Assistant General Manager for Resort Operations, c/o Echo Bay Resort, Dept. SED, Overton NV 89040; tel. 702/394-4000.

Summer Camps

Galilee, Located at Lake Tahoe. Episcopal Church camp for children and adults ages 8 and older. Openings for college students from June 12 to September 8. Needs 3 program counselors (arts and crafts, music, recreation), 1 program counselor/lifeguard. Pays $600/season plus room and board. Also needs many weekly cabin counselors on volunteer basis. "Inquire early, as soon after January 1 as possible. Apply to The Right Reverend Wesley Frensdorff, Camp Galilee, Box 6357, Reno NV 89513; tel. 702/747-4949.

New Hampshire

761 jobs available

Resorts, Ranches, Restaurants, Lodging

The Inn at East Hill Farm, Located in Troy. Family farm resort. Openings from May 22 thru September 7. Needs 6 waitresses (would like someone who plays guitar or piano.) $70/day6-day week plus tips, 1 riding attendant (must have experience training horses or taking riders), $70/6-day week plus tips, and 2 dishwashers, $70/6-day week. Room and board provided. Send resume to Dave Adams. East Hill Farm, Troy NY 03465.

Lake Shore Resort, Located in Northwood. Openings for college students and high school seniors from mid-June to mid-September. Needs 2 waitresses, 3 chambermaids, laundress, general worker, 2 dishwashers, kitchen helper, groundskeeper and tennis pro. Salaries to be arranged. Room and board provided. Apply to E.A. Ring, Lake Shore Resort, Dept. SED, Jenness Pond Rd., Northwood NH 03261.
Fringe Benefits: College credit possible.

Wayside Inn and Motel, Located at Bethlehem. Hotel and restaurant. Openings for college students, teachers and foreign students from June 6 to October 16. Needs 6 waiters/waitresses, 3 dishwasher-kitchen helpers and 3 laundress-chambermaids. Send resume and application request. Apply to Wayside Inn and Motel, Box 452, Bethlehem NH 03574.

Wild Goose Lodges Motel, Located on Lake Sunapee. Resort. Openings for college students, high school seniors and foreign students, minimum age 18, from mid-June to Labor Day. Needs 4 chambermaids, also to do some housework. Room and board provided. Send resume. Apply to Nellie R. Pieczaika, Dept. SED, Box 69, Newbury NH 03255.

Summer Camps

The Aloha Foundation, Inc., Located 20 miles from Hanover (Dartmouth College). Aloha Camp (for girls ages 12-17) and Lanakila (for boys ages 8-14) located at Lake Morey in Fairlee area; Aloha Hive (for girls ages 8-12) located at Lake Fairlee in West Fairlee. Openings for males and females from June 21 to August 18. Needs 75 counselors in the area of arts and crafts, campcraft, canoeing, sailing, swimming, music, archery, photography, ecology. Includes room and board, free laundry service. "Applicants must possess a high degree of skill in their field." Send for application by May 1. Apply to Paul S. Pilcher, Managing Director, Box 258, Fairlee VT 05045; tel. 802/333-9113.

Alton, Located at Wolfeboro, New Hampshire. Camp for boys. Openings for college students, nurses and teachers from approximately June 25 to August 25. Needs specialty counselors: sports and tennis, 2 arts and crafts, 5 waterfront (WSI), 2 boating (SCI), 3 campcraft and hiking, 2 nature, 2 music, 2 drama; kitchen workers (high school). Salaries are $450-750 and up. Room and board provided. Personal interview necessary. Apply to Peter Guralnick, Middle St., West Newbury MA 01985.

Cardigan Mountain School, Located in Canaan. Summer session for children ages 10-15. Needs 20-25 teachers of English, math, and reading (undergraduate degree, minimum) $850 and up. Employment from June 21 to August 8, including orientation days. "Teachers must be able to assist with activities program (many are offered, ranging from waterfront to land sports to crafts) and dormitory supervision. Beautiful and complete school facilities on Canaan Street Lake. Established program with long record of success with youngsters needing remedial English, math or reading help." *Personal interview definitely required.*Apply to Jeffrey D. Hicks, Director, Summer Session, Cardigan Mountain School, Canaan NH 03741; tel. 603/523-7156.

Chase Tennis & Golf Camps, Located in Bethlehem in New Hampshire's White Mountains. Ranch. Openings from mid-June to August 25. Needs 4 tennis counselors, 3 golf counselors, teachers, college students, foreign students all acceptable, $400-1,000/season; nurse (RN), $800/season; 3 kitchen trainees, college students or high school seniors preferred, $500/season. "Apply early and expect to work hard and be a part of the spirit and fun." Apply to Neil Chase, Chase Tennis & Golf Camps, Dept. SED, Box 1446, Manchester MA 01944; tel. 617/526-7514.

Cody for Boys, Located in West Ossipee, New Hampshire. Camp for 150 boys ages 7-16; established 1926. Fifty openings for mature counselors, coaches, and instructors in all athletics (team and individual sports), archery, canoeing, arts and crafts, drama/music, nature, photography, ham radio, riflery, tripping/woodcraft, swimming, sailing, waterskiing, scuba, etc. Salaries $400-800 and up, based on experience. Also needs physician, nurse (RN), waiters, groundsmen, kitchen assistants and secretary. Room and board provided. Contact (winter office) Directors Sandra and Alan J. Stolz, C.C.D., Dept. SED, 5 Lockwood Circle, Westport CT 06880; tel. 203/226-4389.
Fringe Benefits: Free laundry; staff cars allowed. State is tax free for salaries and purchases. Clientele and staff come from all parts of America and of the world. **College credit** available.

Coniston, Located in Grantham on Lake Coniston. YMCA coed camp. Openings for college students and teachers from June 23 to August 22. Needs counselor/program instructors for arts and crafts, archery, gymnastics, riding, swimming, drama, riflery, snorkeling, sailing, canoeing, campcraft, soccer, waterskiing, tennis, ecology, $650-1,100; Program director, unit head, nurse, cook, salary open. Fringe benefits. Apply by April 1 to Robert V. Sanders Jr., Director, Camp Coniston, Dept. SED, Box 1, Claremont NH 03743.

Foss, Located in Barnstead, New Hampshire. YMCA resident camp for girls ages 7-15. Openings from mid-June through August 20. Needs 11 cabin counselors/activity instructors (college students with ability to work with campers in living situation as well as instructing), $500-700/season; 1 waterfront director (college student or teacher for waterfront operation, small craft instruction, WSI), $700-900/season; 1 counselor-in-training director (college student or teacher, leadership development program, values education, camp background necessary), $700-900/season. Room and board provided. Hires physically handicapped; mobility is a must, activity instruction as able. "Applicants from northeast US preferred." Send resume or request application. Apply by March 1 to Ken Goebel, Strafford County YMCA, Dept. SED, Box 1804, 63 Lowell St., Rochester NH 03867; tel. 603/332-7334.

Holiday Trail and Holiday Highlands, Located in Hillsboro, New Hampshire. Privately owned boys and girls camps located in the scenic Dartmouth-Lake Sunappee region. Openings from June 27 to August 26. Needs 40 counselors (college students, teachers): waterfront (WSI, SLS), swimming, sailing, horseback riding, horsemanship, arts and crafts, ceramics, drama, dance, tennis, archery, riflery, pioneering, athletics, secretary, assistant nurse, $600 and up/8 weeks; 2 nurses (RN), $1,000/8 weeks; 5 kitchen staff (college or high school students), $500 and up/season. Room and board provided. Also needs post-season workers, September 1 to September 15. Send for application to Daryl Hawk, Director, Driftwood Point, Dept. SED, Westport CT 06880.
Fringe Benefits: "An interesting and gratifying summer with a congenial group of campers and staff from many states and countries."

Huckins YMCA Camp, Located at C. Ossipee. Resident camp for girls ages 9-15. Openings for college students for 9 weeks, from June 20 to August 23. Needs senior counselors in areas such as waterfront, arts and crafts, $500-600/season. Apply in January and February (deadline is March 1) to Zaven K. Vorperian, Director, YMCA Camp Huckins, Dept. SED, Box 521, N. Conway NH 03860; tel. 603/356-2019.
Fringe Benefits: "While there are benefits such as free medical insurance, the greatest benefits one derives from Camp Huckins are the lifelong friendships begun here, the chance to meet and be with a variety of different people, and the human relations skills learned at camp."

Lincoln, Located in Kingston. YMCA resident camp for boys, and coed day camp. Openings from approximately June 25 to August 25 (9 weeks). Needs waterfront director, college student or teacher preferred, $600-900/season; campcraft/trip director $400-600/season; craft instructor, $300-600/season; riflery instructor, $300-600/season; archery instructor, $300-600/season; 9 cabin counselor/activity instructors, $300-600; college students preferred; program director, $800-1,000/season; CIT director, $600-800/season, teacher preferred. Room and board provided. Apply by April 1. Send for applicaton to Director, YMCA Camp Lincoln, Dept. SED, Box 476, Concord NH 03301.
Fringe Benefits: "This is a small camp with an intense, positive, working atmosphere. There is a coed day camp on the same site." **College credit** possible.

Merrimac, Located in Contoocook, New Hampshire. Private coed camp for children. Openings for college students and teachers from June 27 to approximately August 24. Needs mature group leaders; specialty counselors for pioneering, water safety (ARC), nature, golf, science; instructors for waterskiing, dance, sailing, diving, athletics, riflery, tennis, archery, electronics, ham radio, chemistry, crafts (all phases), riding, judo, wrestling, canoeing, soccer, softball, basketball, fencing, dancing, cheerleading, fine arts, dramatics; ice hockey coaches; figure skating instructors; nurse (RN); kitchen help; bus driver; maintenance person. Salaries are $350-650/8-week season plus orientation. Room and board provided. Apply by March to Robert Bomze, Camp Merrimac,

Dept. SED, 6 Orchard Place, Harrison NY 10528.
Fringe Benefits: "Merrimac offers really great food, interesting staff from all over the world, great campers and professional directors." **College credit** possible.

Merriwood, Located in Orford, New Hampshire. Private camp for girls. Openings for college students and teachers from June 28 to August 18. Needs counselors for arts and crafts, canoeing, archery, riflery, drama, gymnastics, land sports, riding (English), dance, sailing, tennis, waterskiing; boat drivers; water safety instructors; and nurse (RN). Salaries are $500 and up plus travel allowance. Room and board provided. Apply by April to Gary D. Miller, 7 Field Rd., Riverside CT 06878; tel. 203/637-4674.
Fringe Benefits: Free laundry, good working conditions, social atmosphere and close working relationship with director. **College credit** possible.

Merrowvista, Located in Ossipee, New Hampshire. Christian oriented camp for girls and boys, ages 10-17, in separate sessions. Also operates Camp Miniwanca, Shelby, Michigan. Male staff may serve at *either* or *both* camps. Openings for college students, graduates, teachers and high school seniors for varying periods from mid-June through August. Needs workstaff (high school seniors and above); counselors (minimum age 18) with skills in archery, bicycling, canoeing, crafts, photography, rappelling, riflery, sailing, sports, swimming; director (upper college and above) for waterfront, tripping, program, workstaff; food service chef/manager; nurse (RN). Salaries are based on age and experience. Room and board provided. Apply to Ken Bryant, American Youth Foundation, Dept. SED, 3460 Hampton Ave., St. Louis MO 63139.
Fringe Benefits: Travel allowance, laundry and insurance provided.

Monomonac., Located in Rindge, New Hampshire. Christian residential camp for children ages 7-17. Openings for college students, high school students and teachers from June 22 to September 1. Needs 1 director for all waterfront activities, and to initiate a Red Cross Water Safety program, $1,100-1,200/season; 1 unit director for supervision of camping village of 50 campers (June 29-September 1), $650-750/season; 1 arts and crafts director, $800-900/season; 25 counselors to lead and guide cabin groups, possibly for leadership in programs (June 29-September 1), $250-650/season. Room and board provided. Send for application. Apply by April to The Rev. Len Cowan, Director, c/o Christ Church, Dept. SED, 569 Main St., Fitchburg, MA 01420.
Fringe Benefits: "Good working conditions with excellent time-off schedules, interesting work in the out of doors, loving Christian community, bonus for WSI or equivalent."

Moosilauke, Located in Orford, New Hampshire. Private camp for boys ages 8-16. Openings for college students and teachers from June 28 to August 18. Needs general and specialty counselors for tennis, baseball, basketball, canoeing, soccer, outdoor life, sailing, crafts, gymnastics, archery and swimming, $500-1,000. Room, board, laundry and travel allowance provided. Apply by April to Dr. Gordon Porter Miller, 570 Colonial Ave., Pelham Manor NY 10803.
Fringe Benefits: "Laundry, travel allowance, outdoor setting; use of all facilities, one full day off per week." **College credit** possible.

New Hampshire 4-H Camps, Spruce Pond and Bear Hill,

Located in Bear Brook State Park, Allenstown. Agency-sponsored, coed, residential camps for children ages 8-15. Openings from approximately June 24 to August 25. Needs 2-4 program directors, camp administrative experience necessary, $700-1,200/season; 8-10 waterfront staff, college students or teachers preferred, $400-800/season; 15-18 program staff, $400-700/season; 2 trip leaders, college students or teachers preferred, $800/season; 8 unit heads, college students, teachers, and foreign students preferred, $500/season; 20 counselors, college students, high school seniors, and foreign students preferred, $200-300/season; 10 kitchen/maintenance, college students, teachers, and foreign students preferred, $200-800/season. "Qualifications: love of kids and outdoors, willingness to work hard and share with others, understanding of the vital role of camps and staff in the development of youth." Apply to Bruce Matthews, Director, New Hampshire 4-H Camps, State 4-H Office, Moiles House, U.N.H., Durham NH 03824; tel. 603/862-2180.

Pierce Camp Birchmont, Located at Wolfeboro, New Hampshire.

Coed camp for ages 7-16. Openings for high school seniors or college students from June 26 to August 25. Needs sports counselors—tennis, rifle, archery, trampoline and water. Room and board provided. Apply by June 1 to F.W. Pierce, Director, Dept. SED, Mineola Ave., Roslyn NY 11576; tel 516/621-2211.
Fringe Benefits: "Work with all college students and teachers." **College credit** possible.

Pleasant Valley Camp, Located on Lake Wentworth, S. Wolfeboro,

New Hampshire. Resident girls' camp with capacity of 72, plus CIT program. Openings from June 20 to August 21 for the following positions: Program Director, Horseback Riding instructor, Waterfront Director, 3 Waterfront Counselors (WSI), Sailing instructor, Tennis instructor, head cook ($1200), multi-skilled staff. All activity staff has cabin responsibilities. Selections made February to April. YMCA camp emphasizing independence and creativity. Campers select their own activity program. Apply to Barbara E. Damon, Resident Director, 25 Central Ave., Danvers MA 01923.

Runels, Located in Pelham, New Hampshire. Girl Scout camp for girls

ages 7-17. Openings for college students, teachers and high school seniors from June 23 to August 18. Needs 30 counseling staff: unit leaders, counselors, $350-600/season; arts and crafts, $350-600/season; environmental studies $400-600/season; waterfront (WSI), $400-800/season; small craft (sailing, boating, canoeing), $400-800/season; nurse (RN), $700-1,000/season; CIT director, $500-700/season; biking and backpacking, $400-700/season. Apply by June 15 to Camping Services Director, Summer Employment, Merrimack River Girl Scout Council, Inc., 89 N. Main St., Andover MA 01810.

Trinity House, Located in Atkinson. Camp for underprivileged children:

resident camp for girls (ages 6-15) and boys (ages 6-10); day camp for boys and girls (ages 4-11). Openings for college students and teachers from mid-June to end of August. Needs specialty counselors for swimming (WSI), arts and crafts,

nature, sports and campcraft; and unit heads. Salaries are $300-800. Room and board provided. Staff openings for day camp Monday through Friday. Pays $300-450. Apply by June 15 to Susan Noble, Director, Trinity House Camp, Atkinson NH 03811.
Fringe Benefits: Insurance provided. **College credit** possible. "Located less than 1 hour from historic Boston, the New England coast and the White Mountains."

Wa-Klo, Located in Jaffrey Center, New Hampshire. Summer camp for girls from June 25 to August 25. Salaries: $600 minimum/season. Needs 30 instructors: tennis, archery, soccer, volleyball, riflery, riding, basketball, hockey, dance, drama, arts and crafts, gymnastics, swimming (ARC), canoeing, sailing, water skiing. Also needs 2 nurses (RN or LPN, must be able to secure certification in NH), salary open. Room and board provided. Send for application to Ethel T. Kloberg, Owner/Director, Camp Wa-Klo, Dept. SED, 506 Devonshire Rd., Baldwin NY 11510.
Fringe Benefits: College credit possible.

Walt Whitman, Located in Pike, New Hampshire. General coed camp for children ages 7-15. Openings for college students and teachers from June 22 to August 22. Needs staff as follows: 3 waterfront (WSI), 2 sailing, 3 tennis, 2 woodworking, 2 art, 2 music, 2 campcraft, 2 ecology. Salaries are $600 and up, depending on experience. Indicate experience with children. Room and board provided. Apply to Mr. L.C. Soloway, 80-83 Kent St., Dept. SED, Jamaica NY 11432.
Fringe Benefits: "Coed staff; ratio of staff to children is 2:5."**College credit** possible.

Winamac Riding Camp, Located in Bennington, New Hampshire. Private riding and waterfront camp for children ages 6-16. Openings from June 20 to August 20. Needs 6 English riding instructors, 3 Western riding instructors, college students preferred, $400-700/season; 10 waterfront counselors, college students and high school seniors preferred, $400-600/season; 2 riflery instructors, college students preferred, $500/season; 4 athletic instructors, college students and high school seniors preferred, $500/season; 3 ceramics and arts and crafts instructors, college students and high school seniors preferred, $400-500/season; 10 cabin counselors, college students, teachers, and high school seniors preferred, $300-600/season. Room and board provided. Apply to George Athans, Director, Winamac Riding Camp, RFD 2, Mt. Kisco NY 10549.
Fringe Benefits: "Excellent working conditions."

Summer Theaters

New London Barn Playhouse, Located in New London. Summer theater. Openings for college students and teachers from early June through Labor Day. Needs stage manager, technical director, scenic designer, costume designer, box office treasurer, properties coordinator, costume assistant, musical director, percussionist, publicity coordinator, $25-100 plus room and

board; 2 journeymen, $15 plus room and board; 14 acting apprentices, 2 technical apprentices, 1 administrative apprentice, room and board only. Apply by March 15 to Norman Leger, Producer, New London Barn Players, Dept. SED, Box 285, New London NH 03257.
Fringe Benefits: College credit possible. "An opportunity to perform on stage, through open auditions, is available to the entire company."

New Jersey
1,998+ jobs available

Commercial Attractions

Asbury Casino Corp., Located in Asbury Park. Family-oriented amusement center with rides and games. Openings for college students, teachers and local applicants from May 20 to September 13. Needs 10 ride or game operators, $160-$210/week. Lodging available closeby, $25 week and up; eating facilities in area are varied and plentiful. Hires physically handicapped. Send resume or application by March 10 to M. Werfel, General Manager, Dept. SED, Asbury Casino Corp., 701 Boardwalk, Asbury Park, New Jersey 07712.
Fringe Benefits: "We provide an opportunity to meet people of varied backgrounds under good working conditions."

Resorts, Ranches, Restaurants, Lodging

Atlas-Motor Inn and Seashore Food Distributor, Located in Capenay. Motel, restaurant and wholesale food distributor. General positions available. Apply to Harry Satt, President, Madison-Beach Dr., Capenay NJ 08204; tel. 609/884-7000.

Pierre's Holiday Enterprises, Inc., Located on the Boardwalk at Wildwood. Restaurant. Openings for college students, teachers, high school seniors and foreign students from May 15 to September 20. Needs 30 waitresses, 6 bus boys, 6 short order cooks, 2 cashiers, 3 hostesses. New Jersey minimum wage plus tips for some positions. Apply to Pierre's Holiday Enterprises, Inc., 117 E. 23rd Ave., North Wildwood NJ 08260; tel. 609/522-6354.

Summer Camps

American Camping Association, Located at North Plainfield. Members operate organizational and private camps for boys, girls, co-ed and family; resident camps in northeastern states, day camps in New Jersey. "We

For a quick reference, the number of jobs available in each state can be found just below the state heading.

are part of a national organization whose purpose is to assure the highest professional practices for administration and extension of organized camping." Needs college students, high school seniors and teachers for: general counselors; unit leaders; trained and experienced activities counselors for arts and crafts, music, drama, campcraft, pioneering, land and water sports (WSI, NRA); nurses (RN), physicians, business managers, office secretaries, grounds and buildings maintenance, and kitchen staff. Salary depends on position, age, education, and experience. Room and board provided in resident camps. Hires physically handicapped for office work and as counselors wherever terrain and facilities allow. Send resume or for application by June 1 to NJ Section ACA, 5 Mountain Ave., North Planfield, New Jersey 07060.
Fringe Benefits: Scenic locale, interesting people, interesting work and social atmosphere. **College credit** available.

The Appel Farm, Located in Elmer. Art and music center for children. Openings for college students, teachers, foreign students, artists and musicians, minimum age 21, from June 21 to August 24. Nonsmokers only. Needs bunk counselors; water safety instructors (ARC); specialty counselors for dance (modern, ballet, jazz, folk), photography, video/audio and film, arts and crafts (painting, weaving, batik, sculpture, ceramics, printing), music (orchestral and band instruments, jazz, rock); nurse (RN); doctor. Salaries are $600 and up. Room and board provided. Must be motivated and interested in working with children. Apply from January 1 to April 30 to The Appel Farm, Dept. SED, Elmer NJ 08318.
Fringe Benefits: Internships for **college credit** available.

Central New Jersey YMCA Camps, Resident and day camp plus year-round conference center located in Blairstown. Facilities include 500 acres of woods, fields and streams; lake for boating and canoeing; tennis courts; six lane, 25-meter pool; rifle range; and complete set of gymnastics equipment. Coed, for children ages 8-16 years old from the Middle Atlantic region and across the US. Openings from June 15 through August; earlier and later dates possible. College students and teachers preferred. Needs 2 aquatics directors with current WSIs, 2 horseback directors, 2 mini-bike directors, $1,000-2,000/season; 2 AM radio directors, 2 NRA rifle instructors, 2 gymnastics instructors, $800-1,500/season; 2 arts and crafts directors, $1,000/season; 15-20 general counselors $500-1,000/season. Room and board provided. Apply "immediately" to J.H. Wilkes, Executive Director, Central N.J. YMCA Camps, Dept. SED, R.D.#3 Box 41, Blairstown NJ 07825; tel. 201/362-8217.
Fringe Benefits: Use of camp facilities during time off. **College credit** possible.

Dark Waters, Located in Medford. Camp for boys and girls ages 7-13. Openings from June 23 to August 22. Needs cook (college student, teacher, local applicant) to prepare menus, order supplies, cook meals, supervise campers and counselors in kitchen, $1,000-1,500/season; assistant cook (college student, local applicant), $700-800/season; camp nurse, $800-1,000/season; 18 counselors (college students, teachers, high school students, local applicants), $250-600/season. Room and board provided. Applicants "must like children and people in general; must be bright, creative and flexible." Send for application by April 1 to Stephen A. Edgerton, 231 West Winona St., Philadelphia PA 19144; tel. 215/438-9035.

Episcopal Camp and Conference Center, Located in
Branchville. Christian oriented resident camp for children ages 8-16. Openings from June 21 to August 22. Needs program director, college graduate or teacher, $1,000/season; 8 female and 10 male general counselors, 1-2 years college, $600/season (seniors), $300/season (juniors); 4 WSIs, experience required, $800/season; driver, school bus licensed, $600/season; nurse, $800/season. Also needs the following, at $600-700/season, required to have 1 year or more of college and experience in the area applied for: arts and crafts specialist, girls' chief, boys' chief, girl pioneer director, boy pioneer director. Room and board provided. Send resume or phone or write for application by May 20 to The Reverend Phyllis Edwards, Camp and Conference Center, 24 Rector Street, Newark NJ 07102; tel. 201/622-4306, ext. 121.
Fringe Benefits: "This camp is located near High Point, Stokes State Forest and the Appalachian Trail. There is a bird banding station on the property. Employees have the opportunity to play tennis, street hockey and soccer, and to take first aid courses. Staff members are from Great Britain and Germany, as well as the US." **College credit** possible.

Fairview Lake YMCA Camps, Located in Newton. YMCA resident
and day camps. Brother/sister resident camps for children ages 10-16; coed resident unit for 3rd and 4th graders; coed day camp, ages 6-12 . Openings for males and females over 18, from June 28 to August 22. Needs 40 general counselors (responsible for cabin group of 7-9 campers, teaching one program area and assisting in others), $400-700/season; specialty counselors for waterfront, riding, riflery, sailing, arts and crafts, campcraft, archery, dramatics and photography. Bonus for American Red Cross and other recognized certifications. "We are looking for intelligent, mature, outgoing personnel with high energy levels, a love for the out-of-doors, and a love for kids. Previous experience in a camp setting is a plus." Room and board provided. Send for application. Apply before June 20 to W. Daniel McCain, Executive Director, Fairview Lake YMCA Camps, Dept. SED, RD 5, Box 230, Newton NJ 07860; tel. 201/383-9282.
Fringe Benefits: "Site includes 110-acre lake; staff has fishing privileges." **College credit** possible.

Hudson Guild Farm, Located in Andover. Nonsectarian
Neighborhood House Camp serving families, single adults and senior citizens. Program for children (5-15 years of age), parents and senior citizens. Openings from end of June to end of August. Needs program director, single persons and couples with camp, group or teaching experience with specialties in folk music (guitar), outdoor education, recreation and waterfront. Also office clerk, dining room and kitchen workers, cooks and auto driver. Most salaries range from $600-850/season. Room and board provided. Write to Curtis R. Ream, Hudson Guild Farm, Andover NJ 07821.

Fringe Benefits: Located on 550 acres convenient to New York City. Families are of many ethnic and economic backgrounds. Employees have no cabin duties.

Merry Heart, Located in Hackettstown. Coed camp for the physically handicapped. Openings for college students and teachers from approximately June 16 to September 1. Needs 4 specialists, $600-900; 20 counselors, $500-800. Apply by May 1 to Mary Ellen Ross, Director of Camping, Camp Merry Heart, Dept. SED, RFD 2, Hackettstown NJ 07840.

Nejeda, Located in Stillwater. Residential camp for diabetic children, ages 5-15. Openings for college students, teachers and high school seniors from June 29 to August 29. Artistic, musical, arts and crafts and sports skills. Needs 16 counselors, $450-800; salary negotiable. Also needs 2 WSIs. Deadline for applications: April 1. Apply early to Camp Nejeda, 153 Roseville Ave., Newark NJ 07107.

Camp Nomoco, Located near Freehold. Girl Scout camp on a 300 acre site. Openings for college students and teachers from June 28 to August 1. Needs 1 camp director with knowledge of the Girl Scout program, supervisionary and administrative skills, $1,000-2,000/season; 1 program director with knowledge of Girl Scout program and supervisory skills, $600-880/season; 1 business manager with food purchasing skills, $500-900/season, 1 nurse (RN), $700-1,660/season; 5 unit directors with knowledge of Girl Scout program, $300-615/season; 10 specialists in sports, nature, campcraft skills, advance lifesaver, $266-615/season; 1 waterfront director (WSI), $300-615/season; 1 kitchen supervisor (skilled in portion control), $330-415/season. Room and board provided. Send for application. Apply by June to Elizabeth E. Armington, Director of Program Services, Monmouth Coucil of Girl Scouts, RD 1, Farmingdale, NJ 07727.
Fringe Benefits: Located near the Jersey shore (30 minute drive). Staff free 10 am Saturdays to 2 pm Sundays. **College credit** available.

Sacajawea, Located in Sparta. Girl Scout camp for ages 6 to 17. Openings for college students and teachers, minimum age 19, from June 30 to August 8. Needs unit staff, waterfront staff, sports specialists and kitchen staff. Salaries are $300 and up, depending on experience and record. Apply to Betty Ann Marks, Assistant Executive Director, Delaware-Raritan Girl Scout Council, 715 King Georges Post Rd., Edison NJ 08817.

Trail Blazer, Located in New Jersey with 1,000 acres of forest and a large lake. Interracial, interfaith camp for low-income children. Openings for college students and teachers (minimum age 20) from June 20 to August 27. Needs counselors, $500-600/season; lakefront (WSI and senior lifesaver), $650-750/season; 2 dieticians (no cooking), $700-800/season; typist-mimeographer, $550-650/season; pot scrubber-kitchen aide, $500-600/season; nurses, $800-950/season. Mature professional attitude and dedication required. Apply to Jane Brokaw, Trail Blazer Camps, 56 W. 45th St., New York NY 10036.

Vacamas Association, Located on 600 acres in the Ramapo
Mountains in New Jersey; only an hour from New York City. Nonsectarian
social agency camp for boys and girls from low-income families. Needs
counselors, specialists and service staff. No experience required. Men and
women in their junior year of college or higher preferred and given salary
increments. Education, social work, psychology and related majors preferred.
Salaries $300-600, based on qualifications. Write to Camp Vacamas
Association, Irving Topal, Executive Director, 215 Park Ave. S., New York NY
10003.

YMCA Camp Bernie, Located at Port Murray. Resident coed camp
for children, 3rd to 10th grade. Openings for college students from June 20 to
August 17; staff training is the week of June 21-28. Needs 15 cabin counselors,
$450-700/season; 1 riflery instructor and about 4 tripping leaders,
$600-800/season; 1 swimming instructor, $550-700/season; 1 nature and
ecology instructor, $700-850/season; truck driver, $700-900/season. Room
and board provided. Apply by June 15 to Neil VanBodegon-Smith, Camp
Director, Dept. C-SED, Rd. #1, Port Murray NJ 07865, tel. 201/689-1318 or
832-5315.
Fringe Benefits: "At Camp Bernie, there is tremendous individual growth in
staff members. Camp food is good; snacks are provided for staff most
evenings."

New Mexico

648 jobs available

Resorts, Ranches, Restaurants, Lodging

Bishop's Lodge, Located in Santa Fe. Openings for college students
from May through Labor Day, some through mid-October; shorter contracts
not considered. Needs 1-2 lifeguards, $3.50/hour; 3-4 counselors, $4/hour;
10-12 waitresses, 6-8 waiters, $2.65/hour plus tips; 4 wranglers, $3.50/hour; 4-5
busboys, $2.65/hour plus tips; also bartenders, minimum age 21, and desk
clerks. Salaries depend on ability and experience. Apply to James R. Thorpe,
The Bishop's Lodge, Box 2367, Santa Fe NM 87501

Summer Camps

Brush Ranch, Located in Tererro. Private camp for children ages 8-17
(girls) and 8-14 (boys). Openings for college students from June 10 to August 8.
Needs instructors who also serve as boys' and girls' cabin counselors for music,
western riding (boys), English riding (girls), tennis, riflery, fencing, fishing,
certified WSI and synchronized swimming, art, dance, drama and nature. Also
needs 2 full time cooks, 3 dishwashers and minor maintenance. Room and
board provided. Apply by May 1 to James S. Congdon, Brush Ranch Camps for
Boys and Girls, Tererro NM 87573; tel. 505/757-8772.

Fringe Benefits: "Our location is definitely a hidden asset to working at Brush Ranch. The ranch is located on 283 private acres, surrounded by the Santa Fe National Forest. Our proximity to Santa Fe (37 miles) is a plus. Also, a summer at Brush Ranch provides as much education as a semester in college." **College credit** possible.

Philmont Scout Ranch and Explorer Base, Located in Cimarron. Scout Ranch for older Scouts and Explorers with approximately 19,000 campers annually. Openings from June 7 to August 22 for 550 staffers who must be registered members of the Boy Scouts of America, minimum age 18. Majority of staffers hired from outside New Mexico. Needs 160 back country staffers, 140 or more ranger staffers and 250 base personnel staffers. Within these three basic areas, persons are needed for the following positions: cooks, photographers, rangers, security, maintenance, activities, wranglers, group leaders, tent manager, conservation services, museum staff. Especially needs staff for food service, trading posts and snack bars on the camp. Base salary for new employees is (age 18) $270/month. Room and board provided; transportation to and from camp is not. Competition is keen for staff jobs. In 1980 more than 1,400 applications were received. Most staff selections are made by March 15 for each summer. By that time all applicants will have been notified of their status if they have a job, they don't have a job, or they are still being considered. Send a note requesting an application form, mentioning SED in the note. On the back of the form is a brief description of the available jobs and the applicant is asked to note which 3 jobs he is interested in, in order. Apply to Seasonal Personnel, Philmont Scout Ranch, Dept. SED, Cimarron NM 87714.

Tall Pines, Located in Mayhill, New Mexico. Girl Scout camp for girls, ages 6-17. Openings for college students, teachers and high school seniors from June 11 to August 3. Needs 5 program administrators, $45-60/week; 10 program counselors, $30-35/week; riding director, $45-60/week; assistant riding director, $30-40/week; 3 cooks, $45-70/week; kitchen aide, $30-40/week; assistant director, $45-60/week. Room and board provided. Applications considered as received beginning January 1. An equal opportunity employer. Apply by February 1 to Camp Director, Rio Grande Girl Scout Council, 3214 E. Yandell Dr., El Paso TX 79903.
Fringe Benefits: "Practical work experience and unique outdoor living experience." **College credit** possible.

Mary White, Located near Mayhill, New Mexico. Girl Scout camp for ages 9-17. Openings for college students, teachers, high school seniors and foreign students from June 7 to August 1. Needs 6 unit counselors, $325-400; 9 unit assistants, $225-325; directors: riding, program and arts and crafts, $250-450; nurse (RN or graduate), $250-450; 2 cooks, $250-450; business manager, $250-350. Room and board provided. Apply by May 1 to Paula Homer, 2708 Sunset Dr., Dept. SED, San Angelo TX 76901.
Fringe Benefits: "Mary White is a primitive camp, isolated in the mountains; staff lives in log cabins. The camp specializes in hiking and camping out, i.e., backpacking, burro trips, covered wagon trips and outposting."

New York

6,064+ jobs available

Business and Industry

Allied Temporary Personnel, Inc., Temporary services.
Openings throughout the year for college students and teachers who are US citizens. All phases of office work: secretarial, reception, typists and business machine operators. Hourly pay based on experience and skills. No fee to applicants for placement. Apply to Personnel Director, Summer Positions, Allied Temporary Personnel, Inc., 295 Madison Ave., New York NY 10017.
Fringe Benefits: "This organization offers the ability to learn about different industries and fields so that career decisions are helped while still in college."
College credit possible.

Aubrey Thomas Inc., Temporary and permanent personnel agency.
Works with over 200 major corporations serving banking, insurance, publishing, advertising and many other fields in the metropolitan area. Positions available for full-time and part-time help from May 1 to September 15. Needs 250 typists, 250 secretaries, 200 gal/man Fridays, 100 receptionists, 100 word processors, 100 clerk-typists, and 100 accounting clerks. No fee charged to applicants. Can apply in person at following locations: Midtown, 400 Madison Ave., New York NY; tel. 212/486-7800; Wall Street, 150 Broadway, New York NY; tel. 212/732-6100; Westchester, 1 N. Broadway, White Plains NY; tel. 914/428-2020.

Career Blazers Personnel Services, Located in New York City.
Has hundreds of employment opportunities for administrative assistants, secretaries, gal/guy fridays, typists, file clerks, word processors, receptionists and many others. Positions available in publishing, advertising, fashion, film, radio, TV, financial, non-profit organizations, etc. "Highest salaries paid"; full-time, part-time or temporary. Write to Career Blazers Personnel Services, 500 Fifth Ave., New York City NY 10110.
Fringe Benefits: "Diverse fields, employment bonuses, flexible schedules."

The Costume Collection, Located in New York City. Not-for-profit theatrical costume rental service. Openings for teachers and college students. Needs 5-8 full-time workers in July and August to pull costumes for productions, return costumes to stock, and generally assist staff and customers. Also needs students to work part-time during the academic year. Wages are $3.10/hour, 35-hour week. "Graduate or undergraduate students of costume design who wish to apply should send a resume and a letter of application, which must include the name of the university attended, the degree expected, the term being applied for, details of relevant course work, related job experience, if any, and the names and addresses of two people who may be contacted for reference. Students who are eligible to receive federal work-study funds should indicate this information as well." Apply by March 15 to Whitney Blausen, The Costume Collection, Theatre Development Fund, 1501

Broadway, Suite 2110, New York NY 10036.
Fringe Benefits: "In the summer term, field trips are regularly scheduled to the Metropolitan Opera costume shop, Ray Diffen Stage Clothes, Eaves Costumes Company, Robert Joyce Studios, and to costume exhibits at various New York City museums. Also scheduled are informal talks with designers who have productions in these shops at the time." **College credit** possible.

Davidson's Temps, Temporary personnel contractor. Openings for many qualified college students, teachers, high school seniors and foreign students during vacations and holidays. Needs stenographers (minimum 80 wpm); typists (minimum 50 wpm); secretaries (with/without steno), $3.50-4.50; word processing operators (Mag card, Vydek, etc.). High rates of pay with reference to skills, experience and assignment demands. Apply to W.P. Davidson, Davidson's Temps, Dept. SED, 41 E. 42nd St., New York NY 10017.
Fringe Benefits: "Job assignments in New York's finest offices."

North Shore Studios, Located in East Northport. Model services, commercial photography. Needs models (female only), minimum age-18th birthday in 3 months to 36 years old, $5-25/hour; 2 general assistants, college students or teachers preferred, $3.50/hour. Employment not seasonal, but hourly salary when used. "In commercial photography 90 percent of attaining position is beauty of face, then figure. Good manners, proper grooming, good teeth and a healthy disposition are essential. Be yourself, sincere, and study the work you would do in applying for any position." Apply to Alexander D. Jones, Jr., Owner, North Shore Studios, 216 Elwood Rd. E., Northport NY 11731; tel. 516/261-5527.
Fringe Benefits: "Free schooling if accepted as a model trainee (cash value $1100); obtain model portfolio at cost. Good looks, poise and presentation help in a career and can be recognized by the public years after modeling (e.g., Bess Meyerson, former Miss America and head of Department of Consumer Affairs N.Y.C. ran for New York State Senate). **College credit** possible.

Office Help Temporaries, Main office located in Yonkers. Other locations in Westchester-Rockland, Greenwich-Stamford, and New York City. Temporary openings available throughout the year, 1 week to 3 months and all school holidays, for college students and teachers with office skills including secretarial, typing, mag card, keypunching and others. Salaries are $3.10-6 and up/hour. No fees. Telephone for appointment: Greenwich-Stamford, 203/324-2115; New York City, 212/884-2427; Westchester-Rockland, 914/946-1690; Yonkers, 914/965-1333.
Fringe Benefits: "The opportunity to work for various businesses in different fields may lead to unexplored career paths." **College credit** possible.

Wyckoff Heights Hospital. Located in Brooklyn. Non-profit hospital. Temporary and permanent openings year-round for college students and local applicants. Needs temporary and permanent clerical (typing, organized, good phone manner), $240/week; Registered Nurses (NYS license or permit), $288.46/week; respiratory therapists (certified), $275/week. Rent averages $150-250/month. Hospital cafeteria provides meals at reasonable rates, local restaurants also available. Send resume to Anthony Pellicano, Employment Manager, Wyckoff Heights Hospital, Dept. SED, 374 Stockholm St., Brooklyn NY 11237.

Fringe Benefits: 35 hour week, 15 paid sick days, 12 paid holidays, convenient location, excellent salaries.

Government

Department of Labor, Jobs available at the regional office, Room 3580, 1515 Broadway, New York, New York 10036. This office services New York, New Jersey, Puerto Rico and the Virgin Islands. Applications must be made to Washington DC office. See Washington DC office (District of Columbia section) for complete description of jobs available and how to apply information.

National Transportation Safety Board, Jobs available at the regional office in New York. Applications must be made to Washington DC office. See Washington DC office (District of Columbia section) for complete description of jobs available and how to apply information.

Resorts, Ranches, Restaurants, Lodging

Atlantic Terrace Motel Corp., Located in Ocean View Terrace, Montauk, on Long Island. Openings from late June to October. Needs chambermaids, $100/week plus tips; lifeguard, $100/week plus tips; maintenance help, groundskeepers, $110/week; office help, $115/week. Salaries are given out under contract system; part of salary is withheld and given out as a bonus on Labor Day—penalty for premature departure. Housing and kitchen facilities provided. "No person who does not plan to stay until the end of Labor Day weekend should apply." Apply by April 1 to Ralph Jakoby, 286 Vanderbilt Pkwy., Dix Hills NY 11746; tel. 516/427-9389.

Fringe Benefits: "Substantial bonus upon completion of work period at the end of Labor Day weekend."

Blue Water Manor, Located at Diamond Point on Lake George. Resort. Openings for 45 college students and teachers, minimum age 18, from mid-June to Labor Day. Needs waitresses, chambermaids, waiters, cabin boys, secretaries, kitchen help, bartenders, ski-boat drivers, grounds/maintenance personnel and snack bar attendants. Room and board available. Resort experience and talent for staff show and dance band desired. Send self-addressed, stamped envelope for job information and application form. Apply to Dorothy Long, Blue Water Manor, Diamond Point NY 12824.

Driftwood on the Ocean, Located in Montauk. Resort. Openings for college students and foreign students from June 15 to September 15. Apply only if available until September 15. Needs telephone operator-office help, chambermaids, 2 lifeguards and maintenance help, $125 plus tips and free lodging (room with kitchen facilities). Apply to Robert Grau, Driftwood On The Ocean, Box S, Montauk NY 11954.

Golden Acres Farm and Ranch, Located in Gilboa. Family farm resort. Openings for 60 college students, teachers and high school seniors (minimum age 16) from late June (some late May) to Labor Day. Needs waitresses, waiters, bus boys, hostess, bartender, snackbar attendants, cocktail waitress, chef, assistant cooks, kitchen workers, salad maker, baker, baker-trainee, kitchen steward, dishwasher, potwasher, front office clerks, secretary, bellhops/maintenance persons, farm hand, maids, laundry attendant, social director (must know square and folk dancing), nurse, head counselor to supervise teen and children's program, athletic director for adults and teens, general counselors (must swim), arts and crafts counselors, lifeguards, WSI, stable head and assistants (must ride and teach Western riding), craft teacher for adult program, maintenance person, bookkeeper and single musician with electronic equipment. Salary depends on position and experience; most positions have tips plus room and board. A personal interview is required. Send a resume and stamped, legal size, self-addressed envelope. Apply to Mrs. Jerry Buxbaum, Dept. SED, Golden Acres Farm, Gilboa NY 12076.

Lake House Hotel, Located in Woodridge. Kosher, open April to October. Openings from June through October or minimum July and August working 7 days/week. Needs 2 maids, local applicants, college students, high school seniors, foreign students all acceptable, $50/week plus tips; 3 cooks' helpers, local applicants, college students, high school seniors, foreign students all acceptable, $100-150/week; 3 dishwashers, 2 pantry helpers, college students, foreign students acceptable, $100-150/week; 1 baker's helper, college students, high school seniors, foreign students all acceptable, $100-150/week; 2 lifeguards, college students and high school seniors preferred, $70-100/week; 1 or 2 second cook (experienced only), local applicants, college students, high school seniors, teachers, foreign students all acceptable, $125-250/week. "Write, sending as much information as possible. Room and board are provided (Kosher food)." Apply after February 1 to Mr. Kay, Personnel Manager, Lake House Hotel, Box 367, Dept. SED, Woodridge NY 12789; telephone only after June 1, 914/434-7800.

Olympian Village, Located at Lake George, Diamond Point. Resort motel. Openings for 7 college students (minimum age 18) from the last week in June to Labor Day. Needs reservation clerk (general office work) and chambermaids. Apply to Mrs. Henrietta Kopelman, 270 Jay St., Brooklyn NY 11201.

Potter's Resort and Restaurant, Located at Blue Mt. Lake, New York. Family resort. Openings for persons age 18 and older from June 22 through Labor Day. Needs 8 waitresses, 3 dishwashers and 2 chambermaids. Salaries are New York State wage plus tips. Must be able to work until Labor Day. Room and board provided. Send photograph and self-addressed, stamped envelope for reply. Apply by March 15 to Bing Faxon, Manager, Dept. SED, 1612 Treasure Dr., Tarpon Springs FL 33589.

Sugar Maples Resort, Inc., Located in Maplecrest. Summer resort. Openings for 100 people, minimum age 18, during summer and ski season. Needs chef, cook's helpers, pot washer, dishwashers, gardener, porter, carpenter, electrician, shuffleboard attendant, lifeguards, bus boys, bellhops, desk clerks, teen-age social director, maintenance, baker, baker's helper, accountant, office clerks, typists, soda fountain help, salad room help, adult social director, reservation clerk, waitresses, children's social director, telephone operators, gift shop sales, chambermaids, housekeeper, employees' dining room servers and dining room hostess. Enclose self-addressed, stamped envelope with application and a recent photograph. Room and board provided. Apply by April to Sugar Maples Resort, Inc., Dept. SED, Maplecrest NY 12454.

Tennanah Lakeshore Lodge, Located in the Catskill Mountains, Roscoe. Resort hotel. Openings for 30 college students and high school seniors, minimum age 18, from late June through Labor Day. Needs waitresses, front office personnel, dining room hostess, pool attendant, kitchen helpers, groundsmen, bartender, office clerks and bellmen. Salaries are minimum wage and up. Room and board provided. Apply early to Michael Pavelka, President, Tennanah Lakeshore Lodge, Roscoe NY 12776.
Fringe Benefits: Pleasant working conditions, end-of-the-season bonus.

Vegetarian Hotel, Located in Woodridge. Openings for college students, teachers, high school seniors and foreign students from May through September. Needs 4 maids, $71.57/week plus tips; porter, gardener, dishwasher, $95.40/week; cook's helper, $121.70/week; 2 office girls, $65/week; lifeguard, $53/week. Salaries include room and board. Enclose stamped return envelope (foreign students, 2 postal coupons) with application. Apply to Vegetarian Hotel, Box 457, Woodridge NY 12789.

Charles R. Wood Enterprises, Located near Lake George. Includes Howard Johnson's Motor Inn, Storytown Fun Park and Gaslight Village. Openings from May 24 thru September 14. Needs 100-150 ride operators, minimum age 18, $3.10/hour; 20-50 grounds and parking people, minimum age 16 with work permit, $3.10/hour; 30-100 food service personnel, minimum age 18, $3.10/hour and 20-75 shop clerks and motel employees, minimum age 18, $3.10/hour. Send resume or application to Rex D. Billings, Jr., Box 511, Lake George NY 12845. Tel. 518/792-6568.

Summer Camps

American Camping Association, Private and organizational camps for boys, girls, coed and family. Residential camps throughout the northeastern states; day camps in New York metropolitan area and Long Island. Openings for college students and teachers, minimum age 18, with at least one year of college. Needs general counselors; trained and experienced specialty counselors for land sports, water sports, nature, pioneering, arts and crafts, music, drama, WSI, NRA; nurses (RN), physicians, office secretaries, maintenance, grounds, all kitchen staff. Salaries are commensurate with age, education, camp experience and type of position. Room and board provided

for resident camp employees. Visit our office or send SASE for free staff
application. American Camping Association, New York Section, 225 Park Ave.
S., Suite 739, New York NY 10003.
Fringe Benefits: "Some member camps provide traveling expenses and/or
end-of-the-season bonuses. Excellent experience for college students involved in
education and recreation." **College credit** possible.

Association of Independent Camps, Openings at 80 children's
summer camps located in New England and the Middle Atlantic states. Needs
head counselors, group leaders, general and all specialty counselors. Room and
board provided. Apply by July to Association of Independent Camps, Dept.
SED, 157 W. 57th St., New York NY 10019; tel. 212/582-3540.
Fringe Benefits: "Travel expenses paid in part or in full. Learning
experiences—i.e., living and sharing with others; complete camp facilities in a
healthy environment; time for socialization with peers." **College credit** "may
be arranged by student at school."

Baco, Located in Minerva. Openings for college students from June 29 to
August 23. Needs instructors: 1 dramatics, $500-700/season; 1 music,
$400-700/season; 2 nature, $400-700/season; 1 crafts, $400-700/season; 3
hiking/backpacking, $400-750/season; 5 tennis, $400-750/season; 1
photography, $400-600/season; 1 radio, $400-600/season; 2 sailing,
$400-650/season; 2 swimming (WSI), $400-650/season; 2 canoeing,
$400-650/season; 20 all sports, $300-700/season. Room and board provided.
"Applicants should be experienced in related specialty area, i.e. college major,
performer, specific leadership course, intensive interest, member of college
club. Must also have other camp experience and be willing to work as a cabin
counselor and supervise children ages 6-12. Send for application. Apply by April
30 to Mel Wortman, Director, Camp Baco, Dept. SED, 80 Neptune Ave.,
Woodmere NY 11598.
Fringe Benefits: "Travel expense possible. Located on private lake in
beautiful Adirondacks, near Lake Placid, Saratoga, Lake George. Friendly,
family atmosphere, opportunities to teach and participate in camp programs."
College credit possible.

Barker, Located at Cropseyville. Camp of the Troy Boys' Club for low-
income boys, ages 7-14. Openings for college students (minimum age 18) with
one year of college, for 9 weeks during July and August. Needs counselors with
backgrounds in athletics, aquatics, arts and crafts, nature study, archery, BB gun
shooting, special events, singing and drama, boating. Also needs program
director, athletic director, waterfront director (WSI) for lake, driver-maintenance
man, nurse (RN or LPN). Students can be accepted on the college work-study
program. Contact the school financial aid office for details. Salaries begin at
$550/season. Room and board provided. Some weekends off. Send for
application; include resume. Apply by May 18 to Director, Dept SED, Camp
Barker Associates Inc., 1700 7th Ave., Troy NY 12180.

Beech-Wood
Pine-Wood, Located in Sodus (Beech-Wood), Arkport (Pine-Wood). Girl

Scout resident camps for children ages 7-12 (Beech-Wood) and ages 11-18 (Pine-Wood). Openings from the end of June to the middle of August. Needs 2 camp directors for 9 weeks, administrative ability, group leader experience, teacher preferred, $1,700-2,500; 3 assistant camp directors, 8 weeks, group leader experience, supervisory ability, college students or teachers preferred, $800-1,200; 14 unit leaders, 7 weeks, group leader experience, program skills, college students or teachers preferred, $560-1,050; 8 specialists, 7 weeks, WSI for waterfront, riding, arts, tripping, college students or teachers preferred, $560-1,050; 13 assistant unit leaders, 7 weeks, 1 year college and camp experience, college students, teachers all acceptable, $455-600; 4 assistant specialists, 7 weeks, riding, boating, swimming, skills, college students, teachers acceptable, $455-600; 10 unit assistants, 7 weeks, camping experience, college students, high school seniors acceptable, $350-385; 2 clerks, 7 weeks, liking for details and record keeping, college students, teachers, high school seniors acceptable, $455-600; 2 nurses, 7 weeks, RN, LPN or EMT in New York state, $900-1,200; 2 food supervisors, 7 weeks, experience in quantity cooking, $980-1,500; 2 assistant cooks, 7 weeks, cooking experience, $455-800; 6 aides-kitchen and unit, 7 weeks, graduation from high school, $280-350. Send for application or apply by letter with complete resume including Social Security number, dates available and applicable reference letters. Apply by May 15 to Audrey A. Cooper, Camp Administrator, Girl Scouts of Genesee Valley, Inc., 550 E. Main St., Rochester NY 14604; tel. 716/454-7010.

Belle Terre Gymnastic Camp for Girls, Located in South Kortright. Openings for college students and teachers from late June to late August. Needs specialty counselors/teachers (also act as bunk counselors): 6 gymnastics; 1 dance (ballet and jazz); 2 waterfront (WSI, pool and lake); 1 tennis; 2 Western horsemanship; 1 arts and crafts. Salaries are $900 and up, commensurate with skills and experience, plus room and board. Also needs nurse (RN or LPN) and 2 kitchen helpers. "Counselors should seek certification in advanced First Aid if at all possible." Apply early, enclosing complete resume, to Consuelo G. Haus, Director, Belle Terre Gymnastic Camp for Girls, Dept. SED, South Kortright NY 13842; tel. 607/538-9434 or 607/865-4050.

Brant Lake Camp, Located in the Adirondack Mountains, Warren County. Founded 1916. Private camp for boys ages 7-16. Openings for college students and teachers from June 24 to August 24. Needs 12 general counselors, $450-600; 12 specialty counselors for tennis, camping, WSI, riflery, athletics, arts and crafts, $400-800; assistant waterfront director, 2 nurses (RN), $600; director of arts and crafts, supervisor of 9 year old division, $1,000 and up (couple accepted). Room and board provided. Apply by June 1 to Brant Lake Camp, 84 Leamington St., Lido Beach NY 11561.
Fringe Benefits: "Brant Lake offers health care, excellent food, some bonuses, fine colleagues from all over the world, a good social life, great athletic facilities and time to play." **College credit** possible.

Che-Na-Wah, Located in Minerva, in the Adirondack Mountains. Private camp for girls ages 6-16; brother camp on same lake. Openings for college students, college graduates and teachers from June 22 to August 22. Needs group leaders; specialty counselors: athletics, archery, arts and crafts, modern and jazz dance, drama, gymnastics, music (piano), guitar and folk singing, pioneering, photography, tennis, waterskiing; ARC instructors in swimming, boating, canoeing, sailing; and nurse (RN). Salaries are open depending on skill, training and experience. Room and board provided. Apply by June 1 to Mrs. Alice Sternin, Dept. SED, 51 Planting Field Rd., Roslyn Heights NY 11577. **Fringe Benefits:** "Transportation paid from New York City area, and partial travel reimbursement for travel from farther points; American Red Cross First Aid Course given during pre-camp staff orientation; American Red Cross Advanced Life Saving renewal course available; excellent working conditions; friendly, social atmosphere; laundry provided." **College credit** possible.

Eagle Island, Located in Upper Saranac Lake, New York. Girl Scout camp. Openings from approximately June 20 to August 15. Needs program specialists, salaries determined by age and qualifications; assistant director, business manager, directors and counselors for waterfront and sailing; arts and crafts consultant; nurse (RN); maintenance staff; unit leaders and unit counselors. An equal opportunity employer. Room and board provided. "Application deadline is May; better to send applications in January." Send resume and application request to Outdoor Program Manager, Dept. SED, Girl Scout Council of Greater Essex County, 120 Valley Rd., Montclair NJ 07042. **Fringe Benefits:** "Located in Olympic region of New York; on-the-job training; experience of living on an island." **College credit** available.

Echo Lake, Located in Warrensburg, in the heart of the Adirondacks. Private coed camp. Openings for college students, college graduates and teachers from June 21 to August 21. Needs group leaders, $700 and up; instructors: woodcrafts, sculpture, tennis, waterfront (WSI), pioneering and tripping, $600 and up; directors: nature, gymnastics, aquatics, photography, theatre, girls' athletics, folk dance, $700 and up. Apply by March to Staff '80, Camp Echo Lake, Dept. SED, 49 Clubway, Hartsdale NY 10530.

Educational Alliance Camps, Located in Brewster. Specialized camping services for senior citizens and developmentally disabled children; children ages 8-25, older adults ages 60-90. Openings for college students, teachers and high school seniors from June 21 to August 28; pre- and post-season work available in April and September. Needs 4 unit heads, $1,000-1,600; 10 unit assistants, specialists, $500-900; 40 counselors, $200-600; 40 junior staff, $150; 25 kitchen staff, maintenance staff, $75-700; 3 nurses (RN), $1,000-1,500; office workers. Apply to Educational Alliance Camps, 197 E. Broadway, New York NY 10002.

Empire State Speech and Hearing Clinic, Inc., Located in Spencer. Residential camp for ages 6-21. Openings from June 28 through August 11 for counselors with a background in speech and hearing primarily and related fields in general. Salary $400-600/6 weeks. Room and board provided. "Applicants must enjoy working with all types of children (some with limited physical and mental abilities). They should be people planning careers working with children (or seeking experience to decide if this type of work should be a lifetime career)." For information, apply before June 15, Empire

State Speech and Hearing Clinic, Inc., 1408 Lake St., Elmira NY 14901; tel. 607/732-7069.
Fringe Benefits: Credit offered for clinical clock hours.

Department of Environmental Conservation, Located near Albany. Openings for college students and teachers from June 17 to August 31.

Applicant should be a student or teacher in natural resources, biological sciences, environmental studies or education. Should have first aid or water safety instruction. Needs 20 Conservation Education-Labor Camps counselors, $195/week and 20 Conservation Education Camp counselors, $195/week. Room and board provided. Send resume by May 1st to Jim Suozzo, Conservation Corps Administrator, Dept. of Environmental Conservation, 50 Wolf Road, Room 509, Albany, New York 12233.
Fringe Benefits: Experience in educating young people to work in the environment. **College credit** possible.

The Fresh Air Fund, Located in Sharpe Reservation, Fishkill.

Nonprofit organization sponsoring 4 camps for inner city youngsters. Openings for college students from approximately June 22 to August 25. Needs 175 general counselors, $500-650; 14 village leaders, $800-1,000; specialists: 5 arts and crafts, nature, $550-650; 14 waterfront staff (WSI and assistants), $800-1,000. Salaries depend upon experience. Room and board provided. Apply by June 15 to Larry Mickolic, Associate Director, The Fresh Air Fund, 70 W. 40th St., New York NY 10018.
Fringe Benefits: Travel allowance provided. "On days off and during free time, transportation is provided to and from nearby towns. There is a 5-day orientation, and training and guidance throughout the summer by psychologists and therapists." **College credit** possible.

Green Twigs, Located in Roosevelt. Cerebral palsy camp for teenagers

and adults. Openings for college students and teachers from approximately June 25 to August 23. Needs 10 group counselors, $250-500; 6 activity counselors for games, waterfront, nature, music and dramatics, arts and crafts, $500-800. For residential camp, needs 15 residential counselors, $550; residential director, $1,000-1,500; residential nurse, $1,000-2,000. Apply by April or May to Recreation Department, Camp Green Twigs, 380 Washington Ave., Roosevelt NY 11575; tel. 516/378-2000.

Greenwich House, Located in Copake Falls. Settlement house for

coeds, ages 7-12. Openings for college students from June 28 to August 25. Needs 10 general counselors, $150-350; specialty counselors: 2 pioneering, 2 nature, 2 crafts, $300; swimming head, $650; head counselor, $400-800. Apply by April 15 to Morton S. Horowitz, Greenwich House Camp, 27 Barrow St., New York NY 10014.

Hillcroft, Located in Billings. Nonsectarian coed camp for ages 7-14.

Openings for college students and teachers, minimum age 20, from June 25 to August 22. Needs experienced group leaders $550 and up; instructors: 6 WSI, canoeing, gardening, animal care, 2 archery/tennis, dramatics/folk music and

dance, photography, science/hiking, pioneering, $450 and up; 2 nurses (RN), secretary. Room and board provided. Apply to Dennis Buttinger, Jan Ridge Rd., Somers NY 10589.
Fringe Benefits: "Ongoing supervisory support and direction and international guest counselors." **College credit** available.

Huntington Camps for Mentally Retarded, Located in the Catskill Mountains of New York. Camps for learning disabled, brain injured and mentally retarded, ages 6 to adult. Openings for college students and teachers from June 27 to August 23. Needs 30 general counselors, 4 arts and crafts, 2 woodworking, 4 sewing/cooking counselors, 4 music counselors, $400-800; academic teachers, licensed NYS Special Education, $1200 and up; speech therapists, certified NYS Special Education, $1200 and up; head counselor, salary open; 4 unit leaders, $500-800; 4 water safety instructors, $500-1,000; kitchen help and maintenance people; RNs and LPNs; office personnel. Enclose SASE with letter giving details about yourself and position desired. Apply to Camps, 1017 E. 80th St., Brooklyn NY 11236.

Impala, Located in Woodbourne. Resident coed camp for children ages 6-16. Openings for college students from June 25 to August 25. Needs 12 male and female general counselors, $500-600/season; 1 tennis counselor, $500-600/season; 1 WSI counselor, minimum age 22, $800/season; 2 younger WSI counselors, $500/season; 1 pioneering counselor, $500/season; and 2 arts and crafts counselors, $400-500/season. "Applicants should have sincere desire to work with youngsters, enjoy them; be able to participate, show initiative and integrity." Room and board provided. Apply to Fredda/Abe Kerner, Directors, 5405 Avenue S., Dept. SED, Brooklyn NY 11234.
Fringe Benefits: College credit possible.

Jawonio, Located in New City. Camp for orthopedic physically handicapped people, ages 6-25. Openings for college students and high school seniors from June 24 to August 23. Needs 32 general counselors, $400-500/season; 4 kitchen helpers, $600-800/season; nurse (RN), $1,600-1,800/season. Apply to Camp Jawonio, Rockland County Center for the Physically Handicapped, Inc., 260 Little Tor Rd. N., New City NY 10956.

Kennybrook, Located in Monticello in the heart of the Catskill Mountains. Private coed camp. Openings for college students, teachers and foreign students, minimum age 19, from June 24 to August 25. Needs 60 counselors, $500 and up; specialty counselors for swimming, WSI, pioneering, boating, $500-700; 2 tennis instructors, $600; dramatics instructor, $700. Room and board provided. Apply early to Peter Landman, 19 Southway, Hartsdale NY 10530.
Fringe Benefits: "Spending an outdoor experience with children of varied ages as well as staff of similar age and qualifications. Working conditions are excellent." **College credit** possible.

Lenni-Len-A-Pe, Located in Salisbury Mills. Coed camp serving children ages 6-16. Openings for college students and teachers from June 26 to

August 22. Needs 30 general counselors, $350-900/season; 10 group leaders, $500-1,200/season; 40 specialty counselors for pool, lake, waterski, tennis, etc., $300-1,500/season. Room and board provided. Write or call. Apply by June 15 to Director, Camp Lenni-Len-A-Pe, Dept. SED, 3242 Judith Lane, Oceanside NY 11572; tel. 516/764-2112.
Fringe Benefits: "Lenni-Len-A-Pe offers great working conditions, with an established, professional upper staff. Social advantages include being near the Big Apple and many other day-off opportunities." **College credit** available.

Lenoloc, Located in Bear Mountain, New York. Small rustic camp for girls, ages 6-13. Openings from June 25 to August 21. Needs 1 program director, $1,000-1,200/season; head cook, $1,000-2,000/season; 2 arts & crafts directors (college students, teachers, high school students), $400-600/season; waterfront director (college student, teacher), $800-1,000/season; 2 waterfront assistants (college students, teachers), $500-700/season; nurse (teacher), $1,000/season; sports director (college student, teacher, high school student), $600-700/season; 2 assistant sports directors (college students, teachers, high school students), $400-600/season; 2 dance/drama directors (college students, teachers, high school students), $400/600/season; nature director (college student, teacher, high school student), $300-500/season; 3 general counselors (college students, teachers, high school students), $300-450/season; business assistant-secretary, April-October, college credit, part time during off season, full time during on season. Room and board provided. "Learning, caring, growing, sharing is the camp motto" and should be kept in minds of applicants. Send for application by June 1. Apply to Karenne Bloomgarden-Thomas, Camp Director, Camp Lenoloc, Dept. SED, YWCA 395 Main St., Orange NJ 07050; tel. 201/672-9500.
Fringe Benefits: "There is a close, family atmosphere, and a positive self-image is stressed for campers and staff." **College credit** available.

Lincoln Farm, Located in Roscoe. Two adjacent programs: Lincoln Farm Teen Camp for children ages 12-16, and Lincoln Farm Jr. for children ages 7-12. Openings for US and foreign college students and teachers. Needs specialists for 34 craft studios, waterfront (pool and lake), athletic supervisors; leaders for construction, farming, forestry, driver training, typing, science, instrumental and guitar instruction, music, dance and drama; office help, food service workers, mother's helper, bookkeeper, nurse (RN), and groundskeepers and maintenance staff. Salaries are $750-1,500 for administrative staff; $400-800 for specialists; $300-500 for general counselors. Room and board provided. Apply by May to Lincoln Farm, Box SED, Ardsley NY 10502.

Loyaltown, Association for the Help of Retarded
Children, Located in Hunter. Organizational coed camp for trainable retarded people ages 8 through adult. Openings for teachers, college students and high school seniors from approximately June 23 to August 25. Needs 70 general counselors, $350-600; specialty counselors in music, arts and crafts, dance, dramatics, movement, nature, speech, atypical athletics, cooking, sewing, grooming, workshop, $700; swimming (WSI, pool), $500-800; 3 nurses (RN or LPN), $700-1,200. Room and board provided. Apply to A.H.R.C., 189 Wheatley Rd., Brookville NY 11545.

Lymelight Inc., Located in Accord. Camp for mentally handicapped children and adults, ages 10 to adult. Openings begin in June. Needs at least 50 general counselors (minimum age 18 with at least one year of college), $300-600/season (more with BA/BS); 2 specialists in each arts and crafts, minimum $450; 1 specialist each in pioneer, dance, drama, grossmotor (adaptive special physical education), minimum $450; 8 specialists in swimming, minimum $300 with ASL, minimum $500 with WSI. Room and board provided. Must pay $18 medical fee; shirts optional. Send resume or request for application as soon as possible. Apply by March to Stewart Shein, Dept. SED-1, 2273 Sultana Dr., Yorktown Hts. NY 10598; tel. 914/962-2559.

Fringe Benefits: "Lymelight is the largest private summer camp for the mentally handicapped. We offer traveling expenses, end-of-the-season bonus, good working conditions, the opportunity to learn about working with the mentally handicapped in a social atmosphere and flexibility in terms of staff/camper needs." **College credit** possible.

Mogisca, Located in Glen Spey, New York. Girls' resident camp. Openings for college students and teachers from June 20 to August 17. Considers high school seniors for kitchen and stable helpers. Needs 12 unit leaders (minimum age 21), $700 and up; 1 waterfront director (minimum age 21, WSI), $800-1,200/season; 12 assistant unit leaders (ages 18-21), $450 and up/season;; 12 counselors, $300 and up/season; 1 horseback riding director (minimum age 21), $800-1,000/season; 2 assistant horseback directors, $500-700/season; arts and crafts, sports, ecology specialists, $500-800/season; and 5 waterfront counselors (ages 18-21), $400-800/season; 7 kitchen as well as stable helpers, $300-400/season. Room and board provided. Apply to Barbara L. Windrow, Camp Administrator, Morris Area Girl Scout Council, 300 Mendham Rd., Mendham NJ 07945; tel. 201/538-4936.

Fringe Benefits: "This camp has 1,000 acres including lake, athletic field, stables, pool and farm. There is a diversified program—English riding and older girl trip programs. Also, Camp Mogisca provides the opportunity for staff members to gain experience in their fields and to develop their skills." **College Credit** possible.

Normandie, Located in Westport. Waterfront land sports camp with "an international flavor," for children ages 6-16. Openings for college students and teachers, minimum age 19, from June 25 to August 25. Needs general and specialty counselors for waterskiing and boat operation, tennis, baseball, arts and crafts, shop, drama, tripping, waterfront, $350-1,500; waterfront director, $800-1,300; nurse, $700-1,100. Apply early (April 1 deadline) to Camp Normandie, 1199 Park Ave., New York NY 10028.

North Country Camps (Lincoln and Whippoorwill),
Located in the Adirondack Mountains of New York State. Boys' and girls' summer camps. Openings for college students from June 26 to August 23. Needs counselors to live with cabin groups of 4-6 children. Must have trip camping skills, swimming ability, and the skill to instruct such activities as tennis, canoeing, sailing, archery, field sports, crafts or horseback riding. Salaries are $550 and up, depending upon experience. Apply to Peter L. Gucker, Director, North Country Camps, Dept. SED, 96 Everett Rd., Demarest NJ 07627.

Northwood, Located in Utica. Camp for children (ages 6-13) with learning disabilities. Openings for college students and teachers from June 28 to August 18. Needs occupational therapist, salary open; 30 general counselors and specialists in crafts, swimming, waterskiing, sports, video equipment, music, $35-200/week. Room and board provided. Apply by April 1 to Camp Northwood, 10 W. 66th St., New York NY 10023; tel. 212/799-4089.
Fringe Benefits: This camp offers the "opportunity to work with top professionals." Graduate and undergraduate **college credit** available.

Oxford-Guilford Camps, Located in Guilford. Private brother-sister camp for ages 6-16. Openings for 100 college students and teachers for 8 weeks, starting late June. Needs physical education majors and coaches, WSI; specialty counselors for waterskiing, sailing, tennis, land sports, golf, modern dance, gymnastics (apparatus), pianists, nature, photography, pioneering, arts and crafts, ceramics, horseback riding. Salaries are $300 and up, depending on experience and qualifications. Room and board provided. Apply by June to: Barry Kingsley, 51 Simpson Dr., Old Bethpage NY 11804.
Fringe Benefits: Traveling expenses, good working conditions, social atmosphere and end of the season bonus. **College credit** possible.

Point O'Pines, Located at Brant Lake, New York, in the Adirondack Mountains. Camp for girls, 2nd through 9th grades. Openings for college students and teachers, minimum age 20 or 2 years of college completed. Season from late June through late August. Needs instructors for swimming (WSI), sailing, canoeing, boating (prefer ARC certification); many very well-qualified tennis instructors; specialists for waterskiing, diving, athletics, gymnastics, arts and crafts, drama, pioneering, photography, music (pianists), golf, archery, drama, radio, dance; general counselors; nurses (RN and LPN). Salaries include room and board and depend on age, year in school and experience. Apply before June 15 to Andrew S. Rosen, 221 Harvard Avenue, Swarthmore, PA 19081.
Fringe Benefits: Travel allowance, good working conditions, sense of community and extended family (staff-camper ratio 1-3), opportunities for supervision by qualified people.

Pok-O-Moonshine/MacCready, Located in Willsboro, New York 12996, in the Adirondacks. Brother-sister, ages 7 to 16. Openings for college students from June 22 to August 16. Needs Indian crafts instructor, shop counselor, 3 swimming instructors (WSI), baseball, archery, sailing, campcraft, soccer, $400-700. Apply by June to Jack W. Swan, Box 16, Brookfield Center CT 06805.
Fringe Benefits: "Good people to work with; good kids; the opportunity to hike and canoe in the Adirondacks." **College credit** possible.

Summer jobs are loaded with fringe benefits. Check the "Fringe Benefits" section of listings for college credit availability, travel allowance, specialized training programs, and more.

Raquette Lake Boys' Camp, Located at Raquette Lake. Sister camp across lake. Openings for college students and teachers, minimum age 20, for 8 weeks from late June. Needs head coaches and assistants for football, basketball, hardball, soccer, mountaineering, golf; specialists for aquatics (WSI) competitive swimming, tripping, waterskiing, canoeing, sailing, land sports, tennis, archery, arts and crafts, drama; pianists; drivers; boat pilots; kitchen; maintenance; typists; and nurses. All counselors have bunk assignments. Salaries are $300-1,400, depending on experience and qualifications. Room, board, transportation, clothing allowance, laundry, linens and medical provided. Apply to Jerry Halsband, 300 West End Ave., New York NY 10023.

Raquette Lake Girls' Camp, Located at Raquette Lake. Brother camp across lake. Openings for college students and teachers, minimum age 19, for 8 weeks from late June. Needs specialists and department heads for performing arts, fine arts, aquatics, synchronized swimming, gymnastics; counselors for land sports, tennis, archery, arts and crafts, drama; pianists; drivers; boat pilots; kitchen maintenance; typists; and nurses. All counselors have bunk assignments. Salaries are $300-1,400, depending on experience and qualifications. Room and board, transportation, clothing allowance, laundry, linens and medical provided. Apply to Jerry Halsband, 300 West End Ave., New York NY 10023.

Rawhide Ranch, Located in Lake Hill. Coed camp for children ages 8-14. Openings for college students and teachers. Needs 6 cowboy-riding instructors, June 1 to August 24, $750/season; 2 athletic directors, June 24 to August 24, $600/season; 6 cowgirl-riding instructors, June 21 to August 24, $600; 2 lifeguards, June 24 to August 24, $600/season. Room and board provided. "Each child has his/her own horse and takes on new responsibilities. Applicant must enjoy working with children. Contact us as early as possible, give as much information as possible, and don't hesitate to call if you have any questions." Send resume by May 1 to Robert W. Seaman, Owner/Director, Dept. SED, Rawhide Ranch, Lake Hill NY 12448; tel. 914/679-9351.

Regis-Apple Jack, Located in Paul Smith's, in the Adirondack Mountains on the shore of Upper St. Regis Lake near Lake Placid. Nonsectarian friendly coed camps with Quaker leadership; for children ages 6-14 (Regis) and ages 14-17 (Apple Jack Teen Camp). Openings July and August for men and women counselors, minimum age 19, single or married couple. Needs specialists and general counselors, nurses, cooks, maintenance. Teachers, graduate students, undergraduates, and others make up international staff. Informal democratic program. Salaries are $400 and up. Room and board provided. Write to Michael N. Humes, 107 Robinhood Rd., White Plains NY ′ 10605; tel. 914/997-7039.
Fringe Benefits: "Transportation allowance, opportunity to meet campers from all over the US and world, located next to Lake Placid where 1980 Winter Olympics took place." **College credit** possible.

Regis of the Hamptons, Located in East Hampton, New York 11937. Coed overnight camp, ages 5 to 16. Openings for college students and

teachers from June 25 to August 25. Needs 40 general counselors, $300/season. 10 specialists for arts and crafts, drama, etc., $500/season. 6 waterfront, $400-800/season. 4 sailing, $500-700/season. Room and board provided. Apply to John W. Kennedy, Camp St. Regis, 27 Lower Cross Rd., Saddle River NJ 07458.
Fringe Benefits: This is "a happy camp, set on a beautiful salt water site in the fashionable Hamptons area." **College credit** possible.

Sequoia, Located in Rock Hill. Private brother-sister camp for children ages 6-15. Member ACA, 50th season. Openings for college students and teachers for 8 weeks from late June to late August. Needs counselors/ instructors in tennis, pioneering/camping, nature, self defense, dramatics, music, gymnastics, canoeing, sailing, WSI, basketball, horseback riding, waterskiing, crafts (wood, ceramics, fiber), riflery, archery, land and water sports; general counselors; 2 nurses; kitchen help. Salaries are $400-2000. Room and board provided. Apply by May 15 to Camp Sequoia, Attn: CS—Sequoia, Rock Hill NY 12775.
Fringe Benefits: Medical coverage, laundry, "tremendous opportunity for self-growth, awareness, making lifelong friends and developing lifelong skills." **College credit** available.

Te Ata, Located in Harriman State Park, Central Valley, New York. Girl Scout camp. Openings for college students, teachers and foreign students from June 21 to August 17. Needs 6 unit leaders (minimum age 21), $800 and up; 15 assistant unit leaders, $500 and up; 5 waterfront (WSI), $900 and up; counselors (minimum age 21) for backpacking, canoeing, $800 and up; nurse, $800; head cook, $1,200 and up; assistant cook, $800 and up. Apply to Camping Administrator, Lenni Lenape Girl Scout Council, Dept. SED, 555 Preakness Ave., Paterson NJ 07502.

Ten Mile River Scout Camps, Located in Narrowsburg, in the Catskill Mountains. "Largest council owned Boy Scout camping operation in the US." Operates 5 camps, one featuring Kosher food. Openings for 250 college students or teachers with Boy Scout background, married couples, from mid-June to August. Needs specialists for aquatics, archery, camping and outdoor skills, canoeing, ecology and conservation, field sports, handicrafts, horsemanship, riflery; nurses (RN), doctors, assistant camp directors, program directors, Scoutmasters, cooks, bakers, food service, accounting, food ordering, drivers and maintenance personnel. Salaries are $400-1,400/season depending on position and experience. Room and board provided. Apply by June 1 to Director of Camping, Boy Scouts of America, Dept. SED, 345 Hudson St., New York NY 10014.
Fringe Benefits: "Opportunities in working at the largest Boy Scout Council camp; wide variety of positions." **College credit** possible.

Thomas School of Horsemanship, Summer day camp located on Long Island with a full program of horseback riding (specialty), swimming, sports, and arts. Openings for college students and teachers (local only) from June 29 to August 21. Needs 3-5 WSI to teach ages 5-9, 10-15; 3-4 sports counselors to teach skills in team and individual sports (archery, riflery,

wrestling, gymnastics, tennis, karate); 1 crafts program director; 1 ecology program director. Salaries are $400-800/season. All staff live at home. "Many of our riding instructors teach for us year round. Our swim, sports and crafts staff need not know anything about horses. We hire only specialty staff to teach the activities." Send resume outlining special talents and experience, send for application, or phone. Apply to Nancy Thomas, Director, Thomas School of Horsemanship, 250 Round Swamp Rd., Melville, NY 11747. tel. 516/692-6840.
Fringe Benefits: "A really great socially active staff with personality. Also end-of-season bonus." **College credit** possible.

Timbercrest, Located in Randolph on 866 acres. Girl Scout resident camp for girls ages 6-16; "primitive type encampment with 33-acre lake for swimming and boating." Openings for college students and teachers for 6-week program from June 22 to August 20. Needs 8 counselors (some camping experience desired), $300-600/season; nurse (RN), $600-800/season; 2 handypersons (driver's license required), $80-100/week; waterfront director (WSI, some canoeing experience required), $400-600/season. "Room and board are provided but are subject to New York state taxation. Housing is in platform tents for all staff." Send for application by June 15 to Donna Dolce, Camp Director, 7 E. Main St., Fredonia NY 14063; tel. 716/679-1559.
Fringe Benefits: "This is excellent experience for those interested in teaching and recreation or for people who enjoy the out-of-doors. 36-48 hours of time off allotted to each employee per week."

Treetops, Located at Lake Placid. Coed camp for children ages 8-13. Openings for college students, teachers and foreign students from June 25 to August 20. Needs specialty counselors: pottery, music, riding, hiking, drama, carpentry, gardening, weaving, nature, swimming, gymnastics, canoeing, sailing. Salaries are $450 and up/season. Room and board provided. Apply to Colin Tait, Director, Camp Treetops, RFD 4, Winsted CT 06098.

Troutburg, Located near Hamlin, on Lake Ontario. Camp for children. Openings for college students and teachers from approximately the third week of June to the third week of August (8-week season). Needs 3 lifeguards, lifeguard (WSI), $800; 2 SLG, nature/craft director, 10 counselors (college or graduate students), $550/season; nurse (RN or LPN), $800/season. Room and board provided. Apply to Camp Troutburg, The Salvation Army, Box 1010, 60 North St., Rochester NY 14603.
Fringe Benefits: College credit possible.

University Settlement Camp, Located on 88 acres in Beacon. Summer camp for boys and girls ages 7 to 16. Needs 34 counselors (college students, teachers, local applicants interested in pursuing career in social service), June 23 to August 24, $300-700/season; 4 unit supervisors (teachers with graduate work, extensive experience with children), June 18 to August 25, $800-1,100/season; 10 program assistants (high school students interested in gaining experience in social service), June 23 to August 24, $100-275/season; 2 pool staff (college students, teachers, local applicants, WSI), June 18 to August 25, $300-1,100/season. Room and board provided. Hires physically handicapped. Send resume or request application. Apply by June ("but we

accept applications any time") to Maryann Lienhard, Camp Director, University Settlement Camp, Dept. SED, 184 Eldridge St., New York NY 10002.
Fringe Benefits: "Opportunity to work with minority population from New York's Lower East Side, excellent social-work-related supervision, opportunity to learn/improve group work skills." **College credit** possible.

Wabenaki, Located at Lake Stahahe, Southfields. Camp for boys ages 7-14. Openings for college students, teachers and foreign students from approximately mid-June to September 1; includes 1 week orientation. Needs 15 general counselors, waterfront director (WSI), 2 waterfront counselors (SLS), 2 arts and crafts, music, dramatics, hiking, pioneering, nurse (RN). Salaries are based on age and experience. Room and board provided. Apply by April 1 to Ralph Hittman, Executive Director, Boys Brotherhood Republic, 888 E. 6th St., New York NY 10009.
Fringe Benefits: Wabenaki offers "fieldwork experience for future teachers and social science majors." **College credit** possible.

Wendy, Located in Wallkill. Girl Scout camp serving Ulster County and surrounding area for 4 weeks starting July 7. Needs waterfront director (college students, teachers) to supervise pool area and maintain pool cleaning system and supervise other pool personnel, approximately $500 (depending on experience); 2 unit leaders (college students, teachers, foreign students), to supervise unit staff (2), coordinate unit/camp activities, $330-500; 6 assistant unit leaders (college students, teachers, foreign students) to plan and coordinate unit activities, supervise campers and activities, approximately $200 (depending on experience); 1 cook (college student, teacher, foreign student) to prepare menus, order food, supervise assistant cook, cook and serve 2 in-house and one lunch on the road/day, $600-800. Room and board provided. Hires physically handicapped. Send resume or request application. Apply by May to M. Patricia Amitrano, Camp Director, Camp Wendy, Dept. SED, Box 3026, Kingston NY 12401.
Fringe Benefits: "Nestled in Catskill mountains, excellent supervisory staff (environmental education majors with good counseling skills)." **College credit** possible.

Westchester—Putnam Council
Boy Scout Camp, Located in various locations throughout New York State. Camps for boys ages 8-10 (Cub Scouts), boys ages 11-15 (Boy Scouts) and boys and girls ages 15-19 (Explorers). General, specialized and experimental Scouting programs (day and overnight). Openings from July 6 to August 28. Needs instructors in aquatics, sports, nature, crafts and outdoor skills, college students and teachers preferred, $800-1,300/season; 2 nurses, LPN or RN, $1,000-1,300/season; 3 instructors in mountaineering and backpacking, $800-1,000/season; Room and board provided. Applicant should be "motivated, interested in young people, innovating and creative. Stress is on talent and commitment." Send resume or application request. Apply by March 15 to Kenneth C. D'Apice, Director of Camping, 1111 Westchester Ave., White Plains NY 10604; tel. 914/949-6180.

Williams, Located in Suffern. Coed organizational camp for underprivileged children. Openings for college students and teachers from June 24 to August 22. Needs 12 general counselors, $500; 6 specialty counselors for nature, ceramics, art, dramatics, photography, woodshop, $500; WSI, $1,000. Room and board provided. Apply by June to Martin Gordon, 8 Remsen St., Baldwin NY 11510.

Fringe Benefits: "Good opportunity to work with needy, urban children in a beautiful camp setting."

Woodcliff, Located in Kingston. Private coed children's camp for ages 6-16. Openings for 60 college students from last week June 20 to August 26 plus pre-camp orientation. Needs assistant head counselor; division heads; waterfront director; specialty counselors for swimming (WSI), canoeing (SCI), waterskiing, gymnastics, tennis, soccer, athletics, arts and crafts, industrial arts, riding, nature, newspaper, photography, electronics and ham radio, overnight camping and backpacking, drama, dance, music (piano, instrumental), guitar and folk singing, fencing, archery, riflery (NRA instructor); nurse (RN); doctor (New York State license); secretary and bookkeeper; drivers. Salaries $850-1,000. Enclose complete resume of skills and experience with children in letter of application. Room and board provided. Hires physically handicapped. Send resume or phone. Apply by May to Mr. and Mrs. Newton Baum, Dept. SED, 49 East 12 St., Apt. 4C, New York NY 1003. tel. 212/477-0240.

Fringe Benefits: "Travel expenses arranged." **College credit** possible.

Woodmere, Located at Paradox in the Adirondack Mountains. Girls camp. Openings for college students and teachers, minimum age 19, from June 26 to August 24. Needs instructors for tennis, tripping, archery, canoeing (SCI), 3 swimming (WSI), sailing, waterskiing, athletics, nature, drama, arts and crafts, dancing; pianist; nurse (RN). First aid training required for counselors. Room and board provided. Apply by June 1 to Director, Camp Woodmere, 1464 Rydal Rd., Rydal PA 19046; tel. 215/884-5120.

Fringe Benefits: "Transportation, opportunity to work with children, good staff relations, pleasant working conditions, opportunities to participate in activities (swimming, sailing, tennis, etc.)." **College credit** possible.

YMCA-YWCA Camping Services, Located in Huguenot. Three YMCA-YWCA camps of greater New York (Camps Greenhill, Talcott and McAlister), each self-sufficient with own lake, set on 1,000 acres of forests. Openings from June 22 to September 1 (cooks, May to September). Needs waterfront director, unit leaders, arts and crafts director, out-trip director, teachers preferred, $80-110/week; 70 counselors, college students, high school students, foreign students and local applicants preferred, $40-60/week; 20 junior counselors, high school students preferred, $150/season; 6 cooks, $150-200/week; 4 office helpers, $40-60/week. Room and board provided. "We have jobs for people who like working in gymnastics, volleyball, summer resident camps, outdoor environmental education or in our sports center." Send resume, request application or phone. Apply by June 20 to Peter Moffat, Associate Executive, YMCA-YWCA Camping Services, Dept. SED,Huguenot NY 12746; tel. 914/856-4316 or 212/564-1300, ext. 271.

Fringe Benefits: "This work is a very worthwhile experience. Working conditions are excellent." **College credit** possible. Participates in work/study programs with Pace University, Duke University and Vassar College.

North Carolina

2,497+ jobs available

Resorts, Ranches, Restaurants, Lodging

Fontana Village Resort, Located at TVA Fontana Dam, Great Smokey Mountains. 300 cottages, inn, lodge, recreational complex. Openings for 200 persons, minimum age 18. Prefers college students, semi-retirees, teachers; couples considered for full season (April-November). Needs 20 cashier/clerks; 5 craft instructors; 30 general labor (housekeeping, landscaping, laundry, janitorial), 8 reservations clerks, 7 lifeguards (WSI and advance LS), 25 kitchen/dining room helpers; 15 waiters/waitresses (approximately $150/week with tips), 6 buspersons, 5 cooks/helpers, 6 fast food attendants; seasonal managers: crafts, recreation, village pool, movie theater, fast food, dining rooms. Pays federal minimum wage, 40-hour week. Year-round operation, with work commitments: April to November; May 15 to August 15; June 15 to Labor Day; August 15 to November. Must be willing to work for 10-week period *minimum*. Group lodging available for approximately $10/week. EOE. Write for employment information and application by March 15 for spring, April 15 for summer, to A.L. Brack, Personnel Manager, Fontana Village Resort, Dept. SED, Fontana Dam NC 28733.
Fringe Benefits: Meals provided at a discount; recreational privileges granted to all employees; accrued annual leave granted to second-year employees; longer work period available. "This resort is located in a beautiful locale (the Great Smokey Mountains), and employees come here from all parts of the U.S." **College credit** available; "will cooperate in internship or co-op placements."

Lee's Inn, Located in Highlands. "Highest inn in eastern United States." Needs 4 waiters, 3 bellmen, youth counselor, and 10 waitresses, $125/month plus tips; 5 housekeepers, $300/month plus tips. Room and board provided. Work from May 20 to Labor Day, August to late October or open to closing. Apply by March 1 to R.W. Lee, Owner, Lee's Inn, Dept. SED, Highlands NC 28741; tel. 305/293-7098 (winter), 704/526-2171 (summer).
Fringe Benefits: Uniforms provided. "Working at Lee's Inn can be a very rewarding experience, but you have to work."

Osceola Lake Inn, Located in Hendersonville, North Carolina. Resort hotel. Openings for college students and high school seniors from early May to November 1. Needs desk clerks, waiters, waitresses, bus persons, lifeguard, children's counselors, bellhops, kitchen aides, dishwashers, maids, secretary, chauffeurs, maintenance helper, groundskeeper. Room and board provided. Enclose SASE with recent photograph, resume, dates available and references with application. State job preference (first, second and third choices). Apply to winter address: Stuart Rubin, 250 Palm Ave., Palm Island, Miami Beach FL 33139.

Fringe Benefits: Salaries include tips and bonus. "The inn is located in the cool, scenic Blue Ridge Mountains. Staff members have use of the hotel's facilities."

YMCA Blue Assembly, Inc., Located in Black Mountain. Nonprofit conference resort for families, teenagers and adults. Openings for college students, teachers and foreign students from May 26 or 28 to August 26. Needs 80 collegiate staffers working in food service, dining room, swimming pool, craft shop, gift shop, switchboard, etc., minimum wage; 30 supervisory staffers, approximately $1,650/season. "Employees are encouraged to live on the campus in staff dormitories. Meals are provided. Cost for these and other services to staff (insurance, transportation, entertainment, etc.) is $7.50/day." Send for application by April 1. Write: Summer Employment Information, YMCA Blue Ridge Assembly, Black Mountain NC 28711; tel. 704/669-8422.

Fringe Benefits: Three hours of **college credit** are offered on the resort grounds, through the University of North Carolina; the subject is usually psychology or sociology. Travel expenses up to $125 are paid.

Summer Camps

American Camping Association, Southeastern Section,
Located in Tuxedo. Positions available in North Carolina, South Carolina and Georgia. Openings for college students, college graduates and teachers, minimum age 19. Needs cabin and unit counselors; guidance specialists; activity leaders; directors for program, boating, waterfront; dietitians; nurses (RN). Apply to Counselor Referral Service, American Camping Association, Southeastern Section, Box 188, Tuxedo NC 28739.

Blue Star, Located in Hendersonville. Private coed camp. Openings for college students, teachers and foreign students from June 10 to August 25. Needs 100 cabin counselors, $350-750; 20 specialty counselors, $500-1,500. Room, board and laundry provided. Apply by June 1 to The Popkins, Blue Star Camps, 3595 Sheridan Street, Hollywood FL 33021; tel. 305/981-3933.

Carolina for Boys
Rockbrook for Girls, Located in Brevard. Private camps. Openings for college students and teachers from June 12 to August 11. Needs cabin counselors with skills in tennis, golf, swimming (WSI), riding, canoeing, wrestling, pioneering, crafts, hiking, $400 and up; 3 nurses (RN), $800-1,200. Apply to Nath Thompson, Director, Camp Carolina for Boys; Mrs. Teed Lowance, Director, Rockbrook for Girls, Dept. SED, Brevard NC 28712; tel. 704/883-3935 or 883-2491.

Chimney Rock, Located in Chimney Rock, North Carolina. Private coed camp. Openings for college students and teachers from June 22 to August 15. Needs 45 counselors, $500-1200; 12 specialty counselors, $600-1,200; 5 general workers, $100/week plus board; nurse; dietitian. Apply to Barbara Rankin, Box 717, Stone Mountain GA 30086.

Chosatonga for Boys
Kahdalea for Girls, Located in Brevard. Private camps. Openings for college students and teachers. Chosatonga (July 15 to August 20) needs: 32 general counselors, $400-600 for 5 weeks; program specialists, $500-700 for 5 weeks. Kahdalea (June 12 to August 20) needs: 2 nurses (RN) for 10 weeks, $1,000-1,500. Also, other positions open. Room and board provided. Apply to W. M. Oates, Route 2, Brevard NC 28712.

Environmental Adventures, Located in Hendersonville. Camp for young people ages 9-17. Openings for college students and teachers from June 15 through August 15. Needs 10 camp counselors, previous experience with children in camp and a strong natural science background, $600/season. Room and board provided. Send for application. "Apply early since selection process is very competitive." Return application with cover letter, resume and the names and addresses of three references. Apply by May 15 to Dr. Russel E. Bachert, Jr., Box 231, Pleasant Garden NC 27313; tel. 919/674-3465.

Falling Creek Camp for Boys, Located in the Blue Ridge Mountains, Tuxedo, North Carolina. Private mountain boys' camp, Christian centered. Openings for college students and teachers, May 30 to August 25 or June 24 to August 25. Total staff of 80 people; normally 25-30 openings each summer. Average staff age 18-25. Work 9- or 11-week season. First year salary range $500-1,100. Room and board provided. Needs general cabin counselors with teaching level skills in one or more program activities—swimming (WSI), sports, tennis, riding, sailing, skiing, canoeing (white water), photography, archery, hiking, rock climbing, crafts, nature. A few openings for women in riding and craft programs or office work. "Apply early so interview can be arranged—a must for serious consideration." Apply by April to J. Yorke Pharr III, Owner, Falling Creek Camp for Boys, Box 98, Tuxedo NC 28784; tel. 704/692-0262.
Fringe Benefits: "Good fellow workers and youngsters." **College credit** possible.

Golden Valley, Located in Bostic, near the South Mountains and Ashville. Girl Scout camp with 15-acre lake; for girls ages 6-17. Openings for college students and teachers from mid-June to late July. Needs waterfront director (WSI, minimum age 21), $65-90/week; small craft instructor (minimum age 21), $60-85/week; 3 waterfront assistants (must have advanced lifesaving, minimum age 18), $50-70/week; 12 unit assistants (minimum age 18), $55-85/week; nurse (minimum age 21), $55-100/week. Room and board provided. Applicants must "enjoy working with girls in a camp setting with other counselors who are high school graduates, college graduates, and professionals. Program opportunities include swimming, sailing, canoeing, tennis, archery, softball, gymnastics, volleyball, basketball, general camping." Send resume, letter of interest, call or send for application. Apply by May 1 to Ginny Simmons, Camp Director, Pioneer Girl Scout Council, Dept. SED, 324 N. Highland St., Gastonia NC 28052; tel. 704/864-3245.
Fringe Benefits: Accident/sickness insurance, 24 hours off every 2 weeks and between sessions, flexible schedule each session. "Very friendly staff."

Camp is close to Ashville, Boone and Mount Mitchell. **College credit** possible.

Gwynn Valley Camp, Located in Brevard. Independent, non-competitive, coed camp for children, ages 5-12. Openings for college students, teachers and foreign students (will accept married couples), from June 12 through August 20. Needs cabin counselors with program skills and special interest in the younger child, $800-1,200. Room and board provided. Apply by May to Dr. and Mrs. Howard M. Boyd, Gwynn Valley Camp, Dept. SED, Route 4, Box 292, Brevard NC 28712.
Fringe Benefits: "Staff recreation planned weekly; guidance and evaluation in personal goal-setting. Laundry service provided." **College credit** possible.

Hinton Rural Life Center, Located in Hayesville. United Methodist church center "dedicated to working with small churches and groups of rural churches to enable them to be more effective in their ministry." Openings for 10 college students and foreign students from June 5 to August 5. Work includes "1 week of training at Hinton Center and 7 weeks service in a rural church or parish, primarily helping with Vacation Church Schools, recreational programs, work and day camps, outreach, and some social work." Workers given $500 honorarium. Room and board provided. "Employee is responsible for transportation to Hinton Center at the beginning of the project and from Hinton Center at the close. Personal expenses are provided by employee during project." Send for application and return by March 1 to Ann Janzen, Associate for Program, Box 27, Hayesville NC 28904; tel. 704/389-8336.

Kanuga, Located near Hendersonville, in the Blue Ridge Mountains. Coed camp for children ages 8-15; conference center, all ages. Openings for teachers, college students and high school seniors from May 15 to September 1. Needs children's program director; male and female youth coordinators, (minimum age 25); canteen manager; organist and chaplain's assistant; nurse; 12 counselors, preferably with special skills (crafts, etc.); 4 waterfront. Salaries include room and board. Apply by April 1 to Edgar Hartley, Jr., Kanuga, Drawer 250, Dept. SED, Hendersonville NC 28739.

Keystone Camp, Inc., Located in Brevard. Private camp for girls ages 7-17. Openings for college students and teachers beginning in June. Needs CIT leader; waterfront head; 15 activity/cabin counselors for gymnastics, nature, canoeing, swimming (WSI), crafts, tennis/badminton, riflery (NRA), archery, dance (ballet, tap), volleyball/basketball, hiking/camping, golf, drama; 4 forward seat riding counselors; assistant to dietitian. Salaries are $600 and up/season. Apply by March 31 to Stephanie Edwards, Box 829, Brevard NC 28712.

Mountain Lake, Located at Lake Osceola, Hendersonville. Summer camp for boys and girls; 4 or 8 week sessions. Needs 40 cabin counselors (college students, minimum age 19 or teachers, June 19 to August 25), $350-600/season; 10 junior counselors (high school students, June 19 to August 25), $150-250/season; licensed bus driver (minimum age 25, June 19 to August 25), $750/season; 3 nurses (RN, LPN, June 19 to August 25),

$750-900/season; 8 kitchen/dining room workers (college or high school students, local applicants, June 15 to August 27), $85/week. Openings also for instructors (college students, teachers, from June 15 to August 27): 4 swim (WSI), $600-800/season; 2 boating (canoe, sail, playak), $600-800/season; 4 water skiing, $600-800/season; 2 tennis, $500-750/season; 2 arts and crafts, $500-750/season; 1 photography, $500-750/season; 2 overnight camping/ hiking, $500-750/season; 2 riflery and archery (certified), $500-750/season. Room and board provided. Hires physically handicapped as secretary, telephone switchboard operator, nurses aide (paper work, records, insurance forms), mail clerk. Send for application. Apply by April or May to Nanette Savage, Owner/Director, Camp Mountain Lake, Dept. SED, Box 4450, Miami Beach FL 33141.

Fringe Benefits: Partial travel expenses paid; laundry; additional bonus for unit leaders, newspaper editor, certification (ARC, NRA, ACA, etc.). "International staff, interesting work group, opportunity to learn and improve ability, staff participation in all activities." **College credit** possible.

National Wildlife Federation's Wildlife Camp, Located on Kanuga Lake outside of Hendersonville. Coed resident camp for ages 8-13. "The program is educational in focus and emphasizes learning about the natural environment and the culture of the Blue Ridge Mountains. Wildlife Camp has received a presidential award recognizing its distinctive program of environmental education." Openings for college students and teachers from June 13 to August 24. Needs 20 instructors/counselors, minimun age 19, must have or be working toward a degree in natural sciences, outdoor/environmental education, recreation or related fields, $990/season; 1 RN or LPN with relevant experiences, $1,300 maximum/season depending on education and experience. Room and board provided. "Resumes are impressive with a preferred major field of study; previous experience working with children; previous teaching experience; breadth of abilities (environmental interpretation, recreation, outdoor living skills, campfire programs, art and/or music talents, etc.); current certification in first aid, life saving, WSI and CPR." Send for application by February 20 to Kathy Waters, Director, National Wildlife Federation, Dept SED, 1412 16th St. NW, Washington DC 20036.

Fringe Benefits: "Excellent professional experience for those seeking to enter fields of environmental education or interpretation, recreation, resource management, science education; located in scenic and historic Blue Ridge Mountains, opportunity to work with children from all over the US and from abroad." **College credit** available.

North Carolina Outward Bound School, Located in Morganton. Outdoor education for personal growth. "Educational process dedicated to the principle that the individual develops self-confidence, concern for others and self-awareness in the broad scheme of situations when confronted by challenging, shared experiences involving service and adventure." Openings for college students, teachers and local applicants from June through October. Applicants must have training and experience in wilderness emergency care, whitewater paddline, rock climbing, high angle rescue work, backpacking, counseling and outdoor judgment. Needs 20 wilderness instructors. Salaries:

instructors, $600/23-day course; assistant instructors, $400/23-day course. "Applicants should be interested in helping participants learn about themselves and others through physically and mentally demanding Outward Bound courses." Send for application. Apply by February 15 to Mike Fischesser, Program Director, North Carolina Outward Bound School, Box 817, Morganton NC 28655.

Our Lady Of The Hills, Located in Hendersonville. Religious coed camp for ages 7-16. Openings for college students and high school seniors from June 9 to August 20. Needs 2 waterfront directors, $500-700/season; 20 cabin counselors, $225-375/season; 15 specialty counselors for sailing, canoeing, archery, 2 nature lore, $225-375/season; 2 nurses (RN); 2 riding instructors, $350-700/season. Room and board provided. Apply by May 1 to The Rev. J.J. McSweeney, 633 Cooper Drive, Dept. SED, Charlotte NC 28210.

Pinewood, Located in Hendersonville, North Carolina. Private coed camp for boys and girls, grades 2-9. Openings for college students from June 15 to August 19. Needs 70 cabin counselors, $400-450; 15 specialty counselors for archery, riflery, tennis, golf, waterskiing, canoeing, sailing, arts and crafts, drama, dancing, go-carting, riding, swimming, team sports, $450-550; 6 kitchen aides, high school seniors acceptable, $400; 4 cook's assistants/salad makers, college students preferred, $500. Room and board provided. "Only clean-cut, non-smoking persons need apply." Write for brochure/application anytime before May 20 to M. Levine, Camp Pinewood, 1801 Cleveland Rd., Miami Beach FL 33141.
Fringe Benefits: Laundry, travel allowance and gratuities for cabin counselors. **College credit** possible.

Pisgah, Located in Asheville. Girl Scout camp for girls ages 6-17. Openings for teachers and students from June 19 to August 1. Needs assistant director, $750; waterfront director (WSI, CPR), $600; 2 waterfront assistants (WSI, Lifesaving, experienced), $480; riding director (experienced in teaching riding), $580; 2 riding assistants (experienced in teaching riding), $420; head cook (experienced in institutional cooking), $900; 2 cooking assistants, $580; 9 counselors and unit leaders (experienced in camping and working with girls), $360-540; nurse (RN), $690. Room and board provided. Applicant should "enjoy working with girls and camping in the mountains." Send resume or write for application (June 5 deadline) to Barbara A. Orr, Camp Director, Asheville NC 28804; tel. 252-4442.

Sea Gull & Seafarer, Located in Arapahoe. YMCA operated camps for boys and girls featuring seamanship plus all usual camping activities. Openings for college and high school students, teachers and local applicants to work from mid-June through mid-August. Hires physically handicapped, depending on applicant's limitations, ability and positions available suited to the applicant's skills. Needs 100 administrative and senior counselors, $550 and up/season; 100 junior counselors and food service positions, $250 and up/season; 40 dining hall cooks and assistants, $75 and up/week; 7 RNs and graduate nurses, $1,000/season. Salary depends on age, school classification and position held. Room and board provided. Send resume or request application September through May to Don Cheek, Director, Camp Sea Gull, Box 10976, Raleigh NC 27605.

Fringe Benefits: Good working conditions, scenic locale, opportunities to meet interesting people and interesting, rewarding work. **College credit** available.

Southern Conference Camps, Located in Burlington. Church related facility for ages 9-18. Openings for college students and teachers. Needs 1 camp nurse (RN or senior nursing student), $700/season; 1 craftworker (experienced), $700/season; 1 naturalist (experienced) $700/season. Room and board provided. Hires physically handicapped as craftworkers. Send for an application. Applicants should have church affiliation and a commitment to Christian values. Apply by March 31 to Rev. Richard Rinker, Southern Conference Camps, PO Box 2410, Burlington NC 27215.

Fringe Benefits: Mountain valley site with a Christian atmosphere. **College credit** possible.

Thunderbird, Located 17 miles south of Charlotte, North Carolina. YMCA coed resident camp for ages 7-16. Openings for college students, teachers, and high school seniors from June 7 to August 21. Needs 7 aquatic instructors (WSI), 12 waterskiing, 7 sailing, 5 canoeing (whitewater), 3 campcraft-nature lore, 5 riding, 4 riflery, 7 athletic (soccer, basketball), 3 field hockey. Pays $550 and up/season, commensurate with position, references and age. Apply by May to G. William Climer, Jr., Director, Camp Thunderbird, Route 4, Box 166A, Clover SC 29710; tel. 803/831-2121.

Windy Wood, Located in Tuxedo. Coed camp for young children. Openings for college students and teachers from June to August 13. Needs instructor in English riding, tennis, crafts; waterfront director; 16 general counselors; specialty counselors for canoeing, boating, sailing, $55/week with additional if ARC certified; nurse (RN). Apply to William Waggoner, Camp Windy Wood, Box 188, Tuxedo NC 28784.

Summer Theaters

Horn in the West Outdoor Drama, Located at Boone. Outdoor theater with performances for tourist and local audiences nightly (except Mondays) from June 19 to August 15. Openings for college students, teachers, foreign students, and local applicants. Needs principle actors, singers, dancers, villagers, technicians. Salary $30-150. Apartments and rooms available in town and country (university town); costs vary, sometimes negotiable. Hires physically handicapped by individual arrangement. Application deadline March 1. Institute of Outdoor Drama auditions at Chapel Hill, North Carolina. Send resume to Ed Pilkington, Director, Horn in the West, Box 295, Dept. SED, Boone, NC 28607.

Fringe Benefits: "Located in scenic Appalachian Mountains, cool climate; close-knit cast and crew.

North Dakota

168 jobs available

Resorts, Ranches, Restaurants, Lodging

Gold Seal Company, Located at Medora. Tourist attraction, resort. Openings for 150 college students, teachers and high school seniors from mid-May to early September. Needs chambermaids, cooks, waitresses, retail clerks, horse guiding-groundsmen, hourly minimum wage; supervisor, $600/month. Apply to Gold Seal Company, Box 198, Medora ND 58645.

Summer Camps

Triangle Y, Located on Lake Sakakawea at Garrison. YMCA coed camp for children ages 8-16. Openings for 18 college students and teachers from June 6 to August 15. Needs 12 cabin counselors, $675-800/season; directors: riding, boating, CIT, trips, $800-950/season; nurse, $750-900/season. Room and board provided. Apply by February 28 to Triangle Y Camp, c/o Minot YMCA, Minot ND 58701.
Fringe Benefits: College credit available.

Ohio

4975+ jobs available

Business and Industry

CDI Temporary Service, Located in Cleveland. Office, marketing, light industrial personnel. Offers college students, teachers, high school students and other qualified people interesting temporary work at a variety of companies in diversified industries during summer vacation, semester breaks and year round. Work 1 to 5 days, 2 weeks at a time, a month, or for entire summer. Top hourly pay, according to skills, on a weekly basis. Never a fee. Needs all office, marketing, and light industrial skills, e.g., receptionists, typists, secretaries, transcribers, word processors, keypunch operators, figure clerks, bookkeepers, switchboard operators, sorters, stuffers, inventory workers, product demonstrators, market researchers, machine operators, factory workers, assemblers and many others. Suggest contacting office prior to availability. Apply to CDI Temporary Service 6659 Pearl Rd., Parma Heights OH 44130; 355 Richmond Rd., Richmond Heights OH 44143.

Environmental Intern Program/Great Lakes, Located in Cleveland. Openings "all year—summer emphasized." Needs 100 college students for over 30 different disciplines annually—field assistants and indoor research assistant position, 3 years college minimum, $140-250. Will possibly

hire physically handicapped depending on academic training. Send for
application. Apply by March 2 (for summer) to Mr. Jere Tone, Regional
Director, EIP/Great Lakes, Dept. SED, 332 The Arcade, Cleveland OH 44114.
Fringe Benefits: This program offers "excellent learning experiences with
creative professionals; there is the opportunity to attend workshops and
meetings relating to career training as part of participation." **College credit**
possible.

David Hazelkorn, Attorney at Law, Located in Warren. Opening
for law clerk year round. Needs 1 law clerk (law student preferred) for research,
preparation of briefs and pleadings, salary negotiable. Would hire physically
handicapped. Apply with resume by May 1, to David Hazelkorn, 397 Hasmon
NW, Warren OH 44483.
Fringe Benefits: "Learn about the practical practice of law; interesting
people and work." **College credit** possible.

Commercial Attractions

Cedar Point, Inc., Located in Sandusky. Amusement/theme park,
hotel, campgrounds, marina. Openings for 3,300 people from early May to mid-
September. Needs ride hosts and hostesses, refreshment hosts and hostesses,
sales cashiers, ticket takers, groundskeepers, craftsmen, lifeguards, waiters and
waitresses, hotel personnel and many other positions. Salaries are hourly rate
plus bonus. Dormitory and apartment style housing available for 1,900 people.
Send early for application and information to Personnel Department, Cedar
Point, Inc., Sandusky OH 44870.
Fringe Benefits: Ride and beach privileges, dances, movies and bonus.

Cincinnati Concession, Located in Cincinnati. Concession
company. Needs 50 concession stand workers, 10 restaurant help, 20 ride
operators, and 30 golf course concession workers. High school seniors or
college students preferred. Pays $2.00-2.75/hour. Openings year-round, part
time. Apply to Jack Beal, Secretary, Cincinnati Concession, 3400 Vine St.,
Cincinnati OH 45220; telephone (513)861-4981.

Jungle Larry's African Safari, Located at Cedar Point in
Sandusky, Ohio. Zoological park at resort. Openings for college students, ages
18 to 23, from May 1 through mid-September. Needs guides and animal
keepers. All employees must be capable of public speaking and have a love for
the animal kingdom and people. Room ($5) and board available at employee's
expense. Apply by March 1 to Mrs. N.R. Tetzlaff, Dept. SED, Box 7129, Naples
FL 33941.
Fringe Benefits: Uniforms are furnished. **College credit** possible. This
work offers "a great opportunity to learn of the animal kingdom and animal
training."

Sea World, Located in Aurora. Marine life park for entertainment and
education about the sea. Openings from May 17 through September 7. Needs
500 food service attendants, minimum wage; 300 sales clerks, minimum wage;

200 park hosts/hostesses, minimum wage; and 50 tour guides and show people, $3.65 and up/hour. Also year-round opportunities for those with career potential. Would hire physically handicapped people. Apply with application or in person from December to June to Beth Dudas, Sea World, 1100 Sea World Dr., Aurora OH 44202.

Fringe Benefits: "Meet many people ages 16-25 in a social atmosphere. We offer free tickets to local entertainment. Employees can possibly return each season with a pay increase, and will see good advancement opportunities."
College credit possible.

Resorts, Ranches, Restaurants, Lodging

Eddie's Grill & Dairy Queen, Located at Geneva-on-the-Lake. Resort restaurant. 31st season. Openings for 24 college students and high school seniors from June 15 through Labor Day; some from May 26. Needs fountain workers, bus boys, waitresses, counter attendants, $110; fry cooks, clean-up help, $115-135/week. Room and board provided. Apply by July 10 to Edward Sezon, 247 S. Broadway, Geneva OH 44041.

Fringe Benefits: Good working conditions, excellent living accommodations.

Summer Camps

Campbell Gard, Located in Hamilton. YMCA coed camp. Openings for college students, teachers, high school seniors and foreign students from June 16 to August 2. Needs pool director, 4 swimming instructors, 8 specialty counselors, campcraft instructor, craft counselor, 6 general counselors. Salaries are $275-725. Send for application. Apply early (May deadline) to Larry DeLozier, Camp Director, YMCA Camp Campbell Gard, Dept. SED, 105 N. 2nd St., Hamilton OH 45011.

Cheerful, Located in Strongsville. Camp for physically and mentally handicapped children. Openings from late June through late August. Needs 14 counselors, directors: 2 waterfront (WSI), 2 arts and crafts, 2 nature, 2 recreation, $500 and up; nurse (RN), $700 and up. Salaries are for season. Apply to Director, Camp Cheerful, 15000 Cheerful Lane, Strongsville OH 44136.

Circle R Ranch Camp, Located near Cleveland. Western riding camp for girls, ages 9-16. Program includes riding lessons, trail rides, swimming, boating, nature, arts and crafts. Season from mid-June to late August. Needs camp director, assistant camp director, riding instructors, general counselors, waterfront (must be certified by ARC in area applying for), cook, assistant cook, kitchen aides, nurse. "We are looking for people who are interested in singing, drama, special events, sports, guitar, lassoing and pony cart driving. Although Circle R Ranch Camp has a number of activities, we specialize in teaching riding. A great deal of the campers' time revolves around the horses, including overnights, which almost everyone is involved in at one time or another. Sessions last for 6 days and end with a horse show for the parents. Applicants

should be prepared for hard work and long hours, and should enjoy meeting and being with people." Most salaries range from $70-125/week depending on previous experience and position applied for. Room and board provided. Applicants should enjoy youngsters and have a sincere desire to work with them. Send resume, photo and references. Personal interviews desired if possible. Apply by June to Joyce Summers, Program Director, Dept. SED, 38 E. 18th Ave., Columbus OH 43201.
Fringe Benefits: This camp offers "a staff-to-camper ratio of 1:4 and an ideal setting for meeting interesting people. **College credit** has been earned by former staff, depending on their college and curriculum."

Conestoga, Located at Minerva. Coed camp for children ages 7-14. Openings for college students and teachers from June 26 to August 6. Needs 24 counselor-specialists, head counselor, nurse (RN). Salaries are $400-900/season. Send for resume or request application. Apply to James W. Barton, Camp Conestoga, Dept. SED, 1300 Lilly Rd. NW, Minerva OH 44657.

Divine Word Camp, Located 3 miles west of Perrysburg. Openings for college students, teachers and high school seniors from June 9 to August 8. Needs 15 counselors, $550/8 weeks; 20 support staff members, $550/8 weeks; 10 indoor maintenance people, $500/8 weeks; and 4 outdoor maintenance people, $550/8 weeks. Room and board provided. Send for application. Apply by May 15 to James Barney, Administrator, 26581 W. River Rd., c/o Divine Word Camp, Perrysburg OH.
Fringe Benefits: College credit possible.

Echoing Hills, Located in Warsaw. Christian residential camp for physically handicapped and mentally retarded persons, ages 6 and up. Openings for Christian college students and high school students from June to the end of August. Needs 20 counselors, 1 nurse, 1 nurse's assistant, 8 service staff personnel. Salary based on position and experience. Room and board provided. Apply by March 15 to David Jarrett, Camp Director, Camp Echoing Hills, Route 2, Warsaw OH 43844.
Fringe Benefits: College credit possible. "The most important benefit is the valuable experience that comes with working with developmentally disabled persons."

Firebird
Roosevelt, Located in Perry. Separate camps for boys and girls with an 8-week private general program: riding, tennis, sailing, crafts, etc. Openings for college students and teachers from June 20 to August 23. Needs 10 male and 10 female counselors (minimum age 19, skilled in at least 2 camp activities), $600-$800/season. Room and board provided. Apply with resume to Bill Lorimer, Director, Lorimer Camps of Ohio, 2814 Perry Pk. Rd., Perry OH 44081.
Fringe Benefits: College credit possible.

Libbey, Located in Defiance. Girl Scout camp for girls ages 7-17. Openings for college students, teachers and foreign students from June 15 to

August 16. Needs 7 unit leaders, $600-800/season; 14 unit counselors, $375-550/season; pool director, business manager, $550-700/season; 3 pool assistants, $425-500/season; 5 kitchen staff, $340-1,000/season. Apply to Kathy Hay, Maumee Valley Girl Scout Council, 470 One Stranahan Sq., Toledo OH 43604.

Riding Service, Locations at camps throughout Ohio. Riding service for camps; serves children ages 7-16. Openings from mid-June to end of August. "We need 30 horseback riding instructors, minimum age 18 or high school graduate, to live in and teach riding at various camps in Ohio." Instructors teach mainly beginning and intermediate Western riding with formal lessons in riding ring and trail rides. Campers and staff wear hard hats while riding. Past experience in show or teaching are helpful but not necessary. Staff will attend instructors' training clinic in the spring. Salaries are $70-90/week. Room and board provided. "Attitude and willingness to work and learn are more important than experience in this challenging and busy position." Send resume, photo, and three references to: Joyce Summers, Program Director, Dept. SED, 38 E. 18th Ave., Columbus OH 43201.
Fringe Benefits: "A position with the Camp Riding Service provides an opportunity to gain valuable riding instructor skills under the guidance of experienced professionals." **College credit** available.

Ross Trails, Located in Ross. Girl Scout camp for ages 7-17. Openings for June through mid-August season. Needs counselors (high school graduates), $412 and up; unit leaders (21 years old), $562 and up. Also needs nurse; WSIs for pool, lake, small crafts; counselors for riding, biking, backpacking and primitive camping. Room and board provided. Eager to hire staff from out-of-state; Girl Scout experience helpful but not necessary. Apply by April 15 to Camp Administrator, Great Rivers Girl Scout Council, Dept. SED, 4930 Cornell Rd., Cincinnati OH 45242.
Fringe Benefits: College credit possible.

Swoneky, Located north of Cincinnati. Salvation Army resident Christian camp. Openings for college students from June through August. Needs senior counselors, cooks, nurse (RN), lifeguards (WSI), specialty counselors for crafts, nature, $625-1,000. Provides food, lodging and laundry services. Apply to Captain Joseph D. Pritchard, The Salvation Army, 114 E. Central Pkwy., Cincinnati OH 45210.

Valley Vista Sports Camp, Located in Bainbridge. Summer sports camp for boys ages 8-18; facilities include 5 baseball diamonds (3 lighted), 5 basketball courts, 3 lighted tennis courts, 4 dormitories and mess hall. Openings starting June 1 for 8 college athletes to serve as counselors in the areas of

Check application deadline dates in SED listings, but don't wait until the last minute to apply. Send your application early to be among the first considered for a job.

baseball and basketball, $800-1,200/season. Room and board provided. Applicants will be "enforcing strict set of discipline rules, and must be understanding and able to work with younger kids." Send resume or application request. Apply by April 1 to Valley Vista Corp., c/o James Dunkle, Director, Box 524, Bainbridge OH 45612; tel. 614/634-2233.
Fringe Benefits: College credit possible.

Whip-Poor-Will Hills, Located near Morrow. Girl Scout camp. Openings for college students, teachers, high school graduates and foreign students from June 14 to August 9. Needs 20 counselors, $475-800/season; 5 waterfront staff (WSI), $500-750/season; nature and arts program specialist, $600-750/season; 5 cooks and kitchen staff, $350-800/season. Room and board provided. Send resume or application request. Apply to Camp Director, Buckeye Trails Girl Scout Council, Dept. SED, 184 Salem Ave., Dayton OH 45406.
Fringe Benefits: One week pre-camp training for staff. **College credit** possible.

Alfred L. Willson, Located in Bellefontaine. YMCA coed camp. Openings for college students, teachers and high school seniors from June 7 to August 8. Needs 16 resident-program-general counselors, 10 special program counselors (canoe, bicycling, minibike, tripping, horsemanship), $50-90/week; special area directors for arts and crafts, nature, swimming, boating, horsemanship, $50-90/week; 10 kitchen and maintenance workers—cooks, office, dishwashers, general maintenance skills, $30-80/week. Room and board provided. Work-study students welcome. Apply by April 15 to Bruce Boyer, Dept. SED, 40 W. Long St., Columbus OH 43215.
Fringe Benefits: "Close-knit staff." **College credit** available.

Oklahoma

87+ jobs available

Business and Industry

Phillips Petroleum Company, Located in Bartletsville. Large producer of oil, natural gas and natural gas liquids; a major refiner, transporter and marketer of fuels and lubricants; and an important manufacturer and marketer of chemical products. Openings from May to August for students studying mechanical, electrical, chemical and petroleum engineering. Assignments are normally for the Southwest: Oklahoma, Texas, Colorado and Kansas. Students must arrange their own housing. Applicants should have good scholastic standing and the ability to communicate. Send resume and up-to-date transcript to Sherry Richards, Educational Relations, Phillips Petroleum Company, 104 Frank Phillips Building, Dept. SED, Bartletsville OK 74004.

Summer Camps

Cimarron, Located in Oklahoma City. Camp Fire camp for girls, grades 2-12. Openings from early June to late July. Needs CIT director, 3 riding instructors, waterfront director, 2 waterfront counselors and 10 general cabin counselors for archery, riflery, sports and games, crafts and nature. Send resume or request application. Apply by early March to Meredith E. Maddux, Camp Director, Camp Cimarron, 717 NE 21st St., Oklahoma City OK 73105; tel. 405/524-2255.

YMCA Camp Classen, Resident camp in the Arbuckle mountains for boys and girls ages 8-16. Openings for college students from June to August. Needs 40 counselors, $350/season and 10 program specialists (wranglers, waterfront, arts and crafts, etc.), $500/season. Also needs workers for fall and spring weekend campouts. Room and board provided. Send for application or call for appointment. Applications must be received by May. Apply to Mr. Les Long, Director, Camp Classen YMCA, PO Box 1374, Okalahoma City, OK 73101.
Fringe Benefits: Accident insurance provided. **College credit** possible. "Employees will find this to be interesting work in a scenic locale."

Oregon

238 jobs available

Business and Industry

The Bulletin, Located in Bend. Openings for college student from June 10 to August 31 for a daily afternoon newspaper. Needs one student to sub for vacationing reporters, upperclassmen majoring in journalism preferred, $700/month. Bend is a town of 18,000; good apartments and condominiums available on rental basis. Send resume by March 31 to Richard P. Hronek, The Bulletin, 1526 NW Hill St., Bend OR 97701.
Fringe Benefits: On-the-job experience writing news stories. **College credit** possible.

Francisco Martinez, Located in Hillsboro. Agricultural contractor. Openings for students and teachers to work in Oregon and Washington: planting crops and trees for the Forest Service; harvesting strawberries, cucumbers, berries, cauliflower and cabbages in Oregon and Washington. Eight hours/day, five days/week. Good working conditions. Apply to Francisco Martinez, 1787 NE 24th Ave., Hillsboro OR 97123.

Resorts, Ranches, Restaurants, Lodging

Singing Springs, Located at Agness. Summer resort. Openings for college students from May through September. Needs waiters, bus boys, kitchen helpers, $225 plus tips; 2 cook's helpers, $330. Salaries are monthly plus room and board, travel allowance west of the Mississippi. Include SASE. Apply by May 1 to Rudy Valente, Singing Springs Resort, Dept. SED, Agness OR 97406.

Fringe Benefits: Training, travel allowance west of the Mississippi.

Sunriver Properties, Inc., Located in Sunriver, in central Oregon. A 3,300-acre resort community. Positions start early May to mid-June and extend through September and October. Needs cooks, pantry helpers, dishwashers, waitresses/waiters, buspersons, cashiers, hosts/hostesses, cocktail servers, bartenders, maids, housemen, laundry workers, janitors, front desk clerks, front desk cashiers, bellpersons, PBX operators, reservation clerks, night auditors, accounting clerks, tennis court monitors, boatpersons, lifeguards, swim instructors, golf course marshals, golf course maintenance (greens mowers, fairway mowers, rough mowers), trail guides, riding instructors, nature center/naturalists, airport linepersons, grounds maintenance. "A personal interview is a prerequisite to employment. Sunriver does not furnish employee housing; employees may find housing in the surrounding area or in Bend, 15 miles north of Sunriver. Public transportation is available; however, employees should have alternate means of transportation, as the public transportation schedules may not match all work schedules. Applicants with past resort experience are preferred; however, persons with public contact experience will be favorably considered. Local applicants, college students, high school students, and teachers are welcome to apply." Submit resume and request for interview date to Sunriver Properties, Inc., Personnel Department, Sunriver OR 97701; tel. 503/593-1221, ext. 288.

Timberline Lodge, Located in Government Camp. Resort. Needs 6-8 room attendants, $3/hour minimum wage plus gratuities; 6 bus persons (dining room), $2.65/hour plus meals and gratuities. Work any time in May, earliest possible in June until after Labor Day. "Lodge does not provide living quarters for staff. Our employees (80% students) live in village of Government Camp (6 miles from lodge) or other villages down the road. Living quarters range from $150-350/month. Company bus transportation provided from and to Government Camp." Apply by May 1 to Pamela Ashland, Personnel Supervisor, Timberline Lodge, Dept. SED, Government Camp OR 97028; tel. 503/231-5400.

Fringe Benefits: "Employees come into contact with people from all countries because of year-round skiing. We are one of the training sites for the US Ski Teams."

Summer Camps

Cleawox, Located in Florence, on a fresh water lake, one mile from the Pacific Ocean in the Dunes Recreational Area. Girl Scout camp for ages 8-15. Openings from mid-June to mid-August. Needs camp director, assistant director, waterfront director, waterfront assistant, unit leaders, unit assistants, assistant cook, nurse, kitchen aides. Minimum age 18 or high school graduate.

Salary range $300-900. Apply by March 1 to Karin L. Carlson, Western Rivers Girl Scout Council, 2055 Patterson, Room A, Eugene OR 97405.

Kilowan, Located in Salem, 27 miles west in Coast Range foothills. Camp Fire camp. Openings for 40 college students, teachers and foreign students from June 8 to August 16. Needs cabin counselors, unit directors, waterfront director, horse director, nurse (RN), cook. Salaries are $300-700. Room and board provided. Apply by May 1 to Casey Carter, Camp Director, or to Missy Tangeman, Resident Camp Coordinator, Camp Kilowan, Willamette Council of Camp Fire, Box 2352, Salem OR 97308.
Fringe Benefits: "Very good working conditions; one week of pre-camp training." **College credit** possible.

Namanu, Located in Sandy. Camp Fire camp. Openings for 70 college students and teachers from approximately June 15 to August 25. Needs cabin counselors; directors: unit, activity, CIT, assistant camp; instructors for riding, archery; waterfront staff, cooks, $450-1,200. Room and board provided. Apply to Camp Namanu, Dept. SED, 718 W. Burnside, Suite 410, Portland OR 97209.
Fringe Benefits: "Travel expenses (minimal) are paid to some staff members. All employees benefit from skill training and physical improvement— it's a fun, rewarding experience working with youth in a leisure environment." **College credit** possible.

Tyee, Located at Oakland. Camp Fire camp. Openings from late June to early August. Needs 8 cabin counselors, $250-375; crafts specialist, $350; waterfront director (WSI), $500; assistant waterfront, $350; nurse, cook, $700; Program Director/Assistant Camp Director, $800-1,000. Salaries are seasonal and are subject to change. Apply early to Camp Director, Umpqua Council Camp Fire Girls, 2035 NE Stephens, Roseburg OR 97470.

Westwind, Located in Otis. YWCA camp for girls and coeds, ages 8-17; family, all ages, mother-child and single parent-child, ages 3 and up. Openings for college students, teachers and foreign students. Needs riding and waterfront staff, other specialists and kitchen staff from early June to late August; cabin counselors from mid-June to late August. Needs 9 cabin counselors; instructors: riding, 3 riding assistants, 2 waterfront (familiar with motor boats and tides), small craft; directors: seasonal director, assistant camp; specialty counselors: nature (with emphasis on marine biology), archery, CIT, arts and crafts; head cook, 2 assistants, nurse. Room and board provided. Apply by May 31 to Camp Administrator, YWCA, 1111 SW 10th St., Portland OR 97205.
Fringe Benefits: Personal growth, health insurance, 4-day break in mid-season to see area (Oregon coast). **College credit** possible.

Pennsylvania

2,608+ jobs available

Business and Industry

Air Products and Chemicals, Inc., Located in Allentown. Major producer and distributor of diversified products, including industrial and medical gases, catalysts, chemicals, welding products, cryogenic processes and equipment, and environmental systems. Openings for 60 college students who have completed their junior year, or those who are graduating and proceeding to advanced studies: project engineering; research and development; economic evaluation; process design; scientific systems; applications engineering; technical service; plant engineering; accounting; financial analysis; auditing; computer programming; chemical, mechanical engineering; (BS, MS); computer science (BS, MS, with business emphasis); accounting or business administration (BS with computer science minor). Students accepted for summer employment have outstanding academic records and have demonstrated leadership ability. Salaries are varied and competitive. Send resume to Richard J. Ely, Summer Program Coordinator, Box 538, Allentown PA 18105.
Fringe Benefits: The summer student program provides a well-rounded experience for all students involved in addition to experience directly related to career interests. Students are provided with the opportunity to gain broad knowledge about air products. This educational experience is provided through tours, discussions and lectures throughout the summer. Working conditions are excellent. **College credit** available. Full-time career opportunities exist in each area where summer employment is offered.

Allentown & Sacred Heart Hospital Center, Located in Allentown. Hospital work-study program. Openings for college students from June 1 through August 2. Positions available are in anesthesia, dietary, educational development, engineering, financial services, management engineering, medical library, microbiology, nursing, pastoral care, pharmacy, physical therapy, respiratory therapy, surgery, utilization review, volunteer services. Salaries are $155/week. Room and board provided for out-of-region students. "Students must be actively pursuing a prescribed course of study at a recognized educational institution. Each department defines the minimum level of education and experience required. Because admission to the program is highly competitive, application is recommended only to students who meet all admission criteria. Each applicant must complete the work-study application form, submit a transcript of grades and provide a narrative stating goals and expectations for the program." EOE. Would possibly hire physically handicapped. Send for application by March 15 to Susan Knapp, Educational Coordinator, Educational Development, Allentown and Sacred Heart Hospital Center, Allentown PA 18105; tel. 215/821-2026.
Fringe Benefits: College credit possible.

Department of Labor, Jobs available at the regional office, Room 14240, 3535 Market St., Philadelphia PA 19104. This office serves Delaware,

Maryland, Pennsylvania, Virginia and West Virginia. Applications must be made to Washington DC office. See Washington DC office (District of Columbia section) for complete descriptions of jobs available and how to apply information.

Nuclear Regulatory Commission, Jobs available at the regional office in Philadelphia. Applications must be made to Washington DC office. See Washington DC office (District of Columbia section) for complete descriptions of jobs available and how to apply information.

Commercial Attractions

Lipko Comedy Chimps, World Wide Attractions Inc.,
Animal act (chimps) touring the east coast, the midwest and overseas. Openings for high school seniors, college students, teachers and foreign students year round. Needs assistant animal trainer, salary open. Room and board provided. Send resume. Apply to Colonel Jerry Lipko, Box 74, Barnesville PA 18214; tel. (toll free) 800/824-7888, ext. A263. "Just completed 6-month tour of Japan. Must be able to secure passport, international driver's license for foreign travel." **Fringe Benefits:** Travel expenses provided; good working conditions; interesting work. **College credit** possible.

Magic Valley Park, Located in Bushkill. Theme amusement park.
Openings from early June to Labor Day for college and high school students. Needs 3 costume characters (should be fairly tall to wear costumes), high school students preferred, $3 and up/hour; 6 Keystone Kops (must play brass or wind instrument), college students preferred, salary is open; 175 rides, food, games personnel (high school students preferred), $2.85 and up/hour; and 16 (college students preferred) for dancers and singers, $175 and up/week. Apply to Magic Valley Park, Rt. 209, Bushkill PA 18324.

Expeditions, Guide Trips

Mountain Streams and Trails Outfitters, Located in
Ohiopyle. Whitewater rafting. Openings from April to September. Needs several river guides (minimum age 18) for trips on the Youghogheny, Cheat, and Gauley Rivers, $150-250/week. Red Cross cards for advanced lifesaving, first aid and CPR required. "We want competent kayakers and rafters who enjoy working with people. Room and kitchen facilities provided." Apply by March 1 to John Lichter, Personnel Manager, Box 106, Ohiopyle PA 15470; tel. 412/329-4730.
Fringe Benefits: "Working here provides employees with the opportunity to learn, or improve on, the whitewater skills of kayaking, canoeing and rafting. There is the possibility of obtaining weekend work while at school or at another job during the week." **College credit** possible.

Wilderness Voyageurs, Inc., Located in Ohiopyle, in Ohiopyle
State Park. Guided river trips; whitewater rafting. Openings for college students, teachers, high school seniors, foreign students and local applicants from May 1

to October 1. Needs 16 guides, $150-210/week plus room. Raft and kayak guides must be 18 years of age or older, have Red Cross Advanced First Aid training, Red Cross Advanced Lifesaving training and CPR, as well as previous experience in working with people. Whitewater and/or flatwater paddling experience preferred but not necessary. Training program provided. Apply by May 1 to Personnel Manager, Wilderness Voyageurs, Inc., Box 97, Ohiopyle PA 15470; tel. 412/329-5517.

Summer Camps

Akiba, Located in Reeders, near Stroudsburg. Private brother-sister camp for children ages 5-16. Openings for college students and teachers from approximately June 25 to August 21. Needs 50 cabin counselors; specialty counselors for riflery, dramatics, overnight, waterskiing, archery, arts and crafts, tennis; assistant director; athletic assistant; waterfront assistant; nurses; kitchen manager. Room and board provided. Apply to Director, Camp Akiba, Box 400, Dept. SED, Bala-Cynwyd PA 19004.
Fringe Benefits: College credit available.

Association of Independent Camps, Located throughout Pennsylvania. Openings at 80 children's (ages 6-16) summer camps located in New England and Middle Atlantic States. Needs head counselors, group leaders, general and all specialty counselors. Room and board provided. Apply by July to Association of Independent Camps, Dept. SED, 157 W 57th St., New York NY 10019; tel. 212/582-3540.
Fringe Benefits: "Travel expenses paid in part or in full. Learning experiences—i.e., living and sharing with others, complete camp facilities in a healthy environment; time for socialization with peers." **College credit** "may be arranged by student at school."

Beacon Lodge Camp for the Blind, Located in Mt. Union. Children (ages 6-18) and adults (18-senior citizens). Openings for 40 college students and teachers during the summer. Needs Unit Director for Adult Camp; Unit Director for Children's Camp; general counselors; specialty counselors for waterfront (WSI), music, arts and crafts, nature; secretary; nurses (RN); canteen operators. Salaries based on age, experience and education. Room and board provided. Apply by April 15 to Michael Shotzberger, Director, Beacon Lodge Camp for the Blind, Dept. SED, Box 428, Lewistown PA 17044.
Fringe Benefits: College credit available. "Working with the handicapped provides valuable experience."

Blue Ridge
Equinunk, Located in Equinunk, Pennsylvania. Member ACA. Openings for college students and teachers for 8 weeks, from approximately July 1 to August 26. Needs instructors: 10 water safety (ARC), 4 smallcraft (ARC), 10 tennis, 2 golf, 10 physical education, 2 music, 2 dramatics, gymnastics, 2 arts and crafts, photography, science, pioneering, riding; 4 nurses (RN). Salaries are $400 and up. Apply by April to Martin Gelobter, 20 Burton Ave., Woodmere NY 11598.

Brandywine Valley YMCA Camps, Located in Downingtown.
Camp Lookout is a traditional resident camp for children ages 7-12; Circle-Y
Ranch is a Western-style horseback riding camp for children ages 10-16; Camp
Dwight is a teenage camp featuring out-trips in canoeing, backpacking, caving
and rock climbing. "Clientele is generally from Philadelphia area, both urban
and suburban, ages 7-16. There are 4 2-week sessions campers may choose
from." Openings from June 23 through August 23. Needs 15 cabin counselors/
instructors (experienced with horses for Circle-Y, practical experience in
activities listed above for Camp Dwight), college students preferred,
$500-700/season; 10 assistant counselors/instructors, high school students
preferred, $300/season. Room and board provided. "We generally hire staff
first on their ability to relate to the campers they will be working with." Send for
application to Jack Prior, Executive Director, Dept. SED, Box 205, Rt. 322,
Downingtown PA 19335; tel. 215/269-0787.

Bryn Mawr Lake Camp, Located in Honesdale, Pennsylvania. Girls
camp for ages 6-16; family weekends in June; 60th year. Openings for men and
women, college students and teachers, in all activity areas applicable to summer
camp programming, including land and water sports; music and drama; jewelry,
ceramics, leather; the arts; nature; camping; sailing; waterskiing; English riding;
specializing in tennis and gymnastics. Minimum age 19 years. Salaries are
$400-1,500. Room and board provided. Apply by April 1 to Herb Kutzen, 81
Falmouth St., Short Hills NJ 07078; tel. 201/467-3518.
Fringe Benefits: Travel expenses; time off every other evening at 5:30.
"Tremendous learning opportunity from professionals, skilled coaches and
teachers."

Choconut, Located in Friendsville, 17 miles south of Binghamton, New
York, on a private, natural lake. Boys camp for ages 9-14; 8-week camp, 9-week
camp season (late June to mid-August). Openings for 10-15 college students
and teachers, minimum age 18. Needs counselors for 50-60 campers; supervise
basic outdoor activities to help boys help themselves gain self-reliance. High
salaries for the right persons and extra pay for additional work before and/or
after camp. Especially needed are those with carpentry skills and work-project
ability and waterfront (WSI); also natural science, farm animal care, campcraft,
nurse (RN), and general counselors. Room and board provided. "Most jobs are
filled by April, but I sometimes need male personnel all the way until late June."
To apply write S. Hamill Horne, Box 33D, Gladwyne PA 19035.
Fringe Benefits: "A varied job; something different is happening all the time
and all dealing with people, not routine donkey work. Camp counseling gives a
young person much more responsibility than he is likely to have at any other
job." **College credit** available.

College Settlement, Located in Horsham. Agency/environmental
studies camp for coeds, ages 7-12. Openings from June 27 to August 24.
Needs 10 cabin counselors, college students preferred, $650 base/season; 2
environmentalists, college students and teachers preferred, $800/season; 1
registered nurse, $1,500/season. Full job descriptions available upon request.
"Applications are available upon request and should be returned no later than

April 1, if possible. 130 campers, total staff 47 persons, 57 years in operation. Camp is a twelve months operation." Apply to Leonard C. Ferguson, Executive Director, College Settlement Camps, 600 Witmer Rd., Horsham PA 19044; tel. 215/542-7974.

Freedom Valley Girl Scout Council, Located in Valley Forge, 30 miles from Philadelphia in Montgomery County. 3 Girl Scout resident camps; 8-week season for girls ages 6-17. Openings for college students, teachers, local applicants and high school seniors (for horseback riding only) from mid-June to mid-August. Needs 3 program/assistant directors, age 23 or older, to assist and supervise younger staff members, creative programs, $700-900/season; 15 waterfront/boating/WSI instructors to instruct in swimming lessons, diving, row boats, canoes, and other pool activities, $450-900/season; 6 riding director/instructors for English riding program, $450-900/season; 50 counselors/trip leaders for 4 or 8 weeks, $400-800/season (backpacking, cycle and canoe leaders must be 21); 3 business managers, 21 or older, with driver's license, $700-900/season; 3 nurses, 21 or older, RN, graduating RN student or LPN, $900-1,200/season. "Apply as early as possible for best selection for pre-camp planning. Request application, arrange for interview and negotiate for position and salary." Apply to Agnes M. Hepler, Director of Camping, Freedom Valley Girl Scout Council, Dept. SED, Valley Forge PA 19482; tel. 215/666-6141.
Fringe Benefits: Career development and exploration; non-pressure job in the out-of-doors. **College credit** available.

Girl Scouts of Southwestern Pennsylvania, Located near Pittsburgh. Camps Henry Kaufmann, near Ligonier; and Redwing, near Butler. Openings for college students, teachers and high school students from June 15 to August 17. Needs 50 unit assistants, $400-500; 15 unit leaders, $700-800; 9 waterfront assistants and directors (WSI & SLS), $600-700; 3 assistant directors and program directors, $1,000-1,200; 4 maintenance assistants, $400-500; 1 food program director, $1,000-1,400; 2 kitchen managers, $630-720; 10 cooks, $495-585; 10 program specialists, $450-600; 4 CIT instructors and assistants, $500-700; 2 nurses (RN, LPN), $1,200-1,600. Send for application. Apply by May 31 to Camping Director, Girl Scouts of Southwestern Pennsylvania, Dept. SED, 327 5th Ave., Pittsburgh PA 15222.
Fringe Benefits: "Experience; good working atmosphere." **College credit** possible.

Helping Hands Inc. Day Camp, Located in Alburtis. Day camp with two weeks residential, for mentally, physically and emotionally handicapped persons, ages 5-65, of nearby communities. Openings from June to August. Needs 8 senior counselors (college students, teachers), $95/week; 2 activity coordinators to plan arts, crafts and music activities (college students, teachers), $95/week; 8 junior counselors (college students, high school students), $75/week. "Staff can room for 8 weeks at camp at minimal fee. Applicant must be willing to work hard and care for campers." Send for application or call. Apply by May 10 to Beverly Farkas, Executive Director, Dept. SED, 643 Main St., Pennsburg PA 18073.

Hemlock Girl Scout Council Camps, Located in central Pennsylvania, 3 camps for girls ages 6-17 as well as troop camp with core staff program. Openings for college students, teachers and foreign students, precamp training June 19 to June 26; 1 and 2 week sessions, June 27 to August 16. Needs business manager, general counselors, arts and crafts specialists, ecology specialist, English riding director, riding staff, waterfront staff, health supervisor, cook and kitchen people. Send for application and salary information to Director of Educational Services, Henlock Girl Scout Council, Inc., Dept. SED, 350 Hale Ave., Harrisburg PA 17104.

Hidden Valley, Located in Equinunk, Pennsylvania. Girl Scout camp for girls ages 6-17. Openings from June 14 to August 7. Needs waterfront director (WSI), waterfront assistants (senior life), unit leaders, unit assistants, kitchen aides, college students and teachers preferred. "Camp is located on 1,200 acres in Pocono Mountains. Camp skills, backpacking, canoeing and horseback riding are part of the program. Counselors are housed in platform tents with cots." Apply by June to Kay Coriell, Camping Services Manager, Hidden Valley Camp, Rolling Hills Girl Scout Council, Bridgewater NJ 08807; tel. 201/725-1226.

Ken-Crest, Located in Mont Clare. Coed camp for mentally retarded children and adults, ages 8 and up. Openings for college students and teachers from end of June through mid-August, for 7 weeks. Needs camp coordinator, salary open; camp nurse, $85-100; 15 tent counselors, $75-85; specialty counselors for arts and crafts, music, swimming (WSI), recreation, $80-90; swimming (SLS), $75-85. Salaries are weekly. Counselors sleep on bunks, either in tents or cabins. Campers sleep in same area as counselors. Tents are placed on platforms off the ground. Apply by May 1 to Camp Director, Ken-Crest Camp, Dept. SED, Route 29, Mont Clare PA 19453.

Laughing Waters
Indian Run, Laughing Waters located in Gilbertsville, Indian Run located in Glenmoore. Girl Scout camps for girls, ages 6-17. Openings for college students, teachers and foreign students, minimum age 18, from approximately June 20 to August 20. Needs general counselors, WSI, SCI, specialists (arts, sports, environmental education), tripping staff (bike, canoe, backpacking). Salaries are $500-850/season. Nurses (RN) and administration staff salaries higher. "Racially and economically integrated urban camper population. Live in tents." Room and board provided. Apply by March 30 to Camping Services Director, Girl Scouts of Greater Philadelphia, 1411 Walnut St., Philadelphia PA 19102.
Fringe Benefits: College credit available. "These camps offer broad experiences in working with a multiethnic, multiracial, urban population in a rustic, outdoor setting. Also, there is the opportunity to acquire references for future employment."

Log-N-Twig, Located in Dingmans Ferry. Coed Jewish camp. Openings for college students from June 22 to August 22. Needs counselors: 25 general, 4 swimming (WSI), 12 sports, 2 arts and crafts; 2 nurses (RN). Salaries commensurate with experience and maturity. Room and board provided. Apply

to Dr. Morton "Moe" Tener, 7700 Doe Lane, Laverock PA 19118; tel. 215/887-9367.
Fringe Benefits: Laundry service; tips. **College credit** possible. "Good learning situation."

Mosey Wood
Wood Haven, Mosey Wood is located in White Haven; Wood Haven is located in Pine Grove. Girl Scout resident camps, ages 6-17. Openings for college students and teachers from June 15 to August 17. Needs 12 unit leaders, $640-1,000/season; 30 unit counselors, $500-700/season; 2 waterfront directors (WSI), $730-1,100/season; 5 waterfront assistants (WSI), $550-700; 1 sailing instructor, $550-750/season; 2 canoeing instructors, $450-750; and 4 riding instructors, $600-1,100/season. Room and board provided. Apply by May 15 to Camp Administrator, Great Valley Girl Scout Council, Dept. SED, 2633 Moravian Ave., Allentown PA 18103; tel. 215/791-2411.
Fringe Benefits: College credit possible.

Mount Lake, Located in Fannettsburg. Coed camp for ages 6-16. Openings for college students, teachers and foreign students from June 24 to August 22. Needs 10 general counselors, $700/season; 2 WSIs, $800/season; 2 cooks, $150/week; nurse (RN), $120/week. Room and board provided. Apply by May 1 to James M. Close, Mt. Lake Camp, Box 208, Enola PA 17025.

Oneka, Located in Tafton, in the Pocono Mountains. Private camp for girls ages 7-16. Openings for college students from June 26 to August 18. Needs specialty counselors: 6 swimming, 6 boating, 8 land sports, $400-800; 4 crafts, $400-600. Salaries include room and board. Apply by May to Director, Camp Oneka, 2508 Highland Ave., Broomall PA 19008.

Pine Forest, Coed
Timber Tops, Girls
Lake Owego, Boys, Three private camps in northeastern Pennsylvania, in the Poconos. Good food, clean air, nice people. Openings from June 25 to August 22. Needs specialty counselors (minimum age 19) for canoe tripping, sailing and boating, arts and crafts, soccer, athletics, archery, rock climbing, riflery, nature, waterfront (WSI), scouting, tennis, drama; kitchen staff. Salary range $600-1,000. Room and board provided. Apply by June 1 to Marvin Black, 110-A Benson East, Jenkintown PA 19046.
Fringe Benefits: College credit available.

Pocono Highland Camps, Located in Marshalls Creek. Coed camp. Openings for college students, teachers and foreign students from June 25 to August 22. Needs specialty counselors for all land sports, water safety (ARC), smallcraft, sailing, waterskiing, golf, arts and crafts, dramatics, dancing, riflery, riding, tennis, ham radio, pioneering, archery, canoeing, nature, music, song leading, basketball, baseball, soccer, karate, judo, bowling, fencing, photography, wrestling; unit leaders; doctor; nurse (RN). Excellent salaries. Apply to Louis Weinberg, Pocono Highland Camp, 6528 Castor Ave., Philadelphia PA 19149.

Rock Creek Farm, Located in the Blue Ridge Mountains. Camp for children, ages 6-17, with learning disabilities or emotional problems. Openings for college students and teachers from June 20 to August 20. Needs specialty counselors: music, construction, arts and crafts, pioneering, auto mechanics, swimming, nature, woodworking. Also needs group counselors and nurse. Excellent salaries; includes room and board. Apply by May to Bernard Wray, Rock Creek Farm, RD 1, Thompson PA 18465; tel. 717/756-2706.

Susquehannock, Located in Brackney, in Susquehanna County, 15 miles south of Binghamton, New York. Private boys' camp. Openings for college students and teachers from approximately June 21 to August 24. Needs athletic counselors for basketball, baseball, soccer, football, track, lacrosse, wrestling; instructors for waterfront-canoeing, waterfront-sailing; specialty counselors: tennis, waterfront (WSI), campcraft and tripping, arts and crafts, $500-800; English riding assistant, $450-650; nurse (RN), $900. Room and board provided. Apply to E.H. Shafer, Director, Camp Susquehannock, Box 71, Brackney PA 18812; tel. 717/967-2323.
Fringe Benefits: "We provide medical insurance, workmen's compensation insurance, and laundering of camp clothing. The food here is rated 'very good.' Counselors have fishing privileges, the use of boats, and the opportunity to participate in athletic competition. There is a veteran senior staff." **College credit** possible.

Towanda, Located in Honesdale, Pennsylvania. Camp for boys and girls, ages 7-16. Openings for college students and teachers. Needs coaches; general counselors; specialty counselors for tennis, golf, baseball, basketball, WSI, canoeing, sailing, waterskiing, stage scenery, arts and crafts, nature, pioneering, riflery; nurse (RN). Salaries depend on age and experience. Enclose SASE. Apply to Lynne S. Nordan, Dept. SED, 316 Lynncroft Rd., New Rochelle NY 10804.
Fringe Benefits: College credit available.

Tyler Hill, Located in Tyler Hill, Pennsylvania. Private, coed. Openings for college students and teachers from June 28 to August 22. Needs bunk counselors (minimum age 21); assistants in swimming, golf, arts and crafts, tennis. Apply to William Heft, Director, Tyler Hill Camp, Tyler Hill PA 18469. Send Mail to 212-16 82nd Ave., Hollis Hills NY 11427.

Watonka, Located in Hawley, Pennsylvania. Private camp for boys, ages 8-15, interested in science. Openings for college students, teachers and foreign students from June 20 to August 25. Needs 6 cabin counselors, $500-600; riflery instructor, $500-700; minibike riding instructor, $600-800; directors for arts and crafts, $700-900; waterfront (ARC), $900-1,200; program director, $1,000-1,500; 6 science instructors for chemistry, photography, biology, electronics, astronomy, computer science $800-1,200. Room and board provided. Apply by May 15 to Donald G. Wacker, Dept. SED, 43 Franklin St., Cedar Grove NJ 07009.
Fringe Benefits: "Enjoyable, expense-free summer for those who like children and the outdoors." **College credit** possible.

Wayne, Located in northeastern Pennsylvania. Private coed camp.
Openings for teachers, high school and college coaches and college students
from approximately June 23 to August 22. "Specializes in people first; fine
professional staff recruited from throughout US and abroad. Many fun, creative
activities." Needs head counselors and assistant; waterfront director; athletic
director; group leaders; specialists in tennis, camping, nature, golf, sailing,
canoeing, waterskiing, swimming (WSI), soccer, basketball, baseball, ceramics,
batik, macrame, yoga, guitar, ham radio, art, shop, archery. Salaries are
$350-1,500 depending on age, skill and experience. Also needs nurses (RN),
$650-750; doctor; and assistant director. Apply to Camp Wayne, 12 Allevard St.,
Lido Beach NY 11561; tel. 516/889-3217.

Summer Theaters

The Pennsylvania Festival Theatre, Located at University Park.
Equity U/RTA. Openings from early June through mid-August. Needs
apprentice and journeyman actors, technicians, management aides,
$85-115/week; staff positions for designers and management, salaries
negotiable. Send resume. Apply by January 9 to John R. Bayless, General
Manager, Dept. SED, The Pennsylvania Festival Theatre, 137 Arts II Bldg.,
University Park PA 16802.

Prather Productions, Located in Shamokin Dam. Operator of 4
non-equity theaters. Openings for 15 college students and teachers from June
to September, or longer. Needs actors, actresses, singers, dancers, technical
staff, costumers, lighting. Salaries are $50-150/week plus board or room for
candidates with previous professional dinner theater experience. Openings for
college students only as staff assistants who act, $50/week stipend plus room.
Apply by May 1 to T.R. Prather, Prather Productions, Dept. SED, Shamokin
Dam PA 17876.
Fringe Benefits: College credit possible.

Rhode Island

175 jobs available

Business and Industry

Antonio's Restaurant II, Located in Cranston. Italian restaurant
catering to businessmen and family vacationers. Openings from May 20 to
September 5. Needs 4 short-order cooks, experience as chef's helper, college
students and foreign students preferred, $100/week; 30 waitresses/waiters,
some experience needed, college or foreign students preferred, $5/shift; 6
kitchen helpers, high school students preferred, $100/week; 5 bartenders or
barmaids, experience in mixology, college or foreign students or local applicants preferred, $100/week; and 6 bus boys, $12.50/shift or $75/week. Meals
provided for all employees; room provided with some positions. Send resume

and photo by May 1 to Loretta Pompili, Antonio's Restaurant, 1710 Cranston St., Dept. SED, Cranston RI 02920.

Fringe Benefits: "The people employed by Antonio's II will meet and experience different things each day. It will also be a learning experience. We offer a beach resort as well as a clean environment."

Government

US Youth Conservation Corps, Located in Providence. Openings for college students, teachers and graduates from mid-June to mid-August. Needs 12 crew leaders and assistants (applicants should have environmental science background and/or technical (carpentry); must be able to supervise a crew of high school students on conservation work projects; and teaching environmental education. Hires physically handicapped. Room and board is not provided but much work is done in wooded areas and camping on state facilities is often possible. Send resume with application by mid-March to Richard Tierney, US Youth Conservation Corps, 83 Park St., Providence RI 02903.

Fringe Benefits: College credit possible.

Resorts, Ranches, Restaurants, Lodging

Ballard's Inn and Champlin's Marina, Located at Block Island. Resort. Openings for 100 college students, teachers and high school seniors from June 25 through Labor Day. Needs waiters, waitresses, bus boys, dock attendants, lifeguards, kitchen help, cooks, maids, porters, bartenders, snack shop attendants, cashiers, groundskeepers. Salaries are $25-200/week plus board. Send resume with SASE to Paul A. Filippi, Ballard's Farm, Great Road, Lincoln RI 02865.

Summer Camps

Wohelo, Located in Charlestown. Camp Fire resident camp for youth ages 6-16. Fully accredited ACA camp. Openings for college students, teachers and high school seniors. Needs 12 cabin counselors with skills in campcraft, arts and crafts, archery, canoeing, sailing, horseback riding or waterfront. Salaries are up to $500/season. Room and board provided. Apply to Camp Fire Office, 345 Blackstone Blvd., Providence RI 02906.

Fringe Benefits: "Wohelo is located on a freshwater pond, minutes from the saltwater beaches of southwestern Rhode Island. Special sessions are offered for counselors to receive Red Cross Junior Life Saving or WSI certification." **College credit** possible.

South Carolina

109+ jobs available

Business and Industry

Guillermo Corzo, Located in John's Island. Farm contractor. Openings for students and teachers to pick tomatoes. Send for application to Guillermo Corzo, Rt. 4, Box 314, John's Island SC 29455.

Government

Department of Energy
Savannah River Operations Office, Jobs available at the regional office, Box A, Aiken SC 29801. Applications must be made to Washington DC office. See Washington DC office (District of Columbia section) for complete descriptions of jobs available and how to apply information.

Summer Camps

Burnt Gin Crippled Children's Camp, Located in Columbia. State camp for crippled children ages 7-15. Openings for college students, teachers and local applicants from June 6-August 7. Needs 28 counselors to lead and guide cabins of 8 handicapped campers and participate in the general planning of camp programs and activities (minimum age 19 or must have completed freshman year in college), $70-100/week depending on experience; 8-10 activity specialists in waterfront, arts and crafts, dance, drama or music and active games (must be 21 and have adequate training in specialty area and the ability to teach skills), $80-100/week depending on experience; 2 nurses to plan and carry out a program of health and safety (must have RN degree and be licensed to practice in state and have a knowledge of handicapping conditions), $180/week; 4 cooks (must be at least 20 and have had quantity cooking experience), $60-90/week depending on experience; 2 laundry workers (minimum age 16), $60-90/week. Room and board provided. "Working at Camp Burnt Gin is a 24-hour job which requires a lot of hard work and dedication and love of children by the staff member. Previous experience at a camp and with working with handicapped children is helpful." Apply by March 30 to Ms. Lane Pellett, Camp Director, Division of Crippled Children's Care, DHEC, Dept. SED, 2600 Bull St., Columbia SC 29201; tel. 803/758-5491.
Fringe Benefits: "Excellent experience learning about different physical disabilities; very rewarding but hard work." **College credit** possible.

Hope, Located in Clemson. Agency camp for mentally retarded persons, ages 8 and older. Openings for college students and teachers from early June to mid-August. Needs 12 group counselors, 2 unit leaders, 3 waterfront instructors, 3 camping specialists, 2 program directors, camp nurse, crafts instructor. Salaries are biweekly plus room and board. Apply by March 15 to C.R. White, Camp Hope, RPA Dept., Clemson University, Clemson SC 29631.

Pla-Mor, Inc., "Pla-Mor is a well established recreational camp or retreat, located in North Myrtle Beach, South Carolina on Highway 17 South, catering to church-related youth groups, Scouts and other organizations, in one of the fastest growing areas in America. Camp Pla-Mor is a semi-modern camp organized in 1950 for the benefit of young people who care for the better life." Openings for approximately 40 high school seniors and college students from June 1 through Labor Day. "Only clean-cut, high-type energetic persons need apply." Merit will be a consideration in pay. Employees work 6 to 8 hours a day, with one day off a week. Needs 4 or 5 females for kitchen and cafeteria work, i.e., making salads and desserts, serving and clean-up, approximately $70/week; male dishwasher (Hobart machine) and clean-up, approximately $75/week; 1 male maintenance person (general knowledge of plumbing and air-conditioning, mowing and yard work), approximately $75/week; 2 or 3 female dorm/motel cleaners and laundresses (automatic commercial washer/dryer); 18 well qualified, alert beach life guards, minimum age 18, WSI in good standing (preferred) or Senior Red Cross Life Saving; pay is 25% on rentals from umbrellas, chairs and floats—approximately $650-$1,000/season; 2 female pool life guards with life saving credentials, some pool maintenance, approximately $70/week. All females are housed in motel-type rooms and males in small rooms accommodating 2 or 3 persons. Room and board provided. Apply by March 15 to Camp Pla-Mor, Inc., c/o C. Virgil Yow, President, Box 2189 Coastal Station, Dept. SED, North Myrtle Beach SC 29582; tel. 803/272-6649 or 272-8216.

Fringe Benefits: "Camp Pla-Mor is located on approximately 3 miles of beach on the Atlantic Ocean, acclaimed the widest and safest in the world. Entertainment and night-life are nearby. Employees enjoy good working conditions with congenial personnel." **College credit** possible.

South Dakota

156 jobs available

Resorts, Ranches, Restaurants, Lodging

Blue Bell Lodge & Resort, Located in Custer State Park. State Park concessionaire; rustic secluded resort. Openings from middle May to September. Needs 4 housekeepers/laundry persons, minimum $2.75/hour, plus bonus; 6 waitresses/waiters, minimum $1.95/hour, plus bonus and tips; 4 cooks and cook's helpers (cooking experience preferred), minimum $2.75/hour, plus bonus; 4 cashiers and clerks, minimum $2.75/hour, plus bonus. "Salaries are open. We charge $6/day for room and board. Applicants must be interested in working first and playing later." Send resume or application request by April 1; include SASE. Apply by April 1 to Phil Lampert, Manager, Dept. SED, Blue Bell Lodge & Resort, Box 63, Custer State Park, Custer SD 57730; tel. 605/255-4531.

Cactus Cafe and Lounge, Located in Wall. Openings for college students, teachers, high school seniors and foreign students from June to

August. Needs 20 waiters/waitresses (minimum age 21), $14/shift plus room and board; 12 dishwashers-kitchen help, $100/week plus room and board; 4 fry cooks, $22.50/shift plus room and board; 3 bartenders (minimum age 21), $20/shift plus room; 2 hostess-cashiers, $20/shift plus room. "We cannot help foreign students get visas." Apply to Myron L. Beach, Jr., Cactus Cafe and Lounge, Main St., Wall SD 57790.

State Game Lodge, Located in Custer State Park. Resort. Openings for college students from May 20 to October 1. Needs 12 motel-cottage housekeepers, 3 salad makers, 10 kitchen workers, 2 registration desk clerks, 8 sales clerks, 4 service station attendant-lawn worker-maintenance, 2 bartenders, 3 fry cooks, salary open; 15 waitresses/waiters, salary plus tips. Salaries start at minimum wage. Room and board provided. Enclose stamped return envelope for application form. Apply by April 1 to State Game Lodge, Dept. SED, Custer State Park, Custer SD 57730.
Fringe Benefits: End-of-season bonus, top-notch employee-employer relations. Located in beautiful Black Hills. **College credit** available.

Summer Camps

Jaycee Camp for Handicapped Children, Located on Big Sioux River near Baltic. Coed camp for handicapped persons age 4 through adult. Openings for college students, teachers and high school seniors from the first week in June to the first week in August. Needs 2 directors (special education majors), $1,300 and up/season, depending on experience; 24 counselors (some special education majors preferred in music, swimming, nature study, arts), $275/season plus 3.6 credit hours of college work in special education; 10 assistant counselors; nurse (RN); cook, $1,200 and up/season, depending on experience. Room and board provided. Apply early (May 1 deadline) to Jaycee Camp President, Box 1763, Dept. SED, Sioux Falls SD 57101.
Fringe Benefits: There is an opportunity to meet persons (counselors) from different parts of the country. **College credit** available.

Tennessee
1,640+ jobs available

Business and Industry

Southwestern Company, Located in Franklin. Publishers and booksellers of educational and religious books. Summer program for college students, direct selling. No experience needed. Average gross profit per month, per student over past 5 years is $1,100. Apply to Jerry Heffel, The Southwestern Company, Box 820, Nashville TN 37202.

Commercial Attractions

Opryland USA, Located in Nashville. Openings for high school
students, college students, teachers and local applicants April-October
(weekends only during April, May, September and October). Some specialized
areas offer year-round employment. Needs cashiers, area hostesses and hosts,
ride hosts and hostesses, show hostesses and hosts, animal handlers, live show
musicians and performers, merchandise and game hostesses and hosts, cooks,
food and beverage hosts and hostesses, parking lot hostesses and hosts,
security rangers, maintenance hosts and hostesses, landscape laborers,
warehousemen, clerical positions. Minimum age for all applicants is 16; some
positions have a minimum age requirement of 18, others 21. Applicants under
18 must be willing to furnish proof of age (birth or baptismal certificate). All
applicants must have a social security card. "Courtesy and a smile will be 'tools'
used at all times by Opryland USA employees. Our employees must be those
whose personal appearance and personality are of the highest standards. Our
grooming code for men requires a moderate haircut (no long sideburns or
beards). Well-groomed moustaches are allowed." Send for application to Ms.
Kene L. McWhorter, Employment Coordinator, Opryland USA, 2802 Opryland
Drive, Nashville TN 37214.
Fringe Benefits: Good working conditions; opportunity to meet interesting
people, i.e. country music stars; interesting work; social atmosphere. **College
credit** available: "we have structured internship programs for college
students."

Government

Department of Energy
Oak Ridge Operations Office, Jobs available at the regional
office, Box E, Oak Ridge TN 37830. Applications must be made to Washington
DC office. See Washington DC office (District of Columbia section) for
complete description of jobs available and how to apply information.

Resorts, Ranches, Restaurants, Lodging

Lums, Located in Gatlinburg and Pigeon Forge. Restaurants. Openings for
college students, teachers, high school seniors, foreign students and local
applicants from April to October. Needs 15 short order cooks, 30 waitresses
and waiters, 6 dishwashers, 4 busboys, and 4 cashier/hostesses, minimum wage
and up. Send application 2-3 weeks before date available for work. Apply to
Rick Kyker, Manager, Lums Restaurant, Box 409, Airport Rd., Gatlinburg TN
37738; tel. 615/436-7383.

Summer Camps

Hazlewood, Located in Springville (near Paris), on Kentucky Lake. Girl
Scout camp for girls, ages 8-18. ACA accredited. Openings from June 7 to
August 1. Needs 8 assistant leaders, $250-400; waterfront staff (WSI), 5 leaders

(minimum age 21), $400-550; nurse (RN), $400-500. $3 fee charged to register as a Girl Scout. Room and board provided. Apply by May 15 to Dottie Carey, Camp Director, Reelfoot Girl Scout Council, Route 1, Box 436-A, Jackson TN 38301.

Fringe Benefits: Accident insurance; American Campcrafter training; time off weekly; 3 leaders for 24 girls. "Learn *with* the girls and the other staff members. Participate in all camp activities—swimming, canoeing, sailing, cookouts, hiking, singing, tennis, archery, dramatics, nature crafts." **College credit** possible.

Tall Pine, Located in Coker Creek, Tennessee. Camp for trainable and educable retarded people. Openings for college students and teachers from June 23 to August 4, 6-week season. Needs 6 cottage counselors for male campers. Room and board provided. Apply by March 10 to Fred C. Slater, Owner, Tall Pine Camp, Dept. SED, 6221 NW 17th St., Ft. Lauderdale FL 33313; tel. 305/735-0727.

Fringe Benefits: Good working conditions and learning situations. **College credit** offered.

Tellico Mountain, Located in Sweetwater. Coed and Christian oriented. Openings for college students, teachers and local applicants from June 14 to July 16. Needs 30 counselors (Christian young people with love for children and life, college students and teachers preferred), $550 and up/season; 10 program specialists for waterfront (WSI), crafts (at least 2 years experience), riding (experience and references), $600 and up/season; 2 nurses, RN or LPN (college students and teachers preferred), $650 and up/season; and 6 cooks (live-in staff), experience preferred, $700 and up. Room and board provided. Send resume or application by May 30 to Louie Vessar, Director, Tenico Mountain Camp, Rt. 4, Dept. SED, Sweetwater TN 37874.

Fringe Benefits: "Our goal is to have fun. There is an enjoyable atmosphere of wholesome excitement and enthusiasm. Working here for a summer is equivalent to two years in the classroom." **College credit** possible.

Texas

4,673+ jobs available

Business and Industry

Dean BagleyB**agley Produce**Located in Edinburg. Farm labor contractor. Openings for college students, high school students, teachers and local applicants to harvest and process watermelons in the Rio Grande Valley (May and June) and in central and east Texas (July and August). Needs 25 harvestors, minimum wage; 2-4 processors, 10¢ above minimum wage. Work week 60 hours. Workers need own transportation. Send letter giving qualifications and dates available for work to Dean Bagley, Jr., Box 1319, Edinburg TX 78539.

Fringe Benefits: "End-of-season bonus; different culture—bilingual area, 20 miles from Mexico (70% of business done with Republic of Mexico); job could work into office position for right person." **College credit** possible.

Adam Escobar, Jr., Located in San Juan. Farm labor contractor. Needs pickers to harvest citrus fruit in the valley area of Hidalgo County from October 15 to March 15. Crew works 4-5 hours/day, Monday-Saturday. Apply to Adam Escobar, Jr., Rt. 1, Box 18 E., San Juan TX 78589; tel. 781-1900.

Government

Department of Labor, Jobs available at the regional office, Room 739, 555 Griffin Square Building, Griffin & Young Sts., Dallas TX 75202. This office serves Arizona, Louisiana, New Mexico, Oklahoma and Texas. Applications must be made to Washington DC office. See Washington DC office (District of Columbia section) for complete description of jobs available and how to apply information.

National Transportation Safety Board, Jobs available at the regional office in Ft. Worth. Applications must be made to Washington DC office. See Washington DC office (District of Columbia section) for complete description of jobs available and how to apply information.

Nuclear Regulatory Commission, Jobs available at the regional office in Dallas. Applications must be made to Washington DC office. See Washington DC office (District of Columbia section) for complete description of jobs available and how to apply information.

Commercial Attractions

Alamo Village Vacation and Movie Land, Located in Brackettville. Tourist attraction—where movies are made in Texas. Needs sales/cashiers: 2 for Indian Store, 3 for Trading Post, 2 for General; career country western musicians, 1 lead guitar/vocal, 1 rhythm guitar/vocal, 1 bass, 1 drums, 1 piano/vocal; cantina-restaurant, 4 waitresses/vocalist. Pays $400/month. College students preferred. Work May 1 through Labor Day; rehearsals begin May 20. All employees trusted to handle money. "Know what you want. If you do not like people then do not work for a tourist attraction. Be loyal, honest and able to carry out orders. Gentlemen: knowledge of horses, livestock and ground maintenance helpful." Room and utilities provided. Written applications after January 1; send resume and photograph; live auditions/interviews scheduled thereafter. Apply to Happy Shahan, President, Alamo Village Vacation and Movie Land, Box 528, Brackettville TX 78832; tel. 512/563-2580.

For tips on writing your resume and cover letter, filling out an application and applying in person, see "Applying for a Job" at the beginning of this book.

AstroWorld—A member of the Six Flags Family, Located in
Houston, next to the AstroDome. Family theme park with 75 acres. Openings
for college students, teachers, high school students and local applicants from
the last week in May through Labor Day. Needs 1,900 ride operators, food
service personnel, merchandising personnel, parking lot attendants, game
operators, groundskeepers, security officers, $160/week. "AstroWorld has
made arrangements with a large apartment complex near the park to provide a
3-month lease to AstroWorld employees." Send for application. Apply by
August 15 to Mike Glennan, Personnel Manager, 9001 Kirby Dr., Houston TX
77054; tel. 713/748-1234.
Fringe Benefits: "We also have a large special events program which
includes such activities as softball and volleyball leagues, trips to Six Flags
parks, movie nights, and host and hostess parties." **College credit** possible.

Six Flags Over Texas, Located in Arlington. Amusement park.
Openings for 2,400 persons from the last week in May through Labor Day, six
days per week. Needs ride operators, food service, gifts and souvenirs, parking
lot attendants, game operators, groundskeepers, security officers. Salaries are
$1,900/season. Apartments and school dormitories available in the area. Apply
to Six Flags Over Texas, Dept. SED, Box 191, Arlington TX 76010.

Resorts, Ranches, Restaurants, Lodging

Mayan Dude Ranch, Located in Bandera. Needs housekeepers,
assistant cooks, dining room waiters/waitresses, bartenders, lifeguards, office
staff. Must be 18 years of age and have exceptional musical talent (particularly
looking for piano and voice). Salary is $300/month. Room and board provided.
Employment as soon as possible until end of August or Labor Day. "Employees
must be musically talented as we have several shows during the week at which
they must entertain. Must also give work references in their application—not
personal." Apply by January to Judy Hicks, Manager, Mayan Dude Ranch, Box
577, Dept. SED, Bandera TX 78003; tel. 512/796-3312.
Fringe Benefits: "Bonus of at least $1,000 if employee works entire season;
guests from all over the world; wonderful learning experience; outdoor western
atmosphere; general all-around good working conditions."

Summer Camps

Cullen, Located in Trinity. YMCA of Greater Houston Area; resident
camp for children ages 9-14. Openings for college students, teachers and
foreign students from: summer, approximately May 20 to August 20; fall-spring,
approximately September 18 to May 19. Needs 25 summer-cabin counselors,
$60-90/week; 8 summer-activities assistants, $30-50/week; 4 summer-program
area coordinators, $80-100/week; 20 fall-spring cabin and activity counselors
for school outdoor education program, $100-125/week. Room and board
provided. "Apply in February (deadline is May 1). Send complete resume with
references. Make attempt for a personal visit. Obtain various certifications in off-
season, i.e. WSI, canoeing instructor, etc." Apply to Thomas P. O'Connor,
Director, YMCA Camp Cullen, Rt. 2, Box 135-D, Trinity TX 75862; tel.

713/659-2733 or 594-2274.
Fringe Benefits: Red Cross certification in first aid and advanced lifesaving offered. "Christian emphasis." **College credit** available.

Heart 'o the Hills Camp for Girls, Located in Hunt, on

Guadalupe River in Texas hill country. Private camp for girls ages 6-16. Openings for teachers and college students from June 1 to August 15. Needs counselors and instructors in swimming, field sports, canoeing, camp crafts, tennis, golf, archery, riflery, horseback riding, dance, drama, choir, arts, gymnastics, trampoline and photography. Also needs secretarial and kitchen help. Base pay is $500/summer for beginning staff. "Please write for application form and have references available. Counselors must find joy in working with children and teens." Apply to Mr. or Mrs. Whayne Moore, Owners/Directors, Dept. SED, Heart 'o the Hills, Hunt TX 78024; tel. 512/238-4650.

Manison, Located at Friendswood in Galveston County, 5 miles from

NASA between Houston and Galveston. Private coed camp for ages 6-16. Openings for college students, teachers and foreign students year-round— minimum of 1 month to a maximum of 12 months. Needs 30 general counselors, $200-260/month; 10 specialty counselors for waterfront (WSI), wrangler (Western), arts and crafts, tennis, golf, tumbling-gymnastics, archery, riflery, campcraft, nature, $240-300/month. Room and board provided. Apply to Camp Manison, Box 148, Dept. SED, Friendswood TX 77546.
Fringe Benefits: Laundry, uniforms, insurance, staff lounge. **College credit** possible.

Permian Basin Girl Scout Camps, Located in Alpine and

Bakersfield. Openings for college students, teachers, high school graduating seniors and foreign students from early June to mid-August. Needs 20 general counselors, 4 waterfront staff, 4 riding staff, business manager, 7 kitchen personnel, 2 nurses, 2 seasonal directors. Apply to Permian Basin Girl Scout Camps, Box 1046, Odessa TX 79760.

Stewart for Boys, Located in Hunt, in the hill country. Private camp

for children ages 6-16. Openings for 75 college students and teachers from May 28 to August 16. Needs general counselors with skills in Western horsemanship, waterfront (swimming, diving, sailing, skiing, canoeing), music, arts and crafts, drama, ecology, Indian lore, all land sports, archery, hunting and target shooting, riflery (NRA), tennis, photography, sketching; nurses; cook. Employs 2 counselors per cabin of 16 boys. Salaries are $400-1,000/season. "Room and board provided." Apply by April 30 to Mrs. Silas B. Ragsdale, Jr., Camp Stewart for Boys, Hunt TX 78024.
Fringe Benefits: "Most of the campers and staff are really impressed with the quality and quantity of our excellent food—we are proud of it. The associations and friendships are so valuable: during a typical summer we have campers and staff from about 28 states and 14-18 foreign countries. The working conditions are pleasant—the Texas hill country is beautiful and the Guadalupe River is great for all water activities." **College credit** available; "we work with Austin College in Sherman, Texas and would be happy to work with others."

Tejas Girl Scout Council Inc., Located near Dallas. Camp for girls ages 6-17. Openings from June 1 to August 12. Needs 2 assistant camp directors (college students or teachers preferred); 2 business managers and 2 program specialists (college students or teachers preferred); 2 health supervisors (first aider or nurse preferred); 2 waterfront directors (college students or teachers preferred); 6 waterfront instructors and 6 unit leaders (college students, teachers or high school seniors preferred); 4 wranglers (college students, teachers or high school seniors preferred); and 22 assistant unit leaders (college students, teachers or high school seniors preferred). Room and board provided. "Apply early, February on" (May 1 deadline) to Scottie Hubbard, Director of Camping Services, Dept. SED, 4411 Skillman, Box 64815, Dallas TX 75206; tel. 214/823-1342.
Fringe Benefits: "Time off and weekends to spend time in Dallas and nearby cities." **College credit** possible.

Wood Lake, Located on Lake Brownwood. Girl Scout camp for girls ages 6-17. Openings from June 1 to July 24. Needs 4 unit leaders ($65-125/week), 12 unit counselors ($50-75/week), 1 waterfront director ($65-125/week), 2 waterfront assistants ($50-75/week), college students, teachers, foreign students all acceptable; 1 CIT ($65-125/week), college student or teacher preferred; 1 business manager ($75-100/week), college student or teacher preferred. "Indicate current Red Cross certifications (WSI, etc.) and other pertinent training, age, background, and experience." Room and board provided. Apply by March 15 to Zola Moon, Camp Director, Heart of Texas Girl Scout Council, 700 E. Baker, Brownwood TX 76801; tel. 915/646-1516.

Utah

990 jobs available

Commercial Attractions

Lagoon Amusement Park, Lagoon Corporation, Located at 375 N. Highway 91, Farmington. Amusement park. Needs 250 food department workers, $3.10/hour base; 500 ride attendants, $3.10/hour base; and 250 game operators, hourly base plus commission; approximately 150 miscellaneous positions. Higher rates for managerial personnel and for those with special talents. Work from June 1 to Labor Day daily, weekends in April, May, September and October. Apply in February or March to John Freed, Personnel, Lagoon Corporation, Box N, Farmington UT 84025; tel. 801/292-0466.

Resorts, Ranches, Restaurants, Lodging

Flaming Gorge Lodge, Located in Dutch John. Resort. Openings for college students from April 1 to October 31. Needs waitresses, $3.35/hour; 4 store clerks, $3.20/hour; chambermaids, $3.50/hour. Rooms available for

$20/month. Apply by May 1 to Craig W. Collett, Flaming Gorge Lodge, Dutch John UT 84023.

Summer Camps

Utah Girl Scout Council Camps, Openings in 2 camps for 50 college students and teachers from June 1 to August 25, depending on camp. Needs specialty counselors for riding, swimming (WSI), smallcraft, handcrafts, gymnastics; instructors; consultants; unit leaders; assistant unit leaders; health supervisors; maintenance persons; cooks. Salaries are $450-1,200. Room and board provided. Apply by April 15 to Camp Employer, Dept. CLC, Utah Girl Scout Council Camps, 2386 East 2760 South, Salt Lake City UT 84109.

Vermont

458+ jobs available

Resorts, Ranches, Restaurants, Lodging

North Hero House, Located on North Hero Island in Lake Champlain. Country inn, resort. Openings for college students from June 19 to the day after Labor Day. Needs chambermaids, waitresses, combination dock attendant-dishwashers (alternating days), assistant front desk manager, assistant cooks. Salaries are $800/season. Room and board provided. US residents only. Apply to North Hero House, Champlain Islands, North Hero VT 05474.
Fringe Benefits: "Good working conditions—beautiful, completely restored island inn on Lake Champlain; excellent food; full use of facilities (boats, sauna, swimming, tennis, etc.); veterans (returning staff members) receive salary increase." **College credit** possible.

Summer Camps

Abnaki, Located in North Hero on Lake Champlain. Vermont State YMCA resident camp for children, ages 7-15. Openings from June 19 to August 21. Needs 5 male senior counselors ($450 and up/season), 1 male hike master ($600/season), college students, teachers, foreign students all acceptable; 1 male village leader ($600/season), college student or teacher preferred; 1 male or female waterfront director ($850 and up/season), teacher or high school graduate preferred. Room and board provided. Apply by April 1 to Norman F. van Gulden, Director, Camp Abnaki, Box 806, Burlington VT 05402; tel. 802/862-8981.

Aloha Camps, Located in Fairlee. Camp for boys and girls ages 8-17. International, intercultural. Openings for college and foreign students, teachers and local applicants from June 24 to August 20. Needs 150 general counselors in one of several departments. Teaching ability required, experience not necessary. "We are looking for good role models for young people. A love of

children and the out-of-doors is paramount." Pay varies, up to $800/season. Room and board provided. Hires physically handicapped. Send for application. Apply by May 10 to Paul S. Pilcher, Managing Director, Aloha Foundation, Fairlee VT 05045.
Fringe Benefits: Free laundry. "A near 2-1 ratio permits real individual teaching and learning." **College credit** possible.

Dunmore, Located in Salisbury, Vermont. "Camp Dunmore for Girls and Camp Dunmore for Boys are private brother-sister camps on adjoining acreage." Openings for college students and teachers from June 24 to August 24. Needs specialty counselors (minimum age 20) for athletics, tennis, arts and crafts, drama, dance, music (pianist), pioneering, hiking, water skiing, tripping, nature, gymnastics, swimming (WSI) ($450-650), canoeing, sailing, nurse (RN). Room and board provided. "Most positions include cabin responsibility. All counselors are hired for the full eight-week camp season plus several days pre-camp for orientation. We welcome applicants from widespread areas. Salaries are based on age, education, experience and position applied for." Apply to Mrs. George Ross, Camp Dunmore, 400 E. 85th St., New York NY 10028; tel. 212/861-2120.
Fringe Benefits: "Day off weekly except first and last weeks; opportunities for trips, special projects, etc.; social hall open nightly for staffs of both camps; planned staff get-togethers." **College credit** possible.

Farm & Wilderness Camps, Located in Plymouth. Non-traditional camp, 5 sections: 2 for boys (9-14, 11-15), 1 for girls (9-14) and 2 coed (10-12, 15-17). Two areas in Green Mountains. Hiking, swimming, farming; non-competitive; community oriented and Quaker leadership. Openings for college and foreign students and teachers from June 19 to August 25. Needs 10 WSIs for waterfront, $600-900/season; 100 cabin counselors for farming, carpentry, crafts, music, dance, pottery, weaving, backpacking, campcraft, small farm animal care, canoeing, new games, storytelling, (ability to work with children, experience), $500-700/season, 10 cooks (emphasis natural foods and in-camp baking, with crops from camp gardens), $1,000-1,500/season. Room and board provided. Hires physically handicapped. Send resume and request application by June 1 to Ridge Satterthwaite, Farm & Wilderness, Plymouth VT 05056.
Fringe Benefits: "Being part of a dynamic group of people in a long-standing child/adult community." **College credit** possible.

Farnsworth, Located in Thetford, Vermont. Girl Scout camp for girls ages 6-17. Openings for college students, teachers and high school graduates from mid-June to August. Needs unit leaders; unit assistants; waterfront staff; specialists in arts and crafts, riding, canoeing, backpacking, sports, bicycling; cooks; nurse. "Experience with children in groups is a prerequisite." Salaries are $750-900 for unit leaders, $475-600 for unit assistants. Room and board provided. Apply to Nancy Frankel, Swift Water Girl Scout Council, Dept. SED, Box E, 325 Merrill St., Manchester NH 03103.
Fringe Benefits: College credit possible.

Keewaydin Camps, Located on Lake Dunmore, Salisbury, Vermont.

Private camp for boys. Openings for college students and teachers from June 20 to August 25. Needs 5 general counselors; specialty counselors: 2 boxing, 2 sailing, 2 wrestling, 3 nature/ecology, $325-650; tennis coach, $400-700. Room and board provided. Apply by March 1 to A.G. Hare, Jr., 113 Anton Rd., Dept. SED, Box N, Wynnewood PA 19096.

Fringe Benefits: "This camp offers an excellent opportunity for teachers and would-be teachers to gain experience in working with children. There are also overnight canoeing and hiking trips, as well as recreation experience."

Lochearn, Located at Lake Fairlee, Ely. Girls camp for ages 6-15. Openings for college students and teachers from June 22 to August 23. Needs riding director, $1,000-1,200/season; nurse, $900-1,000/season; cook, $1,500-2,000/season; assistant cook, $1,000-1,500/season; riding instructors, $500-700/season; trip director, $500-600/season; kitchen/maintenance workers, $450-600/season; instructors: scuba, swimming, diving, water skiing, gymnastics, sailing, ceramics, trampoline, archery, drama, tennis, arts and crafts, $450-600/season; bookkeeper, secretary, $500-750/season. Room and board provided. Apply to Peter and Mary Shays, Lochearn, Ely VT 05044.

Fringe Benefits: "Caliber of staff; general atmosphere; outdoor-recreational setting." **College credit** possible.

Marycrest, Located in Grand Isle. Camp for girls ages 6-16. Openings for college students and teachers from late June to late August. Needs specialty counselors for tennis, golf, sports, arts and crafts, archery, drama, dancing, waterfront (sailing, canoeing, swimming), $475 and up. Room and board provided. Apply by April 30 to Sr. Virginia Cain, 100 Mansfield Ave., Burlington VT 05401.

Passumpsic, Located in Ely, Vermont. Private camp for boys ages 6-15. Openings for college undergraduates, graduate students and teachers of all faiths, races and nationalities (minimum age 18) from mid-June through the end of August. Needs chef, chef's helper, head counselor, unit leaders; directors: CIT, program, waterfront, land sports; trip leader and trip counselors; specialty counselors for riflery, archery, tennis, soccer, baseball, basketball, street hockey, swimming (WSI preferred), waterskiing, sailing, free diving, boating, canoeing, music, photography, dramatics, arts and crafts, nature, campcraft, fishing, fly tying; kitchen workers, maintenance workers. "Room and board is part of our contracts; additional FICA tax must be deducted from paychecks according to Vermont state valuation of room and board." Apply by June 1 (prefers applications by February 1) to Mr. and Mrs. Jan Kater, Dept. SED, Camp Sunapee Rd., New London NH 03257.

Fringe Benefits: College credit available. "Coop work credit offered on supervised basis."

Thorpe, Located at Brandon. Camp for physically handicapped children (ages 6-14) and mentally retarded adults. Openings for college students and teachers from mid-June to mid-August. Needs 12 general counselors, $500 and up; 12 specialty counselors, $600 and up; nurse (RN or LPN), $100/week. Room and board provided. Apply by February 1 (but will consider later

applicants) to Mrs. Benjamin W. Heath, Director, Dept. SED, RFD 3, Brandon
VT·05733.
Fringe Benefits: Laundry facilities provided. **College credit** possible.
"This camp provides a learning situation for recreation, special education,
recreation therapy and physical therapy majors."

Wapanacki, Located in Hardwick. Summer camp for visually
handicapped youth ages 7-21, "primarily from New York Metropolitan area but
also from many states of the eastern USA; campers are mobile, communicative,
some totally blind, some partially sighted, and some with additional handicaps
such as mental retardation, learning difficulties or mild physical handicaps."
Openings for college students, teachers and high school students from late
June to late August. Needs counselors and activity leaders, $300 and up/
season; RN, salary dependent upon experience. Room and board provided.
"An active program of outdoor recreational activities including swimming,
boating, athletics, nature and trips such as 3-day mountain trail hikes, lake
canoe trips and local overnights. Staff is expected to assist campers with
activities of daily living as well as with recreational activities. They should expect
to spend their time and attention with all aspects of a camper's life at Camp
Wapanacki—recreational, emotional and social. There is only a minimum of
staff free time. We are looking for staff who are experienced or seeking
experience with the recreational and living needs of handicapped youth. Send
resume or application request between January and April to Joe V. Ingram,
Camp Director, Camp Wapanacki, Dept. SED, Hardwick VT 05843; tel.
802/472-6612 (9 a.m. to 12 noon).

Virginia

2,283+ jobs available

Commercial Attractions

The Old Country/Busch Gardens, Located in Williamsburg.
European theme park. Total seasonal staff is approximately 2,000 employees.
Applicants must be at least 16 years-old to be considered for employment. The
park is open seven days a week from the middle of May through Labor Day
and weekends in the spring and fall. Needs ride operators, food and beverage
cashier/servers, attendants, parking lot attendants, security personnel, zoo
attendants, ticket takers, and cash control tellers. Base rate of pay minimum
wage with higher rates for certain areas. Applications must be made in person
at the Personnel Office located five miles east of Williamsburg, Virginia on Rt.
60 East. Will begin accepting applications in January for seasonal employment.
Our office hours are 9 a.m. to 4 p.m., Monday through Saturday. Affirmative
Action, Equal Opportunity employer. Send inquiries for additional information
to Personnel Office, Busch Gardens, Drawer FC, Williamsburg VA 23185; tel.
804/253-3020.
Fringe Benefits: Located near colonial Williamsburg, employee activities
(dances, movies, sports, etc.), variety of positions available; and opportunity to

work with and meet over 2,000 employees. **College credit** possible.

Resorts, Ranches, Restaurants, Lodging

Mountain Lake Hotel, Located at Mountain Lake. Resort. Openings
for college students, college graduates and teachers from June 1 to September
30. Needs 4 front office helpers, 7 waiters, night auditor, hostess, 3 hall boys, 7
maids, 2 bellmen, dock attendant, yard attendant, horse handler, 2 cooks, 8
kitchen helpers. Salary information upon application. Room and board
provided. Apply by July 1 to Dept. SED, Mountain Lake Hotel, Mountain Lake
VA 24136.
Fringe Benefits: College credit possible.

Summer Camps

Easter Seal, Located in New Castle. Camp for handicapped people,
ages 8 and up. Openings for college students, teachers and foreign students
from early June to mid-August. Needs 35 counselors, 12 program staff and 2
nurses. Apply to Director, Camp Easter Seal, Box 5496, Roanoke VA 24012;
tel. 703/362-1656.

May Flather
Potomac Woods, Located in Virginia. Resident Girl Scout camps.
Openings for 115 females and males, minimum age 18, from mid-June through
mid-August. Needs camp director, assistant director (program), unit managers
and assistants, counselors, waterfront, kitchen and maintenance staff. Salaries
are $350-1,200/season plus meals, lodging, health and accident insurance.
Write to Resident Camping Administrator, Girl Scout Council of the Nation's
Capital, 2233 Wisconsin Ave. NW, Washington DC 20007.

Friendship, Located in Palmyra. Private coed camp for children ages
6-15. Looking for energetic young men and women interested in working with
boys and girls from mid-June to mid- or late August. Needs counselors
(minimum age 18) with skills in teaching, riding, swimming, sports, tennis,
gymnastics and other areas. Also needs kitchen workers, program director and
waterfront director. "Room and board provided. Extra costs include weekly
laundry and linen, staff shirt, providing own transportation for days off. Prefer to
receive applications by January 31, but will accept them later." Apply to
Director, Camp Friendship, Palmyra VA 22963.
Fringe Benefits: "This camp offers the opportunity to work with children in
a lovely, outdoor setting." **College credit** possible.

Hanover, Located in Mechanicsville. Coed church camp for children, ages
9-17. Openings from June 10 to August 22 for male and female college
students completing sophomore year (minimum age 19), college graduates and
teachers. Needs 3 lifeguard-waterfront (ARC-WSI), smallcraft (ARC); 30 general
counselors who lead varied trip and resident program. Room and board
provided. Apply by April 1 to John E. Ensign, Director, Dept. SED, 1205
Palmyra Ave., Richmond VA 23227.

Fringe Benefits: "We furnish health-accident insurance, laundry and all snacks, as well as a travel allowance from school, and the opportunity to work with other outstanding college students from the US and 6-8 foreign countries." **College credit** available.

Happyland, Located in Virginia, 75 miles south of Washington, DC. Coed resident camp for children, ages 7-17; coed day camp for senior citizens. Openings for college students from June to August. Needs counselors, lifeguards, craft instructor, nurse. Room and board provided. Apply by March to The Salvation Army—D.Y.S., Dept. SED, 503 E St. N.W., Washington DC 20001.
Fringe Benefits: "Religious atmosphere." **College credit** possible.

Holiday Trails, Located in Charlottesville. Residential camp for children and youth with medical and health impairments, such as diabetes, cystic fibrosis, hearing and speech impairment, hemophilia, cancer. Openings for college-aged and older persons from mid-June to mid-August. Needs counselors, $500-800; directors of waterfront (WSI), arts and crafts, nature, athletics, pool (WSI), nutrition and teenage program. Also needs physical therapist's aides. Personal interviews preferred. Apply early to Camp Holiday Trails, Box 5806, Charlottesville VA 22903.

Mawavi, Located at Prince William Forest Park, Triangle, Virginia. Resident camp for boys ages 6-12, and girls ages 6-18. ACA accredited. Openings for college students, teachers and others from mid-June to late August. Needs cabin counselors and waterfront assistants (minimum age 19), starting salary, $400; waterfront director (minimum age 21, Red Cross WSI), $500-700; unit directors (minimum age 21), $500-600; nurse (LPN or RN), $600-750; driver/maintenance chief (minimum age 21), $600-700; maintenance/kitchen helpers (minimum age 16), starting salary, $350. Room and board provided. Apply to Bryna Selig, Camp Director, Camp Fire-Potomac Area Council, Dept. SED, 1761 R St. NW, Washington DC 20009.
Fringe Benefits: "Coed staff. Opportunity to work with both inner city and suburban children, affluent and poor. If the camp is adequately funded, there will be retarded campers included in one session—a good learning experience for special education majors." **College credit** possible.

Pleasant
Goodwill
Moss Hollow, Located in Virginia. Agency camp for children ages 8-15. Openings for college students and teachers from June 16 to August 30. Needs 4 waterfront directors, $130/week; 12 specialists, $70-100/week; counselors, $65/week; 4 drivers, $100/week; 4 nurses (RN), $150/week; 4 cooks, $130/week. Apply by the end of April to Camps Pleasant, Goodwill, Moss Hollow, Dept. SED, 929 L St. NW, Washington DC 20001.

Shenandoah, Located 14 miles from Winchester, Virginia. Residential camp for mentally retarded children and young adults, ages 9 to late 20s. Openings for 43 college and high school students, and teachers from June 14 to August 23. Needs 20 general counselors (teachers and college students), 2 maintenance counselors, $600-800/season; 8 program specialists in swimming (WSI), canoeing, riding, crafts, gymnastics, camping (teachers and college students preferred), $650-900/season; 12 CITs (high school juniors and seniors), room, board and spending money; nurse (RN or LPN), $750-1,200/season. Apply to Staff Office, Rolf H. Mielzarek, Camp Shenandoah, Concord, Yellow Spring WV 26865.

Skimino—Heritage Girl Scout Council of Virginia, Located in Newport News. Camp for girls ages 6-18. Openings for college students and teachers from mid-June to August. Needs waterfront director, minimum age 21 (WSI), $105-125/week; 2 waterfront assistants, minimum age 18 (ALS or WSI), $70-90/week; 3 unit leaders, minimum age 21 (Girl Scout background preferred), $90-110/week; 6 unit assistants, minimum age 18, $55-75/week. Salaries include room and board. "Applicant must enjoy working in the out-of-doors, sleeping in tents and most important, enjoy working with children." Send for application. Apply by April to Nancy Wagner, Supervisor of Camping, Heritage Girl Scout Council of Virginia, 5 Greenwood Rd. VA 23601; tel. 804-595-9802.

Wingaroo, Located in Goochland. Semi-rustic, residential, coed camp for ages 6-16. Openings for college students, teachers, local applicants from mid-June to mid-August, $400-800/season, negotiable. Needs 2 water safety instructors (WSI); 2 riding instructors (well-versed in balanced seat, prefer previous teaching experience, besides teaching must be willing to help in all phases of stable management); arts and crafts instructor (well acquainted with short term handcraft projects and creative use of natural materials); nature and outdoor camping instructor (acquainted with wilderness camping techniques). Room and board provided. Send for application. Apply by March 15 to Jan Wooton, Director, Camp Wingaroo, Rt. 2, Box 196A, Goochland VA 23063. **Fringe Benefits:** "Excellent learning situation for people who want to work with children." **College credit** possible.

Summer Theaters

Mill Mountain Playhouse, Located in Roanoke. Summer stock with plans for fall and winter productions. Openings for college students, teachers and local applicants from June 1 to August 20. Needs 3 technical assistants (advanced or graduate level skills preferred), $100-150/week; 3 costume assistants (basic skills required), $90-125/week; 30 actors, singers and dancers, $100-150/week; scene designer, $150-200/week; technical director (graduate level skills required), $150-175/week. Room provided. "Employees buy their own meals at numerous area restaurants. Absolutely no actors, singers or dancers can be cast without personal audition. Auditions are held in Virginia and New York in March and April." Send resume by March 15 (actors), May 1 (technical personnel), to Jim Ayers, Producer-Director, Dept. SED, Box 505, Roanoke VA 24003; tel. 703/344-2057. **Fringe Benefits: College credit** possible.

Wayside Theatre, Located in Middletown. Summer theater; "an equity theater, providing the Shenandoah Valley with live, professional performances." Openings from June to September. Needs technical director/ATD (experience required), salary negotiable; properties master/prop staff (some experience required), salary negotiable, costumer/costume staff (experience required), salary negotiable; box office manager/staff (experience required), salary negotiable. Some rooms available in the area. Cost of food and rent are below average. Send resume by April 15 to C. Edward Steele, Managing Director, Wayside Theatre, Middletown VA 22645.
Fringe Benefits: "Wayside Theatre offers the chance to work with prominent directors. It is located in nothern Shenandoah Valley." **College credit** possible.

Washington

312+ jobs available

Business and Industry

Environmental Intern Program/Pacific Northwest,
Located in Seattle. Intern program. Places upper-level undergraduates and graduate students in short-term (3-month) professional positions for career experience. Openings for 120 students all year, but mostly summer. Needs students for over 30 different positions/disciplines used annually: field research and office research positions; 3 years college minimum. Salaries are $140-$250. Would consider hiring physically handicapped students. Send for application. Apply by March 2 to Mr. Bruce Folsom, 731 Securities Bldg., Seattle WA 98101.
Fringe Benefits: "Excellent learning experiences with creative professionals; opportunity to attend workshops and meetings relating to career training." **College credit** possible.

Government

Department of Labor, Jobs available at the regional office, 3144 Federal Office Building, 909 First Ave., Seattle WA 98174. Applications must be made to Washington DC office. See Washington DC office (District of Columbia section) for complete description of jobs available and how to apply information.

National Transportation Safety Board, Jobs available at the regional office in Seattle. Applications must be made to Washington DC office. See Washington DC office (District of Columbia section) for complete description of jobs available and how to apply information.

Resorts, Ranches, Restaurants, Lodging

Kalaloch Lodge, Located on Pacific Ocean in Olympia National Park. Openings from June through September 12. "Must finish the season through September 12." Positions available for reservation and front desks persons, dining room and kitchen, yard and maintenance and housekeeping. Salaries are $3.10/hour starting and up, according to job, experience and performance. "We are building some employee housing at the Lodge." Apply to Kalaloch Lodge, Attention: Manager, Star Rt. 1, Box 1100, Forks WA 98331; tel. 206/962-2271 or 962-3411.

Summer Camps

Four Winds * Westward Ho, Located on Orcas Island of the San Juan Island group. Openings for college students and teachers from mid-June to late August. Needs 16 group counselor/activity leaders, $200-300/month; 2 head counselors, $400-600/month; 2 sailing trip leaders, $300-400/month; canoe program leader, $350-450/month; and 3 activity specialists, $300-350/month. Apply by February 1 to Michael Douglas, Director, Dept. SED, Four Winds * Westward Ho, Box B, Deer Harbor WA 98243; tel. 206/376-2277.

Hidden Valley, Located at Granite Falls, in the Cascade Mountain Foothills. Coed camp for ages 8-16, serving the Puget Sound area, British Columbia and Alaska. Openings for college students, teachers and foreign students from June 21 to September 4. Needs group counselors; pool counselors (WSI); sailing (WSI); canoeing (WSI); dramatics; arts and crafts; tripping and driver/maintenance worker. Salaries are $50 and up/week. Room and board provided. Apply to Bob McKinlay, Dept. SED, Hidden Valley Camp, 8053-132 Ave. NE, Kirkland WA 98033; tel. 206/883-0449.

Institut Francile, Located in Eastsound, Washington. Camp for French language instruction, for children ages 10-15. Openings from mid-June through August. Needs 10 counselors, minimum age 18, 2 years college French, sports or arts skills, college students, foreign students, teachers preferred, $85-100/week; director of French, minimum age 21, teaching skills and experience, teacher or foreign student preferred, salary open; counselor-in-leadership training director, minimum age 21, speak French, counselor experience, $90-100/week; waterfront director, minimum age 21, WSI, French speaking helpful, $90-100/week. Room and board provided. Send resume or request application. Apply by May to M. J. Wintersteen, Camp Director, 7030 Mill Court SE, Olympia WA 98503.
Fringe Benefits: "This camp offers a good chance to practice French with fluent speakers. Living quarters are teepees on platforms with carpet and electricity; heated swimming pool; sailing on open water." **College credit** possible.

Nor'wester, Located on Lopez Island. Coed camp for boys and girls ages 9-16. Openings for college students and teachers from June 23 to August

23. Needs 12 assistant unit leaders, $70/week; 12 unit leaders, $85/week; activity directors: riding, arts and crafts, canoeing, sailing, swimming, mountaineering, riflery, archery, $70-85/week; 5 dishwashers, 3 pantry girls, $60/week; 2 cooks, kitchen manager, $100-120/week; nurse (RN), $100-130/week. Apply by March 30 to David A. Formo, 11201 SE 8th, Bellevue WA 98004..

Pacific Peaks Girl Scout Council, Located in Olympia. Camp for girls ages 6-17. Openings for 60 college students, teachers, high school seniors and foreign students, minimum age 18, from mid-June to mid-August. Needs unit leaders, unit counselors, program specialists, backpacking and canoe trip leaders, riding directors, wranglers, horseback counselors, waterfront directors, waterfront assistants, assistant camp directors, business managers, head cooks, assistant cooks, food packers, nurses. Salaries are $375-1,600. EOE. Apply by March or April to Karen J. Stay, Camping Administrator, Dept. SED, Pacific Peaks Girl Scout Council, 5911 Orchard St. W., Tacoma WA 98467.

Sealth, Located at Vashon Island. Camp Fire camp for grades 2-12. Openings for college students, teachers and foreign students from mid-June through late August. Needs unit counselors, program counselors, unit leaders, waterfront staff (WSI), office staff, cooks and assistants, assistant camp directors, nurses (RN). Salaries are $350-1,100/season plus room and board. Apply to Camp Sealth Director, 8511 15th Ave. NE, Seattle WA 98115.

Totem Girl Scout Council Camps, Located in northwest Washington. Resident camps for girls 7-17, with programs in boating, swimming, aquatics, marine biology, counselor-in-training, canoeing, sailing, cycling, backpacking, horseback trips. Recruiting for resident camps: River Ranch at Carnation, Robbinswold at Lilliwaup, Lyle McLeod at Belfair. Openings from mid-June to mid-August. Needs 2 camp directors, 2 assistant camp directors, 3 health supervisors, 2 trip coordinators, program specialist, naturalist, 13 unit leaders, 28 unit counselors, counselor-in-training director, assistant counselor-in-training director, 3 waterfront coordinators, 6 waterfront assistants, riding director, 2 riding assistants, 3 head cooks, 4 assistant cooks. Salaries depend on previous experience and training. Room and board provided. Send for application to Totem Girl Scout Council, Dept. SED, Judy L. Bittenbender, 3611 Woodland Park Avenue North, Seattle WA 98103.
Fringe Benefits: "Will cooperate in **college credit** arrangements."

Camp Volasuca, Located in Sultan. Coed Christian camp for ages 8 and up, normal children and adults, from moderate to low-income families, mentally retarded and physically handicapped. Openings for college students, teachers, high school seniors and foreign students, from mid-June to the end of August. Special education background is helpful. Needs 8 counselors; 1 craftsperson; 2 WSI; nurse (RN or LPN), negotiable; cook. Salary range from $425-$1,500. Room and board provided. Write before May 31, or as early as February. Send resume or letter of introduction to Major Gilbert A. Saparto, Dept. SED, The Volunteers of America, 2801 Lombard Ave., Everett WA 98201; tel. 206/259-3191.

Fringe Benefits: "This camp offers a good opportunity to receive on-the-job training in the fields of social work and special education. It is located in a scenic mountain area and staff has 3-day breaks between camping sessions to visit scenic areas. Staff members have the chance to socialize with professionals." **College credit** possible.

Zanika-Lache, Located at Lake Wenatchee. Camp Fire Girls camp. Openings for college students and teachers from mid-June to mid-August. Needs cabin counselors, unit coordinators, archery supervisor, CIT director, smallcraft (WSI), swimming (WSI), cook, assistant cook, business manager, maintenance, nurse, assistant director, food pack-out. Salaries are $500-1,000. Room and board provided. Apply by May 15 to Rhonda Hutton, North Central Washington Council of Camp Fire Girls, Box 1734, Wenatchee WA 98801.
Fringe Benefits: "Camp Zanika Lache is located on Lake Wenatchee, a lake situated between Glacier Peak and Alpine Lakes Wilderness areas. There are plenty of opportunities for backpacking, river rafting, canoeing, sailing, etc." **College credit** possible.

West Virginia

124 jobs available

Summer Camps

Bronco Junction, Located in Red House. 176-acre coed summer camp for children with bronchial asthma. Openings for 50 persons from June 7 to August 11. Employs area directors and counselors (minimum age 18 or 1 year college) in waterfront (must be WSI, minimum age for director is 21), nature, sports, gymnastics, arts and crafts, campcraft, music, dance, and drama. Also hires medical student and student nurse counselors, registered nurses, dietician, kitchen helpers, grounds/maintenance personnel. Salary is negotiable. Room and board provided. Write to Bronco Junction, 506 Medical Arts Building, Charleston WV 25301; tel. 304/343-5427.
Fringe Benefits: "Excellent work and learning opportunity for those in recreation, health, or education-related fields." **College credit** available.

Emma Kaufmann, Located 8 miles north of Morgantown, West Virginia. Jewish Community Center; coed camp for children, ages 9-16. Openings from June 20 to August 27. Needs 40 counselors, 20 specialists, $300-600/season; 6 unit heads, $800-1,000/season; 6 head specialists, $700-1,000/season. Apply to Bill Laden, Camp Emma Kaufmann, 315 S. Bellefield, Pittsburgh PA 15213.

Rim Rock, Located in Yellow Spring, West Virginia. Resident camp for girls, ages 7-15. Openings for college students from mid-June to late August. Needs 7 swimming instructors (WSI), 5 riding instructors, 12 unit counselors, 1 archery instructor, 2 crafts instructors, 2 tennis instructors, 2 canoeing instructors, 1 campcraft instructor. Salaries are $500-800. Room and board provided. Apply by May 15 to James L. Matheson, Director, Box 882, Winchester VA 22601; tel. 703/662-4650.

Wisconsin

3,169+ jobs available

Resorts, Ranches, Restaurants, Lodging

Boyd's Mason Lake Resort, Located in Fifield. Family-oriented summer resort. Openings for quality high school seniors and college students able to work from late May to October 20. Needs 5 laundress-cabin maids, 7 waitresses, 3 dishwashers, 2 outside maintenance people, boat dock attendant and a night watchman. From June 1 to September 1 needs a qualified horse wrangler. Salary plus room and board with 2 days off per week for waitresses, dishwashers, and laundress-cabin maids. Off-duty activities include swimming, boating and horseback riding. Room and board provided. For an application and personal response to your questions, please send a SASE after January 1 to Dick Simon, Boyd's Mason Lake Resort, Dept. SED, Fifield WI 54524.
Fringe Benefits: "Boyd's offers good, clean working conditions and 2 days off per week, which give employees a significant amount of time to themselves. Gratuities are shared among employees (we include a 12% service charge on each guest's bill)."

Chanticleer Inn, Located in Eagle River. Resort, motel, condominiums. Openings from June 15 through Labor Day, longer if possible. Needs 10 waitresses, salary plus tips, less room and board; 3 bartenders; 4 yardmen/ waterfront men; 10 chambermaids; 4 kitchen helpers; 2 cooks, salary but must find own room and board. Apply to Jack Alward, Chanticleer Inn, Dept. SED, RFD 3, Eagle River WI 54521.
Fringe Benefits: "Employees may use the resort's facilities when not in use by our guests. They live in and can truly enjoy the great Northwood of Wisconsin. This resort offers excellent experience and the opportunity to meet a wide variety of people." **College credit** possible.

Deer Park Lodge, Located in Manitowish Waters. Summer resort. Openings for college students, teachers and high school seniors (minimum age 18) from the first week in June to Labor Day. Needs 14 waiter/bus boys, 14 chambermaid/laundry personnel, 2 desk clerk/receptionists, 2 playschool teachers, lifeguard/pool attendant, boat dock attendant, 2 stable attendants, waterskiing instructor/driver, cocktail waitress, 5 dishwasher/kitchen helpers, 4-piece dance band. Salaries are $1,500-3,500/season; dance band, salary open. Room and board provided at nominal charge. Apply to Deer Park Lodge, Dept. SED, Manitowish Waters WI 54545.
Fringe Benefits: End-of-the-season bonuses. **College credit** possible. "Employees may use pool, tennis and shuffleboard, and they may attend evening entertainment."

Eagle Knob Lodge, Located in Cable. Resort. Openings for college students, teachers and high school seniors from early May through October 4. Needs waitresses, kitchen help, general workmen, dishwasher, maids. Salaries are $650/month. Room and board provided. Enclose SASE. Letter of application should include references, former employers, earliest starting and terminating dates. Apply by March 1 to Bob Rockstad, Eagle Knob Lodge, Dept. SED, Lake Owen, Cable WI 54821.

Eagle Waters Resort, Located in Eagle River, Wisconsin. Openings for college students, teachers, high school seniors and foreign students with proper visas from mid-May to mid-September, minimum age 18. Needs waitresses, waiters, bus boys, cabin maids, laundry assistants, boat and dock attendants, yard workers, bartenders, student cooks, kitchen workers, play-school teacher, pool attendant, office assistants, cocktail waitress, bellhops. Earn from $1,000-2,000 or more, depending on position. Room and board provided. Also needs social director and/or entertainment group. Salaries are open. Room and board provided; housing is 2 to a room. State available working dates in application. Include SASE. Apply before May 1 to Eagle Waters Resort, Room 100 N.D., 6536 N. Maplewood Ave., Chicago IL 60645.
Fringe Benefits: End-of-the-season bonus. "Staff has its own recreation hall and dining room, as well as use of tennis courts, beach and other recreational facilities." **College credit** available.

Hazen's Long Lake Lodge, Inc., Located in Phelps. Resort. Openings for college students, teachers and high school seniors from early June to Labor Day. Needs waitresses-cabin maids,$60/week; dishwashers, laundress, chore boy/girl, kitchen helper, pastry cook. Room and board provided. Apply by May 15 to N.H. Meyer, Manager, Hazen's Long Lake Lodge, Inc., Dept. SED, Phelps WI 54554.

Lake Lawn Lodge, Located in Delavan, 11 miles from Lake Geneva. Resort. Openings from May to end of September. Needs help for food service, recreation, pool/health club; maids, lifeguards, general maintenance, front desk clerk, bartenders, cocktail waitresses. Hourly wages. Housing not available at resort. Apply to Personnel Department, Box SED, Lake Lawn Lodge, Delavan WI 53115.

Little Swiss Village, Located in Minocqua. Resort, restaurant and gift shops. Openings for college students, teachers and high school seniors from May through September. Needs waitresses, shop people, hostess, cabin help, dishwasher, pantry help, student cook, cook's helper. "Housing is available at $14.50 per week." Send references and give earliest starting and latest departure dates. Apply by April to Harold Hines, Little Swiss Village, RFD 2, Dept. SED, Minocqua WI 54548.
Fringe Benefits: "We have very good working conditions. Our crew has 1 or 2 days off per week and is off daily at 4 p.m. Our business hours (8-3) give employees afternoons and evenings free to enjoy!" **College credit** possible.

Schwartz Resort Hotel, Located at Elkhart Lake. Openings for college students, teachers and high school seniors from approximately May 28 to September 15. Needs 25 waitresses, 8 bus boys, 8 cooks, 8 bellhops, 4 beach guards and 4 pool guards (LSC required), 3 bartenders, 2 yardmen-maintenance, 3 secretaries (shorthand required), 3 desk clerks (typing required), 2 desk clerks with bookkeeping experience, 20 maids, 8 general counselors (specialties helpful), head counselor for day camp program for guests' children; 2 social directors for adults to organize tournaments, games, and other activities (guitar or other talent helpful); 2 social directors to organize and plan activities for teens and tweens. Room, board and tips provided. Apply to Ralph Lawrence, Manager, Schwartz Resort Hotel, Dept. SED, Elkhart Lake WI 53020. **Fringe Benefits: College credit** possible.

Summer Camps

Agawak, Located in Minocqua. Private girls camp, ages 8-16. Openings for 30 college students, teachers and foreign students from June 14 to August 15. Needs specialty counselors for diving, life saving, sailing, small craft, water ballet, waterskiing, swimming (all with WSI); archery, arts and crafts, campcraft, dance, dramatics, golf, riflery, trampoline, tennis, fencing, baton, gymnastics, riding. Also needs tripping director, doctor, nurse, secretary, cook, second cook, baker, kitchen workers, assistant caretaker. Salaries are $500 and up. Room and board provided. Apply by early spring to Oscar Siegel, Dept. SED, 6704 N. Talman, Chicago IL 60645; tel. 312/761-1838.
Fringe Benefits: Transportation allowance, free laundry service and a profit sharing plan are provided. "There is the opportunity to work hard, learn, grow and mature!" **College credit** possible.

Algonquin, Located in Rhinelander. Recreational, educational reading clinic for ages 7-17. Openings for college students and teachers from June 28 to August 15. Needs for camp recreation program: 15 male cabin counselors, $500-800/season; 2 cooks, $1,000/season. Room and board provided. Apply by May 30 to James G. Doran, Camp Algonquin, Dept. SED, Route 3, Rhinelander WI 54501; tel. 715/369-1277.
Fringe Benefits: "Algonquin offers good working conditions with dynamic, fun-type people; swimming; sailing; canoeing; tennis—all kinds of sports; a very positive atmosphere." **College credit** available.

American Camping Association/Illinois Section, Located in Illinois and surrounding states including Wisconsin, Indiana, Michigan and Minnesota. The American Camping Association/Illinois Section is an association of persons involved with camps operated by social agencies and private camp owners. More than 100 camps in Association. Openings for college students, teachers, foreign students and local applicants from late June to late August. Needs persons over 18 years of age who possess a variety of camp leadership skills for positions such as counselors, cooks, waterfront staff, camping and athletic skills teachers, nurses and program directors. Salaries are $500-1,000 for eight weeks or more. Room and board provided. A $2 fee must accompany application. Apply by writing the American Camping Association/Illinois Section, 19 S. LaSalle St., Room 1024, Chicago IL 60603; tel. 312/332-0833.

Anokijig, Located in Plymouth. YMCA coed resident camp with 285 acres, for children ages 8-15. Christian living in a democratic environment. Needs 2 cooks (experienced in mass feeding, dietetics and food management), May 1 to August 31, $81-149/week; program director (teacher with previous camp experience and experience in program administration), June 14 to August 23, $141-159/week; ranch director (teacher or person with advanced training in equestrian programs, including Western style riding, experience in administration and management of staff and horses), June 14 to August 23, $101-119/week; maintenance director (college senior with experience using tractors and light truck, good skills in carpentry, plumbing and electricity), June 14 to August 15, $81-99/week; camp nurse (RN licensed by State of Wisconsin, hospital experience working in pediatrics), June 29 to August 8, $111-129/week; at least 2 senior counselors/program specialists (college students) in the areas of smallcraft, sailing, waterskiing, swimming, land games, horsemanship, campcrafts, nature, archery, Indian lore, arts and crafts, June 14 to August 15, $81-99/week. Room and board is included as a fringe benefit and is added to each employee's total reported earnings. "We are a youth-oriented camp, designed to help youngsters improve their interpersonal relationships, have fun and learn new skills in a Christian environment. All staff are expected to serve as part of the work crew and in a total team effort. Only people with an interest in working with children and who enjoy working in a rustic outdoor setting should apply for these positions." Send resume or write for application by March 1 to David C. Himes, Camp Executive Director, Dept. SED, Racine YMCA, 725 Lake Ave, Racine WI 53043; tel. 414/634-1994.

Campo Fiesta, Located at Boulder Junction in northern Wisconsin on Trout Lake. Private girls camp. Openings for college students, teachers and foreign students, minimum age 19, from June 20 to August 13. Needs 20 cabin counselors skilled and experienced to teach one of the following activities: tripping, waterskiing, sailing, scuba, diving, swimming, riding (hunt seat—show experience preferred), gymnastics, arts and crafts, drama, tennis, archery, riflery, $550-800 depending on skill and experience; office manager, kitchen helpers, housekeeping/laundry, $500-1,000. Room and board provided. Apply early (April deadline) to Mr. and Mrs. N.D. Frisbie, 420 E. Tropical Way, Plantation FL 33317.
Fringe Benefits: Laundry service. **College credit** available. "Ours is only a 7-week season, and the pay is approximately the same as that of most 8-week camps. Our small size (96 campers-35 staff members) and extensive program and facilities have been enjoyed by hundreds of employees over the past 43 years."

Chalk Hills Camp, Located in Amberg. Girl Scout camp. Openings from June 8 to August 12. Needs 1 head cook, knowledge of quantity cooking and planning and supervision of kitchen staff, $900/summer; 3 unit leaders,

---

Most jobs listed in SED note time periods for employment. Be sure you can stay the entire employment season before you apply—some evey pay bonuses if you do!

counselor training and livesaving desirable, college students and teachers preferred, minimum age 21, $680-775/season; 1 nature/crafts counselor, minimum age 20, college students and teachers preferred, $700 and up/season; 6-8 unit assistants minimum age 18, leadership ability, counselor training and lifesaving desirable, college students and high school students preferred, $675 and up/season; and 1 waterfront director, minimum age 21, college students and teachers preferred, $680-775/season and 1 nurse, registered in the state of Wisconsin, $750 and up. "We are interested in a staff member that is knowlegeable in the Girl Scout Program, that will adhere to the principles of the movement, and is concerned that camping is a positive experience for girls—from the beginning camper through the advanced backpacker or canoe tripper. Room and board provided. Send for application by April to Ann T. Bishop, Camp Director, 933 E. College Ave., Appleton WI 54911; tel. 414/734-4559.
Fringe Benefits: Laundry facilities are available for staff use. **College credit** possible.

Chippewa Bay, Located 40 miles north of Eau Claire, Wisconsin. Girl Scout camp. Openings for college students, teachers, high school seniors and foreign students from June 10 to August 20. Needs camp director, assistant director, unit leaders, $660-760; unit counselors, $560-640; arts and crafts specialists, naturalist, $560-700; waterfront director, $660-800; business manager, $600-750; 2 cooks, $900-1,600; nurse (RN, GRN), $850-1,000; approximate salaries. Unit programs include canoeing, sailing, backpacking, creative arts, primitive, and a special unit for EMR children. Philosophy of girl planning with adult guidance. Apply early to Camp Director, Girl Scouts of DuPage County Council, 8 S. 021, Route 53, Naperville IL 60540; tel. 312/963-6050.

Deerhorn, Located in Rhinelander, Wisconsin. Private boys camp for ages 7-15. Openings for college students and teachers. Needs 23 general counselors to instruct archery, crafts, tennis, team sports, swimming, sailing, waterskiing, riding, riflery, golf, soccer, $750-1,000/season; 2 cooks, $1,100-1,400/season. Room and board provided. Apply by April to Don C. Broadbridge, Owner/Director, Camp Deerhorn, 2863 Shannon Ct., Dept. SED, Northbrook IL 60062; tel. 312/272-6080.
Fringe Benefits: Good working conditions, a social atmosphere, learning situations and travel allowance. **College credit** possible.

Edwards, Located in East Troy on Lake Beulah. YMCA resident camp. Openings from June 7 or 13 to August 15 or 24. Needs 16 counselors for coed youth camp, $81-100/week, college students preferred; trip director, $84-120/week, college student preferred; waterfront director, $100-135/week, teacher preferred; assistant waterfront director, $84-120/week; nature director, $81-100/week; crafts director, $81-100/week; assistant cook and assistant office helper, college students preferred. Room and board provided. Apply by March 1 to Kent C. Weimer, Program Director, Camp Edwards YMCA, 1275 Army Lake Rd., East Troy WI 53120; tel. 414/642-7466.
Fringe Benefits: College credit possible. "Camp Edwards is located in

beautiful southeastern Wisconsin, a reasonable distance from Milwaukee, Chicago and Madison."

Harand Camp of the Theatre Arts, Located at Elkhart Lake, Wisconsin. General coed camp for pre-teen and teenage children plus theater activities. Openings for college students and teachers from June 22 through August 18. Needs counselors, specialists for water and sports, 6 accompanists, and dining room help. All salaries $600 and up plus room and board, linen and insurance. Staff lives in cabins that are heated. Apply by May 15 to Byron Friedman, Director, Dept. SED, 708 Church St., Evanston, IL 60201; tel. 312/864-1500.
Fringe Benefits: "Harand is a coed camp. Employees have time off, with many places to go in the resort area. There are learning opportunities that go along with the work." **College credit** available.

Hilltop, Located in Spring Green. Private girls camp, ages 9-16. Openings for college students, teachers and foreign students from June 15 to August 15. Needs specialty counselors: 2 WSI, dance, dramatics, general, 2 riding, music, $600/season; cooks, assistant cooks, $400-800/season. Room and board provided. Apply by May to Mrs. Jan Fritz, Hilltop Summer Camp for Girls, Dept. SED, Spring Green WI 53588.

Holiday Home Camp, Located on Lake Geneva at Williams Bay, Wisconsin. Coed camp for disadvantaged and diabetic children, ages 8-12. Openings from mid-June to mid-August. Needs 2 waterfront directors (WSI), 2 unit directors, laundry worker, $600-700/season; crafts director, college students preferred; 12 counselors, college students and high school seniors preferred. Send resume. Apply to James Myers, Director, Dept. SED, 916 Hollywood Dr., Monroe MI 48161.

Juniper Knoll, East Troy, Wisconsin 53120. Girl Scout camp for ages 6-17. Openings for college students, graduates, teachers and foreign students from mid-June to mid-August. Needs director, program director, assistant director, business manager (minimum age 21 with driver's license), with food service manager, cooks, pack-out staff, nurse, program consultants, waterfront director (ARC, WSI), waterfront assistants, (ARC, WSI, ACS, SCI) group counselors, maintenance assistant. Room and board provided. Apply to Director of Camping and Properties/SED, Girl Scouts of Chicago, 14 E. Jackson Blvd., Chicago IL 60604.

Kawaga, Located in Minocqua, Wisconsin. Private boys camp for ages 8-16. Openings for college students, teachers and high school seniors from mid-June to mid-August. Needs specialty counselors for scuba, sailing, waterfront (WSI), waterskiing, tennis, Indian lore, tripping, small craft (rowing, canoeing), arts and crafts, piano, dramatics, photography, archery, riflery, $400 and up; 4 kitchen staff, $60/week; cook; baker; nurse. Some housing available for married staff. Room and board provided. Apply by April 1 to Ron Silverstein, Director, 2235 Grandview Pl., Glenview IL 60025.

Rodney Kroehler YMCA Camp, Located ten miles south of Hayward on Lac Court Orielles. Openings for period June 7 to August 22. Applicants must be college students or older. Needs 15 cabin counselors-instructors, $800 and up/season; 1 RN/camp nurse, $1500/season; 1 waterfront director, $1,000/season, must be 21 or older. Also needs those with specialized skills in leathercraft at all levels, gymnastics, bicycle motocross, backpacking and outdoor living, sailing, water skiing and land sports. Staff must display originality and ability to adapt to conditions. Seeking patient, mature adults to work with affluent children, coed, ages 9-15, on a 24-hour-per-day basis. Must be prepared to accept role of educators, mediators, surrogate parents and friends to the campers in the development of their character and leadership abilities on a positive basis. Facilities are built for year-round usage. EOE. Apply before March 1 to R.J. Mernitz, Executive Director CCD, Rodney Kroehler YMCA Camp and Lodge, Rt. 6, Box 395, Hayward WI 54843; tel. 715/634-2484.
Fringe Benefits: "Many fringe benefits. Staff members have an equal opportunity to learn new skills and develop personally under excellent working conditions."

Ma-Ka-Ja-Wan Scout Reservation, Located in Wisconsin's northwoods country. Boy Scout Camp for boys ages 10-15; high adventure base offering backpacking and river raft trips; ranch camp with related program. Openings from approximately June 15 to August 15. Needs 2 aquatics directors (WSI), 2 program directors, 2 rifle range directors, provisional scoutmaster, maintenance director, backpacking director, nurse (RN), ranch foreman, chaplain, 2 head cooks, minimum age 21; 2 archery directors, 6 camp commissioners, 3 maintenance and vehicle drivers, 2 ecology/conservation directors, 2 dining lodge directors, 2 wranglers, minimum age 18. Also needs aquatics counselors, handicraft counselors, trading post operators, kitchen personnel, craft specialists. Salaries are $450-1,500/season depending on position and experience. Room and board provided. Scouting background desirable but not necessary. Housing accommodations for families. Send for application. Apply by February 1 to Robert G. King, Administrator, Ma-Ka-Ja-Wan Scout Reservation, Pearson WI 54462; tel. 715/484-2346.

Marimeta, Located in Eagle River, Wisconsin. Private camp for girls, ages 8-15. Openings for college students and teachers, minimum age 19, from June 15 to August 15. Needs specialty counselors for gymnastics, swimming (WSI), sailing, canoeing, waterskiing, tennis, riflery, arts and crafts, golf, archery, $500-800 plus room and board and transportation to and from Chicago area. Counselors must also assume cabin responsibilities. Apply by May 1 to Mrs. Marshall Rabovsky, 645 Lavergne Ave., Wilmette IL 60091.

Menominee for Boys, Located in Eagle River, Wisconsin. Openings for college students, teachers from June 13 to August 13, $500-750/season depending on year of college. Needs 15-20 counselors (interested in counselors specializing in all land and water sports, must have completed one year of college). Hires physically handicapped. Send for application to Alan Wasserman, Camp Menominee for Boys, 1044 Oak Ridge Dr., Glencoe IL 60022.

Fringe Benefits: "Very modern, sportsminded summer camp."

Minne Wonka Lodge, Located in Three Lakes, Wisconsin. Private camp for girls. Openings for 25 college students (at least sophomore) and teachers from approximately June 16 to August 15. Needs specialty counselors for arts and crafts, campcraft, tripping, canoeing, sailing, waterskiing, nature, riding, swimming, archery; typist; and bookkeeper. Salaries are $400-800. Room, board and laundry service provided. Live in cabins with campers. Apply to Mr. and Mrs. C.R. Hanna, Minne Wonka Lodge, 235 Sterncrest Dr., Chagrin Falls OH 44022; tel. 216/248-7207.

Nebagamon for Boys, Located in Lake Nebagamon, Wisconsin. Private camp for boys ages 9-15. Openings for college and graduate students and teachers from June 13 to August 13. Needs cabin counselors; specialty counselors: crafts, photography, nature, wilderness tripping (canoe, backpacking, cycling); food service manager; RN; and waterfront director. Salaries are commensurate with positions. Room and board provided. Contact Bernard Stein, Camp Nebagamon, 7433 Cromwell Dr., Clayton MO 63105. **Fringe Benefits:** "Travel stipend, laundry, excellent recreation—neat employers!"

Nicolet for Girls, Inc., Located in Eagle River. Private camp for girls ages 8-15. Openings for college students and teachers, minimum age 18 or one year college completed, from June 14 to August 14. Needs specialty counselors: swimming (WSI), small craft (SCI or ARC), waterskiing, tennis, arts and crafts, English riding (dressage, jumping), gymnastics, and dramatics. Salaries are $600-1,200 depending on age, qualifications and position. Room and board provided. Nursing, kitchen and stable staff also needed. Apply by May 1 to Dr. Jeff Starz, Associate Director, Camp Nicolet for Girls, Inc., Eagle River WI 54521. **Fringe Benefits:** Laundry provided. "Nicolet offers excellent director-staff communication and the opportunity to develop personal skills and individual interests." **College credit** possible.

Nokomis, Inc., Located in Mercer, Wisconsin. Private camp for girls ages 8-16. Openings for college students, teachers and foreign students from approximately June 18 to August 14. Needs instructors for archery, crafts, music, all water sports (swimming, sailing, canoeing, boating, waterskiing), tennis, riflery, English riding, drama, gymnastics (minimum age 19); nurse (RN). Salaries based on experience and skill. Room and board provided. Apply by April or May to Charlotte L. Mendes, Director, Camp Nokomis, Inc., Dept. SED, 3180 Lake Shore Dr., Chicago IL 60657. **Fringe Benefits:** Travel allowance, laundry. **College credit** possible.

Northwoods, Located in northern Wisconsin near Ashland. Girl Scout camp serving girls ages 10-17; basic Girl Scout camping programs and specialty programs in horseback riding, backpacking, canoeing, primitive camping and arts exploration. Openings for college students, teachers and high school seniors from mid-June to mid-August. Needs assistant camp director (must have car, camp experience, knowledge of Girl Scout program and valid chauffeur's license), $880-1,200/season; 6 unit leaders (experienced in working with groups of children, and preferably in camp counseling or Girl Scouting, and Red Cross Lifesaving and/or First Aid), $720-1,040/season; 12 assistant unit leaders (experienced in working with groups of children, and preferably in camp counseling or Girl Scouting, and Red Cross Lifesaving and/or First Aid), $656-880/season; waterfront director (WSI, experienced in canoeing, and preferably in camping), $760-1,240; 2 waterfront assistants (ALS, prefers camp experience), $656-920/season; health supervisor (RN, LPN, EMT, prefers First Aid training), $720-1,240/season; food supervisor (experienced in quantity cooking, prefers training in food management), $880-1,400/season; 2 cook's assistants (prefers experience in cooking), $800-1,000/season; packout person (physical stamina and basic math skills required), $656-880/season; business manager (chauffeur's license required), $760-1,240/season; bus driver (school bus driver's license required), $656-880/season; horseback riding specialist, $656-880/season. Room and board provided. Equal opportunity/affirmative action employer. Apply by mid-April. Request application of Kay Kramer, Camping Services Director, Girl Scout Council of St. Croix Valley, Dept. SED, 400 S. Robert, St. Paul MN 55107; tel. 612/227-8835.

Fringe Benefits: "Beautiful surroundings." **College credit** possible.

Osoha, Located in Boulder Junction, Wisconsin, 14 miles north of Minocqua. Camp for girls ages 8 through 16. Openings for college students and teachers from June 19 to August 14; secretaries earlier and later. Needs cabin counselors-instructors for swimming, diving, waterskiing, water ballet, canoeing, sailing, English riding, campcraft, vocal music, modern dance, sketching, arts and crafts, archery, badminton, tennis; secretaries; nurse; cook; and kitchen helpers. Room, board and laundry provided. State age and qualifications in letter of application. Apply to Linda Porter, Dept. SED, 854 Prospect Ave., Winnetka IL 60093.

Red Pine, Located 7 miles from Minocqua. Private camp for girls ages 6-16; two 4-week sessions. ACA accredited, 44th season. Openings for college students and graduates from June 16 to August 16 including 5 days pre-camp training. Needs specialty counselors: archery, basketball, canoeing, backpacking, tripping, campcraft, English riding, sailing, swimming (WSI), waterskiing, dance, drama, crafts, gymnastics, tennis; nurse (RN); Food Service assistants; assistant cook; stableperson. Salaries based on age, qualifications and experience. Room and board provided. Apply to Irene Boudreaux, Co-Director, Red Pine Camp for Girls, Minocqua WI 54548.

Camp Roundelay, Located in Minong, Wisconsin. ACA accredited Girl Scout resident camp. Openings from June 28 to August 9. Needs 5 unit leaders, college students and teachers preferred, $100-125/week; 10 general counselors, college students and teachers preferred, $71-95/week; 3 horseback riding instructors, college students and teachers preferred, $85-125/week; 4 waterfront staff, to teach swimming, boating, canoeing, or sailing, Red Cross Instructor's certificate, college students and teachers preferred, $85-130/week; and 1 camp nurse, LPN or RN, $125-145/week. Room and board provided.

Send for application to the Executive Director, Northern Pine Girl Scout Council, 200 Ordean Bldg., Duluth MN 55802.
Fringe Benefits: "Roundelay offers pre-camp and on-the-job training in working with children in an informal setting, in program activities, and in campcraft skills; valuable experience in working with children and in conducting program activities; opportunity to develop good human relations skills. **College credit** possible.

Shewahmegon, Located at Lake Owen, Drummond, Wisconsin. Private camp for boys ages 8-14. Openings for college students and teachers from June 15 to August 15. Needs 14 instructors for crafts, rock polishing, woodshop, riflery (NRA), trampoline, power mechanics, ecology, scuba diving, ARC instructors in sailing-canoeing-power boating, tennis, golf, 3 canoe and campout trip leaders, $500-900/season; medical doctor, RN or LPN, $700-1,000/season; 2 camp maintenance, $500-900/season; assistant cooks, kitchen helpers and kitchen maintenance, minimum wage or more. Room and board provided. Apply by June 15 to William T. Will, Camp Shewahmegon, Dept. SED, 1208 E. Miner St., Arlington Heights IL 60004; tel. 312/255-9710.
Fringe Benefits: College credit possible.

YWCA Camp Talaki, Located in Wild Rose. YWCA resident camp for girls of varied backgrounds, ages 7-17, and women ages 18-80, in separate 1- and 2-week sessions. Openings from early June through mid-August. Needs assistant director, waterfront director (WSI), wrangler, nurse (GN minimum) and head cook. Minimum age for each is 21. Skills and experience required in appropriate area. Salaries are $85-110/week, depending on position and experience. Also needs unit leaders (minimum age 21) and general counselors (minimum age 19). College students, teachers or other social service area people preferred. Salaries are $75-90/week, depending on position and experience. Also openings for high school students as kitchen aides, $65-70/week. Salaries based on 1980 rates and may vary slightly by 1981. All positions include a one-week paid training period at camp. Room and board provided. Send resume, send for application or phone. Application deadline is May. For specific job information and application, contact Jan Susa, Camp Director, YWCA of Greater Milwaukee, Dept. SED, 610 N. Jackson Street, Milwaukee WI 53202; tel. 414/271-1030.
Fringe Benefits: "Talaki offers use of facilities between camping groups; tremendous social setting and potential for personal growth; opportunity for skill development in working with groups of people; contact with a wide variety of people; beautiful surroundings; modern plumbing; housing in buildings." **College credit** possible.

Tiwaushara, Located in Redgranite. Girl Scout camp for girls ages 9-14. Openings from June 10 to August 1 or 15. Needs 10 counselors, $590-625; 3 unit leaders, $550-700; 1 business manager, $500-625; 1 waterfront director, $550-700; 2 cooks, $600-750; 2 waterfront assistants (one with boating), $525-675; health supervisor, $750-950; program director $750-950. Room and board provided. Apply by May 15 to Ann Fuerbringer, Camp Director, 307 N. Main St., Fond du Lac WI 54935; tel. 414/921-8540.

Fringe Benefits: "A one-week training session 'to do the job' is included. There is time off during the week and on weekends. The staff is entitled to use any equipment that is not in use by campers." **College credit** possible.

Towering Pines

Woodland, Located at Eagle River, Wisconsin. Camp for boys (Towering Pines), camp for girls (Woodland). Openings for men, women and married staff in an unusually varied program, for a single 7-week season from June 20 to August 19. Needs specialists in tripping, nature lore, tennis, sailing, all land and water sports, crafts, riding, marksmanship, performing arts. Also needs man capable of sailing a 34-foot sloop on Lake Superior; department directors; nurse; and cooks. Starting salaries are $500-800. Room and board provided. Apply to John M. Jordan, Dept. SED, 242 Bristol St., Northfield IL 60093.
Fringe Benefits: Laundry, travel allowance. **College credit** possible.

Union League Boys' Clubs Camp, Located in southeastern Wisconsin, near Salem. An ACA accredited resident camp for children ages 6-14; 7 weeks of boys and 1 week of girls. Openings for college students, teachers and other qualified adults. Minimum age for staff is 19. Dates of employment; cottage counselors, June 15-August 16; all other staff, June 14-August 16. Bonuses paid to cottage counselors for first aid and/or lifesaving skills certified by the Red Cross. All staff receive 2 days off every 2 weeks plus room and board, in addition to their salaries. Needs 16 cottage counselors, $675; nurse or EMT, $750; assistant cook, $750; tripper/assistant driver, $750; naturalist, $750; assistant waterfront director, $900; unit leader, $900. Apply to Frank J. Matkovich, Camp Director, Union League Boys' Clubs Camp, 2157 W. 19th St., Chicago IL 60608; tel. 312/829-6840.
Fringe Benefits: "Good experience working with inner-city youngsters from the Chicago area. Dedicated workers needed." Swimming, fishing, boating, sailing, sports, and camping activities offered.

Waupaca For Boys, Inc., Located in Waupaca, Wisconsin. Camp for children ages 9-14. ACA accredited, 30th year. Openings for college students and teachers, minimum age 19, from mid-June to mid-August. Needs instructors in swimming (WSI); specialists in waterskiing, tennis, golf, riflery (NRA), archery, crafts (woodworking), photography, horseback riding, baseball, wrestling, nature; swimming director (WSI); nurse (RN); and caretaker. Salaries open. Room (cabins with washrooms and showers attached) and board provided. Apply by February to Camp Waupaca for Boys, Inc., 6850 N. Crawford Ave., Lincolnwood IL 60646; tel. 312/676-0911.
Fringe Benefits: Laundry, medical insurance and travel allowance provided.

Windego, Located in Wild Rose, Wisconsin. Girl Scout camp for girls ages 9-17. Openings for college students, teachers and foreign students from mid-June to mid-August. Needs unit leaders; counselors; English riding instructors; Western riding instructors (CHA, HSA); specialty counselors for arts and crafts, CIT training, campcraft, sailing, canoeing, natural science, sports; swimming instructors (WSI); cooks; nurse. Salaries are $630-1,200. Room and board provided. Apply by May 30 to Illinois Shore Girl Scout Council, Inc., Box

544, Dept. SED, Wilmette IL 60091.

Fringe Benefits: "This camp offers the chance to meet people from many different areas and backgrounds, to learn how to live with others and to work with children." **College credit** possible.

Wyoming

2,967+ jobs available

National Parks

Hamilton Stores, Inc., Located in Yellowstone National Park, Wyoming. General merchandising. Openings for 500-600 college students, teachers and high school seniors, minimum age 18, from late May through mid-September. Needs sales clerks, fountain clerks, dishwashers, grocery stock clerks, maintenance workers, kitchen helpers, housekeepers, cashiers and security guards. Federal minimum wage. Also needs cooks (for employees' dining rooms), office workers, construction workers; salaries based on experience. Room and board provided at a minimal daily charge. Write after January 1 for application and descriptive brochure. Apply by August 1 to Personnel Department, Hamilton Stores, Inc., Box 2700, Dept. SED, Santa Barbara CA 93120.

Fringe Benefits: Five-day week, seven-hour day for most positions; family style meals (not a cafeteria) with excellent quality and no limit on quantity; no charge for meals on days off; uniforms furnished. **College credit** possible.

TWA Services/Yellowstone, Located at Yellowstone National Park. Concessionaire. "We have over 2,000 openings from late April to October in food service, lodging, reservations, accounting, vending, gift shops and transportation." Minimum age 18. Employment information sent with application. Equal opportunity/Affirmative Action employer. Please write to TWA Services, Employee Services Office, Yellowstone National Park WY 82190.

Yellowstone Park Service Stations, Located in Yellowstone National Park, Wyoming. Concessionaire. Openings for college students and teachers (US citizens only, minimum age 18) from May 1 to October 31; minimum period June 10 to Labor Day. Need 85 male or female gasoline service station attendants, 6 warehouse/office/clerical help, 8 journeyman automobile mechanics, 8 mechanic's helpers. Wages for all positions are based on hourly rates, with none being less than the federal minimum wage. Apply by May 1 to Employment Department, Box 11, Dept. SED, Gardiner MT 59030.

Resorts, Ranches, Restaurants, Lodges

Absaroka Mountain Lodge, Located in a small valley at Cody, 12 miles from Yellowstone Park. Rustic mountain lodge, resort and dining room with 13 cabin units serving families. Openings for college and high school students from May 1 to October 1. Needs 2 cooks, $200-300/month; 5 maids/ kitchen helpers/waitresses (girls rotate weekly for variety), $150-200/month plus tips. "Apply only for the period you know you can work. We are a small resort next to a mountain stream and we specialize in quiet and relaxation. Everyone must pull together to make it work for all of us. The ability to get along with others is essential." Room and board provided. Send resume including SASE and dates available to work, to Mike Rueffert, Manager, Box 7, Cody WY 82414; tel. 307/587-3963.

Fringe Benefits: Training and laundry service are provided. "If you fulfill your working agreement by staying the period we agree upon and your work and attitude are satisfactory, you will receive a bonus at the end of the season."

Blackwater Lodge, Located near Cody, 15 miles from east entrance of Yellowstone Park. Resort. Openings from April 25 to October 15. Needs 2 food-cocktail waitresses, $130/month plus tips; cabin maids, kitchen help, $250/month; breakfast cook (will train), dinner cook (will train), salary open. Room, board and use of horses provided. Send resume and dates available for employment. Apply to Mrs. Thomas Ivanoff, Blackwater Lodge, Box 1162, Cody WY 82414.

Bill Cody's Ranch Inn, Located between Cody and Yellowstone National Park. Resort. Openings for college students and teachers, minimum age, 19. Must be serious, mature workers, available to work for at least 3-months between May 1 and October 1. Needs cook's assistants, office assistants, cabin maid/waitresses, cabin maid/laundry workers, $125-300/month, depending on experience and ability. Horse wranglers must have basic horse care knowledge and Western and mountain riding experience, horseshoeing ability helpful, $125-300/month depending on experience and ability. Room and board provided. Openings for winter resort program, December 10-March 20. Needs cabin maids, waitresses, cooks, Alpine and Nordic ski guides. Salaries and details upon request. Please specify which season you are applying for and dates you are available to work. Please include resume, photo and references. Apply by March 15 (summer program) and November 15 (winter program) to Mrs. William Cody, Bill Cody's Ranch Inn, Box 1390, Cody WY 82414.

Fringe Benefits: "Bill Cody's is a small, prestigious resort (Best Western Golden Crown Award, 4-Diamond rated AAA). There are only 18 employees on our staff; they have the opportunity to meet vacationers from all over the world. Employees receive tips, end-of-season/contract bonuses and riding privileges."

College credit possible.

Deer Creek Ranch, Located in Cody. Small dude ranch. Openings for college students from June 20 to approximately October 10. Needs cabin maid-waitress. Salary is $200/month. Salary includes room and board. Apply to Hope W. Read, 125 E. 72nd St., New York NY 10021.

Flagg Ranch Village Resort, Located in Grand Teton National Park, 2 miles south of Yellowstone National Park. Openings for store clerks, maids, waitresses, buspersons, kitchen work (all types), gas station attendants, maintenance personnel and general workers from May 1 through September 30 and/or December 15 through March 30. Salaries are $310/month. Room and board provided. Enclose SASE. Apply by March 30 to Eddy Dentino, Flagg Ranch, Moran WY 83013.

Fringe Benefits: "We are located in Grand Teton National Park. We pay some employees bonuses or travel expenses; training provided in all departments, to benefit those who have not had previous experience in the jobs they are hired for." **College credit** possible.

Flying L Skytel, Located on the Cody Road to Yellowstone National Park in Cody. Western guest ranch/resort with private airstrip, elevation 5,670 feet. Openings from May 1 to December 1. Needs 2 cooks, 4 cabin maids, 5 waitresses, 3 wranglers, 1 yard man and 2 out-of-door steak cookout men. Salary open, depending on ability and honesty. Room and board provided. "We send a mimeographed list of company policies for the consideration of all personnel. Living facilities at the ranch are excellent." Apply to Cecil A. Legg, Box 1136, Cody WY 82414.

Fringe Benefits: Uniforms, utilities, recreational activities, i.e., horseback riding, heated pool, tennis, fishing, all furnished and classified as reimbursed wages plus a cash stipend.

Goff Creek Lodge Motel, Located in Cody. Resort. Openings for high school or college students from May 15 to October 15. Needs 8 waitresses or waiters (prefers waitresses), 8 cabin maids, 8 kitchen helpers, 4 assistant cooks (will train), 4 wranglers (must have some knowledge of horses), 2 chore and yard persons (male or female). Salaries are $150-250/month plus tips. Room and board provided. Send resume, recent photo, and dates of employment. Will hire some to start work in July. Apply by March 1 to Gloria T. Schmitt, Manager, Goff Creek Lodge, Box 155, SED 1, Cody WY 82414.

Fringe Benefits: "Employees have use of horses and the chance to work in the mountains for the summer."

Hatchet Motel and Restaurant, Located in Moran, Wyoming, near Grand Teton National Park. Openings for college students, teachers and high school students from mid-May to early September (June 15 to August 25 minimum). Needs waitresses, kitchen helpers, relief persons, maids, desk clerks, station attendants, cooks and grounds maintenance. Salary plus tips. Room and board provided. Salaries range from $250 to $500/month. Send SASE with inquiry. Apply by March 1 to Leland J. Luther, 1415 Jackson St., Great Bend, KS 67530.

Fringe Benefits: "Good working conditions; beautiful area."

H F Bar Ranch, Located in Saddlestring. Dude ranch. Openings for college students, teachers and high school seniors from June 1 through September 10 or later. Needs waiters/waitresses, room attendants, dishwashers/pantry helpers and transportation personnel. Must stay entire season. Room and board provided. Apply to H. S. Horton, President, H F Bar Ranch, Saddlestring WY 82840; tel. 307/684-2487.

Fringe Benefits: Staff may participate in guest activities.

Medicine Bow Lodge and Guest Ranch, Located in Saratoga.
Dude ranch in the mountains of Medicine Bow National Forest. Needs 2
housekeepers, 1 kitchen helper/waitress, 3 wranglers (must ride well), 1 kiddie
wrangler (must ride well). Salaries are $200/month, plus tips, college students
and high school seniors preferred. Also needs 1 cook, mimimum $450/month
plus tips, college student or teacher preferred; 1 cook's helper, minimum
$200/month plus tips, college student, high school senior or teacher preferred;
counselor for preschoolers. Needs some employees as early as May 15, others
first week in June. All needed through week of Labor Day. Open year round.
Occasionally will have fall and winter openings. Knowledge of snowmobiling
and/or cross country skiing required. Room and board provided. Apply by May
15 to Manager, Medicine Bow Lodge and Guest Ranch, Box 752 P, Saratoga
WY 82331.
Fringe Benefits: "Free use of horses in free time." **College credit**
possible.

One Bar Eleven Ranch, Located near Saratoga. Ranch. Openings
for college students and high school students from June 1 to September 1.
Needs 3 ranch hands to drive tractor, repair fence and ride cattle,
$400-600/month. Room and board provided. Send resume. Apply by March 1
to J.E. Rouse, Box 646, Saratoga WY 82331; tel. 307/327-5571.
Fringe Benefits: "Travel expense to and from ranch will be refunded to
applicant at end of season if employee stays full season and has proven
satisfactory."

Pahaska Tepee, Located 50 miles west of Cody, Wyoming, at the east
entrance to Yellowstone National Park. Resort, hotel, ranch, restaurant. Buffalo
Bill's original hunting lodge. Openings for 50, between May 1 and September
30. Needs waitresses, $250/month plus tips; station attendants, gift shop clerks,
cabin maids, yard crew people, kitchen help, $250/month; cooks, salary open.
Salaries include room and board. Apply early to Ted Leavens, Pahaska Tepee,
Box 2370, Cody WY 82414.

Parkway Motel, Located in Jackson. Thirty-nine-unit motel located in a
destination summer/winter resort area serving families, senior citizens, young
couples and business persons. "We cater to middle- and upper-middle-class
travelers including many foreign visitors." Openings from May to October for
college students, foreign students and local applicants. Needs 4 housekeepers
who are neat, clean, well organized and able to work with others. Salaries are
$3.50/hour, 6 days/week, 6 hours/day. Housing is available, board not
included. "Persons applying should be willing to make a firm commitment from
May through September and should be individuals who take pride in doing a
good job." Send letter requesting application to Tom Robbins, Dept. SED, Box
494, Jackson WY 83001; tel. 307/733-3143.
Fringe Benefits: "This is an ideal area for persons interested in the
outdoors as we are located near Grand Teton and Yellowstone National
parks."

Shoshone Lodge, Resort motel. Located in the Shoshone National

Forest, 48 miles west of Cody, Wyoming, and 4 miles east of Yellowstone National Park. Openings from May through Labor Day or later. Needs 1 breakfast cook/waitress, $200-275/month plus tips; 1 dinner cook (will train), salary open depending on experience and ability; 3 waitresses, $175/month plus tips and 3 cabin maids/laundry workers, $200-250/month plus tips. Room and board provided. Coin laundry on premises. Send applications to Betty Woodruff, Manager, PO Box 790, Cody WY 82414; tel 307/587-4044.

Siggins Triangle X Ranch, Located 38 miles southwest of Cody. Openings for qualified teachers, college students and high school seniors during summer season (June 1 to September 1) and fall season (September 1 to November 20). Available positions include: cabin maid/waitress, cooks, assistant cook, kitchen assistant, lawn/maintenance, floaters, youth program counselor, wrangler/guide, housekeeper. Salaries vary according to position and experience. Room and board provided. To receive our application form, send SASE with your letter of application. Apply to Mrs. Stanley D. Siggins, Siggins Triangle X Guest Ranch, Dept. SED, Cody WY 82414.
Fringe Benefits: "Employees have use of ranch recreational facilities (horses, swimming pool, tennis court, recreation lodge) and the chance to receive tips."

Triangle C Ranch, Located in Dubois, Wyoming. Dude resort in the mountains. Needs 3 cabin maids/kitchen helpers, 3 corral workers, $200/month plus room and board. Work mid-June to Labor day; will keep some personnel on through November. High school seniors preferred. "Our employees are encouraged to participate in the ranch activities. They are allowed to ride our horses. We do not give specific days off." Apply to Ken Kidneigh, Owner, Triangle C Ranch, Dubois WY 82513; telephone (307)455-2225.

Valley Ranch, Inc., Located 40 miles southwest of Cody. Openings for 15 persons, minimum age 19, from May 1 to October 31. Needs cook, assistant cook, 2 waiter/waitress, dishwasher, 3 wrangler/guides, laundry worker, head housekeeper, 2 cabin maids, arts/crafts/recreation director, gardener, chore person, irrigator/ranch hand. Salaries are $325-400/month. Room and board provided. Apply by April 1 to Manager, Valley Ranch, South Fork Star Route, Cody WY 82414.

Wapiti Valley Inn, Located 18 miles west of Cody on the road to Yellowstone Park. Resort. Openings for college students and high school seniors from May 1 through October 15. Needs 10 waitresses, 4 cooks, 10 cabin maids, 5 maintenance workers, 3 wranglers. Salaries are $250/month plus tips. Room and board provided. Apply by March 15 and no later than May 15 to Christel Bauer, Wapiti Valley Inn, Wapiti WY 82450; tel. 307/587-3961.
Fringe Benefits: This resort offers "a family atmosphere, comfortable living quarters, use of heated pool, horseback riding privileges and a chance to meet interesting people."

Summer Camps

Girl Scout National Center West, Located in Ten Sleep. Girl Scout camp. Openings from June to late August. Openings on the support staff: 1 support services coordinator, 1 business manager, 1 administrative assistant, 1 commissary manager, 1 cook, 1 assistant cook, 2 nurses, 1 riding coordinator, 1 backwoods coordinator, 1 trading post manager, 2 handypersons, 5 trail crew members and 1 visitor center hostess; Wyoming trek staff: 1 program director, 2 camp coordinators, 1 hostess, 1 group coordinator, 2 archaeology consultants, 3 backpacking consultants, 3 environmental education consultants, 2 geology consultants, 1 riding director, 7 riding instructors; special events staff: 12 directors, 7 assistant directors, 6 commissary managers, 2 equipment/tack managers, 3 riding directors, 11 riding instructors, 8 troop advisors; teachers: college instructors and certified high school teachers. College students, teachers and foreign students preferred. Salaries are $450-1,200. Send resume or send for application by April to Sharon Denayer, Program Director, Girl Scout National Center West, PO Box 95, Ten Sleep WY 82442.
Fringe Benefits: This camp offers "beautiful scenery; opportunity to meet and work with people from all over the US and from several other countries; educational opportunities; fascinating and challenging work experience."
College credit available.

Teton Valley Ranch Camps, Located in Jackson Hole. Summer camp for boys and girls ages 10-16. Separate seasons for boys and girls. Boys' season June 15 to July 27; girls' season July 27 to August 31. Program of horseback riding and backpacking with extensive in-camp program in Jackson Hole. Needs 12 cabin counselors, season only, college students, teachers, local applicants, $250-350; 3 dishwashers, local applicants, high school seniors preferred, $350 plus/season; 1 maintenance and clean-up person, college student, high school senior, local applicant acceptable, $600/season; laundry person, $600 plus/summer; 1 lapidary instructor, working knowledge of lapidary, including ordering; 1 crafts counselor, $500 plus/summer, local applicants, college students, teachers acceptable; 4 riflery/archery counselors, pay varies with experience, college students and teachers preferred; 1 ham radio operator, pay varies, college students, teachers, local applicants acceptable. Room and board provided. Send for application. Apply by March 20 to Stuart Palmer and Matt Montagne, Directors, Teton Valley Ranch Camps, Dept. SED, Box 8, Kelly WY 83011; tel. 307/733-2958.
Fringe Benefits: These camps offer "partial travel expenses; a week of orientation; friends and fine country."

Canada

207 jobs available

Resorts, Ranches, Restaurants, Lodging

Prince of Wales Hotel, Located in Waterton Lakes National Park, Alta, Alberta, Canada. Resort hotel. Openings for 100 college students, teachers and high school seniors from June 1 to September 10-16. Needs chief room clerk, room clerks, night clerk, auditors, front office cashiers, information clerks, bellmen, elevator operators, housekeeper, housemen, maids, cleaners, chef, first cook, second cooks, cook's helpers, baker, salad-pantry workers, kitchen workers, kitchen storekeeper, dining room hostess-cashier, dining room cashiers, waitresses, bus boys, head bartender, bartender-waiter, gift shop senior and junior clerks, night watchman, full-time string trio, laundry workers. Talented students given additional consideration as are hotel and restaurant majors. "Our guest entertainment programming is an important part of our schedule." Salaries are described and listed in Employment Circular sent when applying. Applicants must be Canadian citizens. Apply to Mr. Ian B. Tippet, Assistant General Manager, Glacier Park, Inc., 1735 E. Ft. Lowell, Suite 7, Tucson AZ 85719.

Summer Camps

John Bosco Camp, Located in Saskatchewan. Wilderness camp. Openings from May 1 to August 31. Needs 60 employees, 16 years of age or older, good healthy willingness to work, dedication, loyalty; college students, teachers, high school students, foreign students and local applicants acceptable; pay is negotiable. Room and board provided with some positions. Housing available in the area. Send resume or send for application by June 1 to John Boutin, Camp Director, Box 217, Dept. SED, Smeaton, Saskatchewan Canada S0J 2J0.
Fringe Benefits: "Learning situations, good working conditions, scenic locale, opportunity to meet interesting people, interesting work, social atmosphere." **College credit** possible.

Pine Valley Camp, Located in Ste. Agathe des Monts, Quebec. Private coed camp for children 7-16. Needs "college students and teachers ready for a challenge with bright, exciting young people, in an outdoor environment, with a commitment for full season only." Openings for cabin group counselors (minimum age 20); activity instructors (minimum age 20) for basketball, baseball, football, tennis, archery, swimming, canoeing, waterskiing, arts and crafts, gymnastics and nature lore; unit directors (minimum age 24); waterfront director (minimum age 24); program director (minimum age 26). Experience and references required. Personal interviews will be arranged. Room and board provided. Apply by April 1 to Mr. R. Lazanik, MSW, Director, Dept. SED, 5165 Sherbrooke St. W., Suite 316, Montreal, Quebec Canada H4A 1T6; tel. 514/489-8722.
Fringe Benefits: "Pine Valley Camp offers excellent salaries, transportation expenses, laundry service; also wonderful friendships, a chance to meet and live with Canadians and a chance to see Montreal (we're only 1 hour away)." **College credit** available.

Stephens, Located at Kenora, Ontario, 7 miles southeast on Copeland Island. Coed YMCA resident and wilderness camp with canoe tripping for ages 8-16. Openings for 11 college students from June 1 to September 15. Needs 5 counselors, $50/week; 6 canoe trippers (male and female), $70/week. Room and board provided. Apply by June 1 to Grant Platts, YMCA Camp Stephens, 301 Vaughan St., Winnipeg, Manitoba Canada R3B 2N7.

Walden, Located in Palmer Rapids, Ontario. Children's summer camp. Needs general camp counselors (male and female) and specialists (male and female) in swimming, sailing, canoe tripping, water skiing, crafts, ceramics, musical theater and tennis, $500-800/season; college students preferred. Also needs unit heads and heads of all specialties listed above, $800-1,200/season, college students or teachers preferred. Room and board provided. Apply to Ted Cole, Director, 3995 Bathurst St. #206, Downsview, Ontario Canada M3H 5V3; tel. 416/635-0049.
Fringe Benefits: "Walden offers a social atmosphere and a chance to work with children in the out-of-doors." **College credit** possible.

White Pine, Located on Lake Placid, Haliburton, Ontario. Private, coed, decentralized, group centered camp for children ages 8-16. Openings for 36 college students (at least juniors) and teachers from June 21 to August 17. Needs 6 section heads (village directors), cabin counselors; activity instructors and head specialists (experienced) for swimming, sailing, waterskiing, canoeing, riding, canoe tripping, arts and crafts, gymnastics, tennis, woodshop, copper enamel, ceramics, photography. Salaries are $500-1,000 and up/season. Salary depends on experience and references. Room and board provided. Interviews available: Toronto, Buffalo, New York, Los Angeles, Cincinnati, Pittsburgh, Boston, Chicago, Detroit. Enclose SASE. Apply by May to J. Kronick, 8 Rollscourt Dr., Dept. SED, Willowdale, Ontario Canada M2L 1X5.
Fringe Benefits: College credit possible. "White Pine can provide you with: a chance to develop and use your 'people' skills in working with children and other staff; an opportunity to have fun and spend a summer in the out-of-doors; an ability to meet challenges and develop new skills while receiving support and supervision; surroundings where you can meet staff from many other countries; and above all, a summer you'll never forget!"

West Indies

Summer Camps

Antigua Adventure, Located at Antigua in the West Indies. Water sports camp for ages 13-18. Openings for college students and teachers from June 30 for six weeks. Needs specialists in all water activities: sailing, scuba diving, waterskiing, swimming, marine biology; also in tennis, drama, dance, yoga, karate, guitar. Camp or group work experience required. Salaries are $200-600. Apply to Walter Bush, Dept. SED, Antigua Adventure, 480 W. 246th St., Bronx NY 10471.

U.S.A

Summer Camps

Boy Scouts of America, Staff positions are available to qualified students and teachers in more than 500 local camps throughout the country. A background in Scouting is preferred, but not necessary. Needed are those with backgrounds in conservation, wilderness backpacking, handicrafts, nature, aquatics, archery, commissary, first aid and administration. Salary is based on background and position. Contact should be made as early as possible. See Boy Scouts of America in your local telephone directory.

Camp Fire, Inc., Camp Fire councils in all parts of the country employ college students, graduate students, teachers and other mature adults to work on the staffs of resident camps. Positions available for qualified applicants at least 18 years of age include cabin counselors, unit directors, activity directors, cooks, nurses, business managers and maintenance personnel. Camp director and assistant camp director positions are available for those with at least three previous years' experience in an administrative position. Write to Camping Services, Camp Fire National Headquarters, 4601 Madison Ave., Kansas City MO 64112. Give your age, experience, dates available and part of the country in which you prefer to work; you will be referred to councils having job openings in that area. See also many Camp Fire camps listed throughout *Summer Employment Directory*.

Girl Scouts of the U.S.A., Nearly 600 camps are operated by Girl Scout councils from coast to coast and offer a chance to enjoy an expense-free summer with full maintenance plus salary, in a relaxed and informal atmosphere. Needs college students in all fields, as well as nurses, dietitians, teachers and graduate students. Write to Recruitment and Referral, Girl Scouts of the U.S.A., 830 3rd Ave., New York NY 10022 for information. A camp directory will be sent if you give the name of the state in which you would like to work. See also many Girl Scout camps listed throughout *Summer Employment Directory*.

Young Men's Christian Association, Many opportunities for young men and women in the field of camping, both resident camping and day camping. College students are given first consideration. Gain valuable experience in leadership training and in working with children of all ethnic backgrounds. YMCA camps are located from coast to coast. For further information, contact your local YMCA or the National Council of YMCAs, 291 Broadway, New York NY 10007. See also many YMCA camps listed throughout *Summer Employment Directory*.

Young Women's Christian Association, There are varied and interesting YWCA summer opportunities throughout the United States for college students. These include positions in resident and day camps and in other program areas such as swimming and informal group activities. Interested persons should write to the Executive Director or Camp Director of the YWCA in the location in which they wish to work. A listing of YWCAs with a resident camping program is available from the Data Center, National Board YWCA, 600 Lexington Ave., New York NY 10022. See also many YWCA camps listed throughout *Summer Employment Directory.*

Late Arrivals

Camp Aliso Conservation School, Located in Santa Barbara. US Forest Service Youth Conservation Corps school. Openings for college students, teachers and local applicants from June 15 to August 28. Needs 1 camp director/work coordinator (requires 1½ years general experience and 3½ years related specialized experience to qualify), $7.30/hour and 8 work leaders (requires 1½ years general and ½ year specialized experience), $5.27/hour. Apply by March 1 to Gary Nichols, Manpower Coordinator, US Forest Service, Los Priepos Star Route, Santa Barbara CA 93105.

Appalachia Service Project, Inc., Located in Nashville. Openings from May 31 to August 13 for college students and teachers. Needs 30 for summer staff to coordinate work camps for church youth groups, $800/season and 1 truck driver to distribute supplies to various work camp centers, $800/season. Room and board provided. Send for application. Apply by March 1 to Ruth Benedict, Co-Director, Appalachia Service Project, Inc., Dept. SED, PO Box 840, Nasvhille TN 37202.
Fringe Benefits: "Opportunities for ministry and service to Appalachian families." **College credit** possible.

Belle Terre Gymnastic Camp for Girls, Located in South Kortright. Openings for college students and teachers from June 24 to August 22. Needs specialty counselors/teachers (also act as bunk counselors): 6 gymnastics, 1 dance (ballet and jazz); 2 waterfront (WSI, pool and lake); 1 tennis; 2 Western horsemanship; 1 arts and crafts. Salaries are and $1,000 up, commensurate with skills and experience. Room and board provided. Also needs nurse (RN or LPN), 2 kitchen helpers. "Counselors should seek certification in advanced First Aid if at all possible." Apply early, enclosing complete resume, to Consuelo G. Haus, Director, Belle Terre Gymnastic Camp for Girls, Dept. SED, South Kortright NY 13842; tel. 607/538-9434 or 607/865-4050.

Birch Trails, Located at Irma. Girl Scout resident camp; 7-, 10- and 14-day sessions for ages 9-18. Openings for college students from June 12 to August 19. Needs assistant camp director, unit leaders, unit assistant, arts and crafts/nature specialist, waterfront staff; nurse. Unit programs include canoeing, backpacking, bicycling, creative arts, one mentally handicapped group. Philosophy of girl planning with adult guidance. Apply to Vicki Wright, Camp Director, Birch Trails Girl Scout Council, 14 N. Third Ave., Wausau WI 54401.

Brook Bound Lodge, Located in Wilmington. Openings from June 20 to Labor Day. Needs 2 college students for food preparation, waiting on tables, chambermaid, weeding and picking vegetables and light maintenance, $40/week and share of tips. Room and board provided. Send resume by May 1 to Mrs. Wayne Fajans, Dept. SED, R1, Box 190, Wilmington VT 05363.
Fringe Benefits: "Room and board is worth so much in this resort area. Our employees are accepted as one of the family and have use of all facilities. Working conditions are good with time off between noon and 4 pm to enjoy the

beautiful area. Excellent opportunity to learn about cooking and general maintenance. Association with our guests is interesting, pleasant and advantageous."

Greentop, Located at Lantz. Camp for physically disabled children (ages 6-18) and adults (18 and up). Needs 14 cabin program leaders and 26 counselors. "Counselors work with cabin groups and in activity areas; water safety instructor required for swimming; crafts and sports require experience with children. Room and board provided. Experience working with children and adults desired." Also needs clerical, business and kitchen personnel and nurses/LPNs. Needs counselors for adult camp session from mid- to late August, usually 2 weeks. For children's camp, work from late June to mid-August. Apply to Chad M. Casserly, Director, Camping Recreation, The League for the Handicapped, Inc., 1111 E. Cold Spring Lane, Baltimore MD 21239; tel. 301/323-0500.
Fringe Benefits: Transportation from Baltimore to camp.

Happy Valley, Located in Ojai. US Forest Service Youth Conservation Corps camp. Openings for college students, teachers and local applicants from June 15 to August 28. Needs 1 camp director (requires 1½ years general experience and 3½ years related specialized experience), $7.30/hour; 1 environmental awareness coordinator (requires 3 years general experience appropriate to position), $5.90/hour; 2 night counselors (requires 1½ years general and ½ years specialized experience), $5.27-5.90/hour; and 4 work leaders (1½ years general and ½ year specialized experience), $5.27/hour. Apply by March 1 to John Boggs, Manpower Coordinator, US Forest Service, 1190 E. Ojai Ave., Ojai CA 93023.

Indians Ranch Camp, Located in King City. US Forest Service Youth Conservation Corps camp. Openings for college students, teachers and local applicants from June 15 to August 28. Needs 1 camp director (1½ years general experience and 3½ years related specialized experience), $7.30/hour; 1 environmental awareness coordinator (3 years general experience appropriate to position), $5.90/hour; 2 night counselors (1½ years general and ½ year specialized experience), $5.27-5.90/hour; and 4 work leaders (1½ years specialized experience), $5.27/hour. Apply to March 1 to Frank Stewart, Manpower Coordinator, US Forest Service, 406 S. Mildred, King City CA 93930.

Kohl's Ranch, Located in Payson. Ranch resort. Openings for college students, minimum age 19, from Memorial Day through Labor Day. Needs 4 chambermaids, 4 waitresses, 4 yardmen. Apply to Michael Mikol, Kohl's Ranch, Payson AZ 85541.

Legend City, Located in Tempe. Openings from April to September. Needs ride operators, food and beverage, security, maintenance and cleanup personnel; cashiers and bartenders. Salaries start at $3.10/hour. Hires physically handicapped. Apartment rentals, $100-150/one bedroom apartment. Send for application. Apply by April to Taryn Jewell, Legend City, Dept. SED,

1200 W. Washington, Tempe AZ 85281.
Fringe Benefits: "Opportunity to meet interesting people and work in a
social atmosphere. Scenic locale."

Little Notch, Located in Fort Ann, New York, near Glens Falls and Lake
George. Girl Scout camp for ages 7 to 17. Openings for college students,
teachers and foreign students from approximately June 21 to August 24. Needs
nurse, $1,000-1,200; unit leaders, $600-720; counselors, $450-585; waterfront
director, $600-720; nature consultants, arts and crafts consultants, $600-720.
Apply to Frances Plummer, Administrator of Camp Development and
Properties, Hudson Valley Girl Scout Council, 750 Delaware Ave., Delmar NY
12054.

Meadow Mountain Ranch, Located in Allensparks. Girl Scout camp
for girls ages 8-17. Needs 1 camp director, $1,500-2,100/9 weeks; 1 program
director, $600-1,000/9 weeks; 8 unit leaders, $450-650/9 weeks; 16 unit
counselors, $300-500/9 weeks; 1 arts and crafts counselor, $400-600/9 weeks;
2 handymen, $450-700/9 weeks; 2 riding counselors, $300-500/9 weeks.
College students and teachers preferred. Work early June through mid-August.
Request application form from: Camping Services Director, Mountain Prairie
Girl Scout Council, 2627 W. 10th St., Greeley CO 80631.

New Jersey 4-H Camps, Two camps. The Lindley G. Cook Camp is
located in Stokes State Forest and is situated on 120 wooded acres. The
Beemerville 4-H Camp is located adjacent to High Point State Park on the
former site of the Rutgers Dairy Research Center Farm. Openings for college
and high school students and local applicants from mid-June to mid-August.
Needs 2 aquatics supervisors (WSI and advanced lifesaving certification),
$300-360/month; 4 lifeguards (advanced lifesaving certification),
$220-260/month; 2 small craft instructors (advanced lifesaving certification),
$240-260/month; 2 chefs, $350-550/month; 2 health directors (RN, LPN, EMT
or advanced in first aid and CPR), $360-550/month; 4 wranglers
(horsemanship experience), $240-260/month; 1 animal science instructor
(experience working with large animals), $240-260/month; 1 county horse
instructor (horsemanship experience), $240-260/month; 2 nature instructors,
$240-260/month; 2 energy science instructors, $240-260/month; 2 craft shot
managers, $240-260; 2 cooks, $240-280; 2 assistant cooks, $200-240/month.
Room and board provided. Hires physically handicapped. Send for application.
Send application by May 1 to Kevin J. Mitchell, Program Associate, New Jersey
4-H Camps, RD 6, Box 250, Sussex, New Jersey 07461.
Fringe Benefits: Sleeping quarters are in a separate building from the
campers' quarters. Free laundry facilities available at the camps. Time off on
Saturday afternoon and evening, all day Sunday, and most weekday evenings.
Camps are located in a rural setting.

Nippersink Resort, Located in Genoa City. Hotel. Openings for
college students, teachers, high school seniors and foreign students from May 1
to October 1. Needs 8 governesses, 25 waitresses, 15 pool attendants, 25
waiters, 8 cooks, 20 bus boys, 20 general kitchen workers, 12 bellhops, 5 clerks,

10 porters, 4 bartenders, 30 maids, 10 children's counselors, 16 social staff workers, 8 snack shop workers, 4 bar boys. Room and board provided. State any musical talents. Apply by May 15 to Bud Urban, Nippersink Manor Resort, Genoa City WI 53128.
Fringe Benefits: "Employees are invited to nightclub floor shows and bi-weekly pool parties; free golf, free tennis." **College credit** possible.

Old Colony Council, Located in South Carver. Openings from June 20 to August 20. Needs 25-50 college and high school students and teachers for general duties (summer camp certifications necessary in some areas), $500-$2,000/season; 1-5 for environmental education-nature, ecology, etc. teaching to school groups, salary is negotiable; 1-5 openings for general staff/teachers for a small group rehabilitation program with 14-17 year old juveniles, $170-200/week. Room and board provided on premises. Certain educational and administrative and secretarial positions can be competently filled by handicapped applicants. Send resume or application by June 1 to Kevin P. Mullen, Director, Old Colony Scout Reservation, PO Box 931, Dept. SED, South Carver MA 02366.
Fringe Benefits: College credit available. Located 15 minutes from Cape Cod. Great experience for potential career interest.

Eddie Lee Robinson, Located in Florida City. Farm labor contractor. Needs workers to harvest tomatoes in Florida. Work 5 hours/day, 2 days/week. Send for application to Betty Jean Rolles, 945 NW Lucy St., Florida City FL 33034.

Sacandaga 4-H Camp, Located in Speculator. Openings from June 24 to August 16. Needs 4 college students or teachers for program coordinator, $125/week; 10 college students, teachers or high school students for course counselor, $60-90/week; 10 high school students or local applicants for junior counselors, $50/week and 1 teacher for camp director, $200/week. Room and board provided. Will hire physically handicapped. Send resume by April to James Batsford, Dept. SED, Old Courthouse, Fonda NY 12068.
Fringe Benefits: Located in Adirondack Mountains; campers from a variety of backgrounds. **College credit** possible.

St. Nicholas, Youth Conservation Corps Camp, Located in Frazier Park. Openings from June 15 to August 28. Needs 1 camp director to manage the entire camp work and education program, $7.30/hour; 1 environmental awareness coordinator, $5.90/hour; 2 night counselors, $5.90/hour; and 4 work leaders, $5.27/hour. Room only is provided for the camp director and night counselor positions. Send for application. Apply by March 1 to Marilyn G. Shaw, Administrative Assistant, US Forest Service, Dept. SED, Star Route, Box 400, Frazier Park CA 93225.
Fringe Benefits: The job activities are carried out primarily in Southern California pine forests as well as a high desert environment. The work involves an excellent opportunity to develop supervisory skills working with youth and gain experience in forest related employment.

Santa Lucia Conservation School, Located in Santa Maria. US Forest Service Neighborhood Youth Corps. Openings for college students and teachers from June 15 to August 28. Needs 1 environmental education coordinator (3 years general experience appropriate to position), $5.90/hour and 3 work leaders (1½ years general and ½ years specialized experience), $5.27/hour. Apply by March 1 to Mike Foster, Manpower Coordinator, US Forest Service, 1616 Carlotti Dr., Santa Maria CA 93454.

Shady Oaks Cerebral Palsy Camp, Located in Lockport. Employs 75 high school seniors, college students and teachers. Seeks general counselors, head dorm counselors, specialty counselors in arts and crafts, athletics and nature lore, WSI, program director, secretary, nurse, and cook. Season: late June to August. Room and board provided. Apply by the end of May to Camp Director, Shady Oaks Camp, 159th St. and Parker Rd., Lockport IL 60441.
Fringe Benefits: "Excellent social atmosphere; many field trips in the Chicago area." **College credit** available.

Southwestern Historical Wax Museum, Located in Grand Prairie, a Dallas suburb. Needs ticket sellers, gift shop cashiers, ticket takers, snack bar cashiers, security guards. High school seniors preferred. Work last week in May through Labor Day. "All applicants will be required to work weekends and holidays. When applying, ask questions concerning job you are applying for. No vacations allowed during summer operation." Apply to Southwestern Historical Wax Museum, 601 E. Safari Pkwy., Grand Prairie TX 75050; tel. 214/263-2391.

Squanto, B.S.A.,
Child, B.S.A., Located in Plymouth. Two residential camps operated by Old Colony Council, B.S.A. In addition to traditional Boy Scout programs, outdoor environmental education, day camps, specialized camps, etc. are offered year round. Openings for teachers/instructors, certified rifle marksmanship instructors, WSI certified waterfront personnel, etc. Scouting background helpful but not required. College work-study certification a plus. Salaries negotiable. Interviews year-round. Write or phone for further information. Apply to Kevin P. Mullen, Assistant Ranger, Director of Special Programs, Camp Squanto Environmental Education Center, Box 931, S. Carver MA 02366; tel. 617/224-2010.
Fringe Benefits: "Located in historic Plymouth, gateway to Cape Cod."

Star Lake Camp, (The Salvation Army), Located in Bloomingdale, New Jersey. Summer employment opportunities available for teachers, nurses, college students and high school seniors from mid-June to mid-August. Needs lifeguards, campcraft, arts, 7 crafts, nature, recreation, counselors, kitchen, dining room, secretary, and nurses. Salary range $350-1,000. Room and board provided. Requests for applications will begin to be accepted mid-January. Contact Captain Guy Klemanski, Camp Director, The Salvation Army, 50 West 23rd Street, New York NY 10010.

The Student Conservation Association, Inc., Located near Charlestown. "SCA places volunteers in national parks and forests where they learn firsthand the work of resource management agencies and at the same time do work that the agency could otherwise not afford." Openings for college students and teachers for 10-12 weeks during the year. Needs 300 college students for park and forest assistants, no salary, travel and uniform grants, free housing and food allowance; 300 high school students to participate in a work group, no salary, food and tents provided and financial aid is available; 15-20 work group supervisors (must be over 21, have first aid card, and experience in use of hand tools and trailwork); 10-12 urban work group supervisors. Salary information for work group supervisors and urban work group supervisors sent with the application. There may be some park and forest assistant positions open to physically handicapped persons, depending on the handicap. Send for application. Apply by March 1 (volunteers), February 1 (supervisors) to Scott Izzo, Program Director, The Student Conservation Association, Inc., Box 550, Dept. SED, Charlestown NH 03603.

Fringe Benefits: "Whether working as a volunteer or as a work group supervisor, SCA offers the valuable learning experience of participating in a natural resource management agency. High school participants also enjoy living and working in a spectacular area with a group of peers from all over the country. Many park and forest assistants do arrange to receive credit from their schools."

Tecumseh, Located in Pittstown. Coed camp for children, ages 6-14, on 365 beautiful acres. Openings for 65 persons for 9 weeks during summer. Needs counselors: general, program, nature, pioneer, crafts, athletic, waterfront, $500-1,300; camp secretary, cooks, nurse, dining hall, kitchen and maintenance personnel, $300-1,400. Room and board provided. Serves New Jersey youth with a special Christian ministry to the underprivileged. Member of ACA. Apply to Divisional Youth Secretary, The Salvation Army, Box 679, Newark NJ 07101.

Towanda, Located in Honesdale PA. Camp for boys and girls, ages 7-16. Openings for college students and teachers. Needs coaches; general counselors; specialty counselors for tennis, golf, baseball, basketball, WSI, canoeing, sailing, waterskiing, stage scenery, arts and crafts, nature, pioneering, riflery; nurse (RN). Salaries depend on age and experience. Enclose return stamped envelope. Apply to Lynne S. Nordan, 316 Lynncroft Rd., New Rochelle NY 10804.

Plan ahead with these informative directories from Writer's Digest Books:

1981 Internships. Edited by Kirk Polking.
You'll find over 15,000 opportunities for temporary positions, offering exposure to a variety of careers, including architecture, business, communications, science, and many more. The listings are provided by the directors of intern programs at major firms throughout the U.S. Listings tell the length and season of each position, rates of pay, desired qualifications, a description of the duties and training involved, the location, guidelines for applying, interviewing, and researching positions, and much more.

ISBN 0-89879-036-0   280 pages/Paperback **6.95**
ISBN 0-89879-051-4   Hardcover/**10.95**

Directory of Overseas Summer Jobs 1981
This brand new edition lists more than 50,000 jobs in locations around the world. From Australia to Yugoslavia. Includes length of employment, rates of pay, visa and work permit regulations, plus who to contact for each position
ISBN 0-901205-85-0   168 pages/Paperback/**6.95**

Summer Jobs in Britain 1981
More than 30,000 jobs in Scotland, Wales, England, the Channel Islands, and Northern Ireland: The jobs listed here range from farm hand to office worker to lorry driver. Includes complete information on applying for each job, and lists visa and work permit procedures.
ISBN 0-901205-87-7   159 pages/Paperback/**6.95**

Travellers Survival Kit Europe
Inside information about the best, the least expensive, the most popular in accommodations, transport, food, drink and entertainment. Tips on local news media, communications, customs duties, and handling emergencies.
ISBN 0-901205-72-9   192 pages/Paperback/**6.95**

1981 Adventure Holidays
Exciting alternatives to the standard package tour! Tells where in the world to enjoy hang gliding, yoga, sailing, skiing, rafting, jungle trekking, or any of hundreds of adventure holidays. Includes complete information on each activity listed.
ISBN 0-901205-88-5   231 pages/Paperback/**6.95**

Kibbutz Volunteer
Listings of the more than 200 Kubbutzim give complete information on Kibbutz life in Israel. Details in each listing include name, address, accommodations, what's free, languages spoken, types of work available, and more. Plus tips on the law, customs, eating and drinking, and seeing the country.
ISBN 0-901205-73-7   126 pages/Paperback/**6.95**

Buy these books at your favorite bookseller, or order direct from the publisher.
For mail orders, add $1.00 for the first book; 50¢ for each additional book for postage and handling, and enclose check or money order for the full amount.

Writer's Digest Books, 9933 Alliance Road, Cincinnati, Ohio 45242
Prices Subject To Change Without Notice